Doing

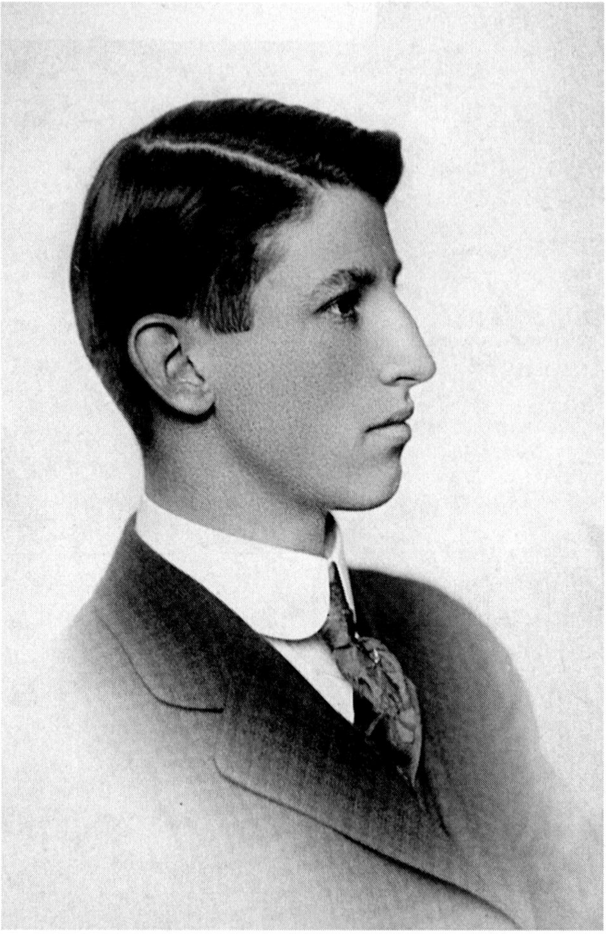

Doing My Bit Over There

A U.S. Marine's Memoir of the Western Front in World War I

EVERARD J. BULLIS

Edited by David J. Bullis

McFarland & Company, Inc., Publishers
Jefferson, North Carolina

Frontispiece: Everard as a young man (courtesy Robert G. Bullis).

Library of Congress Cataloguing-in-Publication Data

Names: Bullis, Everard J., 1896–1964, author. | Bullis, David J., 1953– editor.
Title: Doing my bit over there : a U.S. Marine's Memoir of the Western Front in World War I / Everard J. Bullis ; edited by David J. Bullis.
Other titles: U.S. Marine's Memoir of the Western Front in World War I
Description: Jefferson, North Carolina : McFarland & Company, Inc., Publishers, 2018 | Includes bibliographical references and index.
Identifiers: LCCN 2018029951 | ISBN 9781476674292 (softcover : acid free paper) ♾
Subjects: LCSH: Bullis, Everard J., 1896–1964—Diaries. | World War, 1914–1918—Personal narratives, American. | United States. Marine Corps. Marine Regiment, 5th. | Belleau Wood, Battle of, France, 1918. | World War, 1914–1918—Campaigns—Western Front. | Soldiers—United States—Diaries.
Classification: LCC D570.9 .B875 2018 | DDC 940.4/5973092 [B] —dc23
LC record available at https://lccn.loc.gov/2018029951

British Library cataloguing data are available

ISBN (print) 978-1-4766-7429-2
ISBN (ebook) 978-1-4766-3278-0

© 2018 Everard J. Bullis. All rights reserved

No part of this book may be reproduced or transmitted in any form or by any means, electronic or mechanical, including photocopying or recording, or by any information storage and retrieval system, without permission in writing from the publisher.

Front cover image of Everard J. Bullis postwar (author collection); *background* a close up view of the Belleau Wood showing the hard fought ground captured by the American Army in 1918, Schutz Group Photographers, Washington, D.C. (Library of Congress)

Printed in the United States of America

McFarland & Company, Inc., Publishers
  Box 611, Jefferson, North Carolina 28640
  www.mcfarlandpub.com

For my Grandfather,
who did his bit—
and to all those doing their bit.
—David J. Bullis

Acknowledgments

First, I would like to thank SSG Steven C. Girard (Ret.), World War I Marine Corps Archivist/Historian, for his interest in the book and for his provision of pictures. I greatly appreciate them.

Marilyn Sears deserves many thanks for reviving my sluggishness in finishing the book. It doubtless would not have been completed in a timely manner without her encouragement.

Deborah Taylor's generous help at the last minute in printing and other necessary details helped me meet my due date. I give her my sincere thanks. She is much appreciated.

Thanks go to my son, Ryan, for his expertise with the computer, in saving and restoring my "lost" manuscript. His contribution saved me much labor and he has done sundry other things.

My sister Deanna deserves great credit in introducing me into the use of the computer. I was sorely lacking in this skill, and she provided and patiently instructed me in its use. This was of no little consequence in continuing my work on the book.

Don Bullis came to my aid at a time when I was under pressure in getting many photos ready. He brought them up to specification. He has my thanks.

French historian Gilles Lagin was exceeding generous in providing appropriate photos and a map. I am very grateful to him and for his enthusiasm in providing what I needed for the book.

And finally, my esteem goes to Barbara Bullis, who eagerly came to my assistance in the final stages of completing the book. She, well qualified, acted as assistant and secretary. Her help cannot easily be measured. And the word *help* seems such a simple word to describe her willing labor and aid. But its inherent meaning describes her contribution quite well. From the dictionary, *help* is the simplest and strongest of these words (synonyms) meaning to supply another with whatever is necessary to accomplish his ends—and so has she been to me.

—David J. Bullis

Table of Contents

Acknowledgments vi
Preface 1
Introduction 3

Part I: Belleau Wood

1. Up to the Battle 15
2. Fire and Smoke and Screams and Blood 17
3. Such Was Belleau Wood 26
4. Friendly Fire 31
5. The Inevitable Question 37
6. Idling on the Marne 41
7. Belleau Wood Is Ours 44
8. Shell-Shock 48
9. The Naked Battalion 55
10. Hell's Angels 57
11. The Big Parade 60

Part II: Soissons

12. The Pick of French and U.S. Troops 65
13. Hesitant to Kill 69
14. Sniper's Duel 74
15. The Cave of Blood 80
16. Lieutenant Max Is Killed 83
17. Gas! 87

18. The Ladies from Hell	90
19. The Doughboy's Dream	94
20. Sergeant Dan Daly	100
21. Bedlam in Freeville	107
22. A Display of Might	110
23. Something Big Is Coming	115

Part III: St. Mihiel

24. A Private Speaks	121
25. Privates, Jacks and Queens	126
26. Over the Top	130
27. Outpost	135
28. A Farewell to Arms	142

Part IV: Blanc Mont

29. The One Way Trail	146
30. Into the Storm	156
31. A Warrior's Boast	164
32. He'll Need Those Tags	168
33. Miss Duffy	172
34. A Souvenir	178
35. A Salute	182
36. The Salvation Army Girl	186
37. They Never Failed in Assignments	192
38. The War Is Over!	195

Part V: Looking Westward

39. Let the Big Boys Take Over	198
40. Shipwrecked!	202
41. Officers First	209
42. Look, Marie	216
43. Hilarious Celebration	219
44. The Worst Battle	224

45. Joe Erwin	227
46. Red Tape	228
Notes	233
Index	235

Preface
David J. Bullis

My grandfather's memoir of his experiences in the Great War came into my hands a few years ago. After reading it, I saw a book. I then set myself to the editing of his work. I established chapters, named chapter headings, cut it into parts, (which for the most part were already in place), added punctuation, and ordered paragraphs, all the while maintaining the integrity of the text.

His story is the story of four major battles the Marines fought in World War I: Belleau Wood; Soissons; St. Mihiel; and Blanc Mont. And these are foundational in learning of the Great War in 1918. In the pages of the book, we see a firsthand account of front line battle. My grandfather won a Purple Heart, and in the book describes what he went through in surviving his wound. We also see historic figures—General Pershing, Captain Frank Whitehead, and Major George Hamilton—names that should be remembered for their historical import.

To be sure, historians will have great interest in my grandfather's work. Marines also will be interested in this historical piece. Men and women who love history will find it to their liking. Even those who don't read it for history's sake will read it with anticipation. And it would be good reading for high schools, colleges, and universities. As a final note, the centennial of the above battles is 2018.

Introduction
David J. Bullis

This is not a history book—nevertheless, it is historical. It is a story of adventure, of hardship ("War is hell," as the general said), humor, camaraderie, and doing one's "bit."

Doing one's bit, as it then was commonly called—that was the motivation of a certain young man in 1917. Driven by patriotism, a love of country, and indignation toward the enemy, he wanted to fight.

Before he came of age, and when he learned in the news of General John J. "Black Jack" Pershing leading a troop into Mexico, giving chase after Pancho Villa, he asked his father if he could enter the service. His father said, "No." So he bided his time.

But when war was declared against Germany in April of 1917, now twenty, he made up his mind to go. He at first thought as an officer:

> I am excited. The Army intends on opening a Reserve Officers Training Camp at Fort Snelling; so I submitted my application. … three recommendations.… Major George Sheppard, George Brack, and Mr. Andrew Boss…: a wounded hero of the Spanish-American War … a banker in St. Paul's largest bank; and a nationally known Educator. Well, they ought to be good enough for anyone.

But they weren't. He was only twenty; he needed to be twenty-one.

> Well, so long to becoming an officer. I won't wait.…

So he joined the Marines June 9 of 1917.

> I left work at noon and proceeded to look at enlistment posters. I viewed them all, and, at last, being enticed by an alluring tropical scene of a serviceman dressed in "whites," on a palm studded beach with cute girls dancing in native costume, I climbed the stairs.…

Then he had to spring the news on his family.

> At supper that night.… Mother was standing across the table from me: Dad in his place at the head of the table: Lillian on my right: and on my left, Ruth, Vera … and last, Esther.

I blurted out, "I enlisted today."
... Mother's worried exclamation followed, "Enlisted?"
Then dad's voice, "In what?"
Then a medley of questions from the girls, from mother, and from dad....

It seemed that all of St. Paul, Minnesota, turned out to send off the 53 new recruits:

> We assembled on the street, and soon paraded up 6th Street to Rice Park, where there were to be "going away" ceremonies. It was my first parade in the Marines, and it was long remembered.... It was hard to return the many greetings of "Hi, Ev," that I received along the way. Many of my parents' friends were there, the women smiling and waving, only to break into tears as we passed.... At Rice Park, we were crowded into the center around the speaker's podium by several thousands of people. We were to be honored by two of St Paul's leading citizens, who in turn gave us long, tiresome speeches: "Hero's," etc., "going to war." The train on which we were supposed to leave was scheduled to depart at 8:00 p.m.; but 8:30 came; then 9:00 o'clock passed; and we were still standing. James J. Hill, past president and builder of the Great Northern Railway, one of the speakers, had held the train for us. Bishop Ireland, who was still extolling our "bravery," finally came to a halt in his speech; and we moved out. I leaned from the window and waved my last good-byes to mother, dad, and my sisters, until I could see them no more.

Everard J. Bullis was born October 10, 1896, and died January 25, 1964. I remember him well, the few times I saw him. And the foremost thing I remember is that he fought in World War I. I will never forget the day he pulled down the knitted collar of his sweater to reveal an ugly scar. And my worst memory was the day I asked him how many men he killed: a somber cloud swept over his face, and I knew that I had asked the wrong question. And I felt bad. After all those decades, he was still pained by his memories.

He was proud of being a

Young Everard with his father, John J. Bullis (courtesy Robert G. Bullis).

marksman, and, one day, during hunting season, as my dad (John J.) told me, my grandfather decided to go hunting. He refused to take more than one bullet; but the friend he borrowed the gun from insisted that he take two bullets, the second for the *coup de grace;* and off he went. He returned with a 4-point buck, killed with the one bullet. But he was so sorrowful over killing the deer, he never hunted again. Killing was too painful to him.

The etymology of the name "Everard" is quite interesting. In Old French it is *Everart*; in Old High German it is *Eberhard* < *eber*, wild boar + *hard*, strong: literally, strong as a wild boar. In the middle ages certain warriors etched wild boars on their battle helmets; thus, by association, a warrior. Beowulf is said to have such a helmet. The Anglo-Saxon spelling for *Everard* was *Eoforheard*. Because of the courage and fierceness of the wild boar, the Marines would have been suited as such. But nothing can replace Devil Dog. The Marines earned the name.

The first evidence I found that he kept a diary is in a letter home while he was in boot camp. In another letter, he states that he had finished the first volume, and was going to start another, entitled, "Doing my Bit Over There." This was started before he embarked on the ship to go overseas (on the *Henderson*). But he did not finish this while in France. As for *when* the second volume was completed was in a notation about a relative, a lieutenant in the First World War, and a major in the Second World War. Thus, the second volume was not finished until after World War II. And it took him years to finish it. My Uncle Bob and Aunt Pat both confirm that he was typing up the memoir around 1955, and that he worked on it for years, finishing it a few years before his death. The manuscript is both typewritten and in script.

I did not know of its existence until a few years ago. And the story I heard made me shake my head. My grandmother, a widow of long years, had my grandfather's war memorabilia, including the memoir. She asked my dad and stepmother if they wanted it, she was going to throw it away. My stepmother quickly responded, "I'll take it." When I learned of its existence, and, after reading it, I saw a book. I made a copy and quickly began editing. Rather than put it in a book in its rough form, I took liberties with it to make it more readable. I punctuated it, touched it up, divided it into chapters, named chapter titles, and turned it into a book. And so it is. I hope by this means many will be able to read it, and that it will last for time to come. It is a good story, and is instructive about the Great War in 1918, at least from one private's perspective.

It is a lengthy memoir, and it begins at his youth, as a sort of prologue. His earliest memory of war was sitting on his father's shoulders watching a parade of soldiers returning from the Spanish-American War. There were other incidents and wars as he grew up, that he said, "It seems all my short life, there have been 'wars and rumors of wars.'" Due to the length of his memoir, we cannot include it all in this book. It has too much detail (though quite absorbing). Therefore I am sharing some excerpts, so that the reader can get to know Everard before he goes into battle:

Arrival

At last, we pulled into the Reading terminal of Philadelphia, and there detrained ... and soon we were aboard a trolley, headed south down Broad Street to the Navy Yards. As we approached the yards, I caused uproar in the car when I yelled—"See the battleships!" as I jumped to the window. The battleships looked grand and tremendously large to me; but I was shortly to learn that they were passé, too small for duty; outclassed by newer, much larger and finer ships. But to me, from the Midwest, they represented our great and mighty Navy that I was soon to be a part of.

Taking the Oath

The bunch sat around all day, expectantly awaiting the "swearing in" ceremonies, and discussing the event to come.... The group repeating the oath in unison, Major Beaumont made it quite impressive, and it left a sober minded bunch of Marines in silence. We were committed; and viewed our future in silent wonder.

A Close Shave

One afternoon, we were marched to the camp barber shop.... "Sit there." So I sat on the upended box. He threw a sheet over my uniform, and began. The clippers made fast work of it. In a moment he was done—"Next!" he yelled, and I emerged to a cheering crowd, grinning foolishly.... They sure didn't advertise this on their damned recruiting posters.

A Lesson Learned

I was assigned to camp police duty, and my job was to clean the main street in front of the tent of the camp commander, Major Beaumont. I had a "come to me" broom and a large street-cleaners cart, with instructions to sweep the street. I took the brush and cart, and moved out.

At the first pile of horse droppings I came to, I stopped, looked at it, thought a while, then dropped the brush and started to leave. But somehow, or other, the major was there, and in a fatherly voice inquired as to what the trouble was. I told him that in civilian life I was not required to sweep streets, nor did I intend to start now.

I'll say this, the major understood. He quietly explained that it was necessary to do many things that were obnoxious and disgusting to us; that if we intended to be good Marines, we did that which was asked of us, and took pride in doing a good job of it.

I smiled, and said that I was wrong, picked up the brush, and with the cart did a good job of it.

I can thank the major for quietly explaining to me the duty of a Marine. Do what you are told to do without question, and without feeling belittled or disgraced by it.... I never needed another "lesson" while in the Marines.

The Infamous Swagger Stick

They still, though, tried to emulate the top kickers. He was the fashion plate.... The swagger stick gave us an idea; and soon almost every boot carried one on liberty. Then a great many girls were seen carrying them. On questioning them about it, they told us that Sergeant or Corporal So-and-so of the Marines had presented it to them for "services rendered": and so the swagger stick habit died a horrible death.

A Tradition in the Corps

Facing the battalions was the regimental commander, a colonel, and his staff and reviewing guests. At times, the colonel's place was taken by a brigadier general, who was a tradition in the Corps. He was Tony Waller, the man who led the Marines in the fracas known as the Boxer Rebellion in China in 1900.

The Rifle Range

There are four ratings; the Marksman, at $2 per month extra pay; the Sharpshooter, at $3; and the Expert, who wins a $5 boost in pay per month. Then those who shoot Expert three years in a row, there is the Gold Expert rifleman's badge. But that is a rare and coveted medal for the rank and file, and rarely ever seen ... during the preliminary days I was one of the best shots in the company ... the day we shot for record, I was nervous as a leaf in a wind storm and completely lost my nerve ... and I had to be content with a Marksman's pay.

A Mascot

The Marines had an English bulldog known as Sergeant Major Jiggs, which only traveled with Marines. He never stayed long at a post, but was apt to turn up anywhere Marines are stationed. He had long been with the Corps, and I understand had a regular warrant (a certificate of appointment) of sergeant major of Marines. He was in Philadelphia at the Marine base while I was in Boot Company, and when we boarded the train to go to the range, he went along.

Sounds of War

At night, we could hear the boom of the big guns at Indian Head, a naval gun testing base about four miles upriver. And this made the war more real to us. And we could see the red phosphorous disk on the butt of the shell, as it coursed high above us in the sky.

Green Bunch of Recruits

As I look back now to June when we were the rawest of boots, I can note a miracle on members of company F. We were a green bunch of recruits, awkward, clumsy, and in poor physical condition; today, we are smart, well trained, and in superb physical condition.... The training has been rough and tough, but we are the better for it; my 120 pounds has now increased to 145; but still they call me "Slim."

Old Timers and Unsung Heroes

In the barracks, their personal items were always kept in a military manner, and his bunk was always the picture of neatness. He was a quiet, orderly individual, wrapped up in his memories, easy to get along with, and unobtrusive.

When in his drinks, he became sentimental, and one would find him going through his "ditty" box, laying out his medals in a neat row, and musing over them. Once in a great while we would get them to talking about the medals, and then would get a story seldom heard in life: true, no doubt, for the condition of the man indicated that. They were campaign medals from the Boxer Rebellion in China, where the Marines fought under Tony Waller; from the Philippine Insurrection; from the war duties chasing bandits in the San Dominican troubles; from like conditions in Haiti, Nicaragua, and finally down to the recent Mexican troubles at Vera Cruz. They were the unsung heroes of numerous wars and near wars, and they wore the many-colored ribbons of the campaigns on their chest; neither understood nor appreciated by the civilians about them.... The professional meets requirements; he is a good soldier, and does his job well. On assignments he does just that, no more and no less. He is punctual, obedient, and obeys commands without questioning why. He is puzzled by the new Marine; the Marine motivated by patriotism, and wonders what makes us tick. He is contemptuous of our morals, and frankly says "You won't be a Marine, until you have had a 'dose'; and further, no sane Marine doesn't drink the "gut rot" they lean towards.... A certain few had pooled their monies, and purchased a "bawdy" house in lower Philadelphia. The "girls" paid them a good income for the arrangement. They called it their "club," and couldn't understand why we weren't interested in visiting the place with them.

On Leave

October 6, 1917. Mother and Dad arrived today, and put up at the Hotel Waltonian. I met them there, and we spent Saturday and Sunday together—what a treat to see them! Gardner came along, and we all spent the afternoon at Fairmont Park and sightseeing in Philadelphia. For supper, we returned to the Waltonian and had the best meal I've enjoyed for months. When the waiter brought the check, Gard dived in his pocket and handed Dad fifty cents and said, "'Here, I guess this will cover my share."

The waiter pretty near lost his dignity, but Dad said straight faced, "No, Gardner, this is on me." But I split a rib laughing and had a hard time giving any explanation.... We had a good visit that evening in the hotel; and when it was time to go, Mother was in tears, and it was hard to leave; so that night I slept on a davenport in their room.... I had to leave.... I took one last look up at their room, to see them standing in the window, waving good-bye.

Escort Duty

The escort was required to walk one pace in front and one pace to the right of any person; he was not allowed to carry any package or bundle for the person; and he was instructed only to answer "Yes" or "No" to questions, and not to discuss any yard business with the individual.

On my first tour of this phase of work, I was assigned to escort a middle-aged civilian to the submarine base and present him to a lt. commander on duty there. I started out at a fast walk, with the civilian following behind: but I noticed he preferred to stroll instead, and was inclined to talk. I told him what my duties were and that I would have to obey the instructions, thinking that would stop him; but he just grinned and talked away, regardless. I refused to discuss any questions as to what boats were in or anything about the yard. So then he started on me.

"You haven't been in service long, have you?"

"No, Sir."

"Where's your home?"

"St. Paul, Minnesota, Sir."

"How do you like the service?"

"Fine, Sir."

"What do you think of all the ships, aeroplanes, and submarines?"

And then we got confidential and walked abreast to our destination, while I raved about aeroplanes, battleships, and submarines, even getting so rash as to express a desire to ride in each before the war was over, he grinning and encouraging me all the while.

As we approached the pier and submarine base, I resumed my correct position. Recognizing an officers' group ahead of me, I prepared to salute and present my companion—when I was startled to see the officers snap to attention, and salute my guest. To make matters worse, they addressed him as Admiral ----. He was the admiral in charge of submarine operations: and my heart sank into my boots, and I feared what would happen to me.

The admiral turned toward me, winked, and said, "Thank you; you are excused now." He returned my salute, and I left with a solemn vow about the next time.

Vice Patrol

October 14th. Another interesting experience was being the member of a vice patrol. This took place outside of the yards in Philadelphia in and around what was known as the worst "China Town in the U.S.A...." This area contained the burlesque theaters, numerous Chinese dumps, the living quarters of old and retired seamen, the haunt of Philadelphia gangs, and the red light district. It was a squalid area, with mediocre business activity by daylight, but everything booming at night.

It seems gobs[1] and Marines had been sampling its wares, with the resultant increase in the hospital rate, as well as numerous disabled servicemen. The Secretary of the Navy therefore, Josephus Daniels, put it "out of bounds," and thus the vice patrol.... The patrol was accompanied by two plain clothes detectives from the Philadelphia Police Department.... The men of the area avoided us; but not the girls. They came in droves, only to be herded away; that is, all except two teenagers that the detectives knew. We were forced to stand about while the "dicks"[2] openly loved them up and took liberties with them. It was revolting to us, but apparently did not affect the men and women on the stoops; for they watched, too, as though it was a commonplace occurrence.

Finally, one girl made a play among us, but was rudely shoved aside by each, until she came to ----, who had a weakness for her and tried loving her up, only to be roughly told to move along by the rest of us. ----, however, did succeed in making a date with the "broad" for the night; and we carried on. Our faith in the dicks was lowered as we disgustedly moved along.

We were taken to the so called "clubs," and were warned not to "poke our noses" in. So we just watched. They were all darkened buildings, with one dick going to the door and giving a secret knock. Soon a trap in the door was opened and the dick was engaged in talk, but not admitted. It was quite mysterious and ominous; but what was hard to understand was why the police department permitted them to operate. The dick explained that these buildings housed gambling operations managed by the gangsters.

A Letter from Miss L. Sweet, January 31

My Dear Mrs. Bullis,

Ever since your son spent an evening at our house, I have had it in mind to write to his mother and tell her about it! It was a very simple occasion, but as I sat there enjoying his conversation, I couldn't help thinking how much it would mean to his mother just to have the chance to have the look at him, that we were having. I hope my impulse doesn't sound wild on paper. Impulses are rather unreliable leads to follow.

In the first place, how much we liked him! We, being my mother, brother, and myself. He was the first in uniform we have entertained, as yet—and he has set a high standard for future guests. Of course, he is just a boy, but such a manly, simple one. Well, he arrived a little before six—looking very nice and tall in his long army overcoat! We were much unenlightened on the Marine Corps, and very much interested in what he could tell us about it, and his army experiences; so there was plenty to talk about.

After supper, I suggested going skating, hoping that he liked that sport as much as I do. He seemed quite ready for it, so we went up to the rink, where he managed to find a pair of skates that fitted, and we skated about an hour. As we were about to put our skates on, I heard one small boy say to another, "There's a soldier!" Whereupon the other corrected him in a very superior tone, with—"That's a *Marine*." I was impressed by the small boy's observation, for it is all I can do to tell the difference in uniform between the Marine Corps and the Army in the day time, to say nothing of after dark.

I just thought a word from someone who had seen him might be pleasant for you to hear, and would give you news of him from a little different angle, than his letters. He seemed in good health and spirit.

Most Sincerely,
Louise Sweet
1518 Oneida St.
Utica, New York

Transferred to 140th Co., Replacement Battalion, Quantico

It was sudden, without any preliminaries, without any warning: this morning, April 10, I had been told that the number of men going to officer's training school at Quantico had been cut, and I was one of them. Now, at 11:20 a.m. I was transferred to an overseas replacement battalion. About 8:00 a.m., I was called to the office, where Captain Norris gave me official notice; I had failed to get the appointment. Blunt and to the point, he told me that due to the reduction in the number going, I was cut from the list. Well, nothing to do but get out of the office. I was stoical and resigned.

As I left the office, the first sergeant, Van Dyke, who had always been fair and square with me, followed me into the hall and said, sympathetically, "It's tough luck; but you will go to the second school."

I wasn't much impressed by the *second* school, and I suppose I showed my disappointment, for he then asked if he could do anything for me.

I said, "No, I'll go back and carry on."

I was then asked if I would like a transfer to an overseas detail.

I said, "That's what I enlisted for, and I sure would appreciate anything you can do for me."

With that I returned to my quarters, checked the guard list, found I was assigned to guard duty, and got ready.

My guard station was No. 3 pier, and I was silently walking my beat when I was startled to see a Marine running toward me, frantically waving his arms to "assemble on center," and motioning me to take off the gun. It was highly irregular, and against regulations, but I began to run in his direction.

As we met he was out of breath, but somehow I got the drift that I was wanted quick, and that I'd better accept the replacement as intended. I ran all the way to the guard house, about three-quarters of a mile away, and dashed into the guard room, where the sergeant of the guard yelled out—"See the officer of the day…" I was notified that I was transferred.

As I tore down to the mess hall, I found they had prepared a special plate for my benefit, and I enjoyed the meal set before me. All the K.P.'s and the cooks stood around talking as one. While I ate, I noticed a detachment forming on the porch, so I rushed through the meal—said good-bye and so-long to the cooks and K.P.'s—and hurried to fall in.

As I appeared, Boyd held my pack, which I shouldered; Kiser handed my piece, and—"Fall in!"—a quick roll call—"All present and accounted for! Right face; forward march."

And we were off. No time for good-byes. It's just as well.

Excerpt from a Letter Home, April 10

Well, I weigh 170 when dressed for the street (without overcoat), so must weigh about 160 stripped. But they still call me "Slim." Guess I'll have to put on forty pounds of weight before I come back.

I can certainly tell you I almost cried for joy when we left Philadelphia, for I knew my dreams were coming true. And believe me, I saw tears in the eyes of a good share of the fellows left behind. We know we are going over within a very short time, but we haven't any idea as to where. Anyway, it is for service.

I will be well on my way to the "Big Fight." The order for this outfit to sail was for the 15th, but there has been quite a little delay. So, I expect it won't be long till we do sail. Nelson was in Philadelphia last Sunday, and he heard that the USS *Henderson* docked there, so I guess that's the one we will go on.

Yesterday, the battalion had a final review and inspection by Brigadier General John A. LeJeune, the commandant down here. Well, we were some sized force; and believe me, when we swung into columns of platoons, preceded by the band and the Stars and Stripes, and passed in review, the blood was racing through my body and chills run up and down my spine. I felt like a warhorse for fight. We carried our heavy marching order. It certainly felt good to know that your next step was to be aboard the transport and on the way to do your bit.

As you know, this is to all, a finale to the first volume of my Marine life; to be continued in another volume entitled, "Doing My Bit Over There."

Boarding the Ship

We pulled into Philadelphia in the late afternoon, and detrained on the navy yard siding, where we once again formed companies and the battalion. We marched through the gate and proceeded down Broad Street to the pier, where the USS *Henderson* was berthed.

As we marched past the Marine parade ground, it was lined by the men of the First Regiment, and I caught fleeting glimpses of men I knew. Many wept unashamed; and the many calls of "Hi, Slim," "Hello, Bullis," and other greetings, I had to leave unanswered as we marched along at order.

At the pier, the men filed aboard in orderly fashion, and went to the quarters assigned them. After we were aboard, I was paged from the pier, and I went topside to answer. Many friends were there standing and waving up at me, including Mr. and Mrs. Frazier, who had been so kind to me. But I was stubborn, and refused to leave the ship; I had cut my ties, and I didn't want to go through with that ordeal a second time. And I waved good-bye, and went below to my quarters.

In the morning of April 23, 1918, I arose to the noise of the propeller shaft turning, and rushed to the deck above. The ship was gradually backing out, with the help of tugs, to mid-channel, and finally edged forward on its way. On the pier, a group was waving good-bye, and I stood there till the yard faded from view.

A Letter from Mrs. Emma Lowener, May 5

My dear Mrs. Bullis,

I received your most beautiful letter on arriving home from town about half an hour ago and felt as though I had to answer it at once. When I saw the postmark I thought at once of your boy and that he had probably gotten home on a furlough for a few days before going over and had found a few minutes to drop me a line.

I cannot express to you how fond we were of your dear boy. While he was with us only briefly, I felt as though I had known him a long time. I have entertained an awful lot of boys, but I never found any I liked as well as him and his friend.

I was so disappointed when I heard they couldn't spend the following Sunday with us; I just had to cry. I don't feel as though I did anything out of the ordinary, and really no more than any woman should do, but to help the boys be happy: think what they are giving up. I haven't any boys of my own, but I am willing to do most anything for someone else's. I wrote each of the boys a letter, but do not know whether they received them or not.

I have a very lovely daughter who will soon be nineteen years of age, and can realize what a sacrifice you have made letting your dear boy go; if she had to leave us. Her boy friend is going to … on Monday next; so you know how we feel at the present time. I can only hope and pray for a safe and speedy return for them all.

It seems a dreadful thing that Christian people have to be slaughtered down, for nothing that I can see. And while we are worrying, I have never heard one boy say anything but that he wants to go over and get it over with. I only have sixteen boys at various camps with whom I correspond and send goodies to.

Now, my dear friend, I again thank you for writing to me. And at any time you and your husband come east, I would be more than glad to have you both as my guests. I will also pray for your boy. And when you hear from him, don't forget to tell him he has a friend in Germantown, whose door is open for him at any time and who would be glad to hear from him. And should he ever come in this direction, I will be more than glad to have him again. He sure has proven himself to be what we thought he was. You have one boy you may be very proud of. My only sorrow is we haven't more like him.

Wishing you and your family the best of health, and would be pleased to hear from you again. I am

Yours truly,
Mrs. Emma Lowener

Excerpt of a Letter from Mother, May 5

When I was a girl about eighteen or nineteen years of age, I, too, wanted to cross "the Pond," as New Yorkers used to say, but my opportunity never came; but, instead, I "went West." And I just did my "bit" here in Minnesota.

And I never considered before how important my bit was. But when I realize I raised a Soldier, to fight for liberty and justice: and four lovely girls to fill up my life with such sunshine and pride, and to help make this world sweeter and better; then I know my bit was also important.

And that other life that was with me—but a few brief years—and that passed on into a larger and fuller one (how full, little we know); a life spent just doing the small, common, every-day things, the best I knew how, I found is truly worthwhile. So, Boy dear, don't get discouraged in your part, whether in the "rear ranks," or else-where; you are filling your place in the big game of life.

"France at last"

While we stood in ranks on the deck, some Marine spotted a pin point of light to the east, and at the discovery there was no subduing the men, as cheer after cheer went up: a lighthouse on some point of France. We watched that light grow brighter, and as the light increased in size so did the beginning of day. In about an hour's time the light

Everard with parents, John J. Bullis and Celeste Bullis (courtesy Robert G. Bullis).

faded and the sun appeared. What an approach to France. A blimp appeared and searched the sea about us for submarines; then an aeroplane and numerous small craft of the French Navy; thus we were well escorted up the bay to Brest, France. We dropped anchor outside the harbor of Brest on May 6th, and lighters appeared at the side of the ship, and work details began unloading supplies. On May 7th, we hoisted anchor and with the aid of tugs steamed in to the inner harbor and docked alongside a pier.

France at last. Now what is ahead of us? God knows, we don't; but hope that He will be merciful to each and every one of us.

Part I: Belleau Wood

1

Up to the Battle

We left Coublanc[1] in quick time and proceeded to Grandchamp, where the other companies were joining in the dark. Together we swung on the road to Vaux Andigny.

June 6

There wasn't much talking, as the fellows were deep in thought and about three o'clock in the morning we came into Vaux Andigny, and were halted in the outskirts and dismissed. We were told the train would be in about 7:00 a.m., and that we should "bed down" anywhere.

I located Nellie,[2] and with two others went into town to find billets. On the far side of town we found a vacant room, made ourselves comfortable, and turned in for a couple hours of sleep. We were up at 6:00 a.m. and sought out the kitchens; we ate at the first one we found, and wandered around until we heard the "toot" of an approaching train; then hurried to our respective companies.

Soon we were "high-balling" on our way, we didn't know where; but it was evident that we were needed. The usual horse-play was lacking in the men. The war didn't seem real; it was still far away, until we passed through Colombey les Belles, and we had our first sight of war's destruction. The town was still burning and many buildings were in ruins. The town had just been visited by enemy bombers, which was a reminder to us that we weren't in the rear area any longer.

Late in the afternoon, we pulled into St. Denis[3]: and we learned another important lesson. A large number of us were sitting with our legs dangling in the doorway of the car, when all at once the train drew up to the loading

---

The remainder of the text is Everard J. Bullis' combat memoir, edited and with notes by David J. Bullis.

platform of the depot—and we were trapped. The platform was at the same level as the car floors, with only about four or five inches between. The train came to a jerking halt, and we were pinned in. Fortunately, none of us were hurt; and after quite a wait, the train jolted and slowly backed away. We were out, but a lesson learned: don't dangle your legs from the cars.

We were in the outskirts of Paris, and in the distance we could see the Eiffel Tower and a maze of large buildings. After a short wait, we were on our way again. We soon came to a wood, where we thought was enough privacy to get that relief that is necessary. Consequently, the car doors were filled with men, their breeches down, in a squatting position. When the train cleared the forest, we crossed a viaduct near a factory, and the area below there was filled with women, all shouting and waving at the troops—only to have a view of bared butts to wave at. As we passed out of sight, the echoes of our audience lingered with us.

When darkness settled, we were cautioned, "All lights out," and, "No smoking," as we were nearing the front. We were still a good many miles from any Germans, and we wondered how they would notice what we did at that distance. But, then, "orders are orders"; so we didn't question them. At any rate, the orders started the men to thinking, and there was little else done.

About 9:00 p.m. we pulled to a stop in Meaux.[4] We heard that this town marked the peak of the Germans' success in the first drive on Paris. We detrained, and formed the battalion. We then marched through Meaux, up a long grade, into a shelter of a tree-arched road. And we were lined up and given instructions, of which I was assigned a squad of men and told to take them off the road and get some sleep.

2

Fire and Smoke and Screams and Blood

June 7

    I slept fitfully that night. There seemed to be an unusual amount of traffic on the road which disturbed my sleep and toward morning a burst of machine gun fire brought me erect. Others heard it, too, and men all around were getting up. It seems an aviator flying high overhead was responsible; but he was merely warming his guns as he flew toward the lines.

    The road was alive with trucks and cars, and I moved in that direction to see what was doing there. The men crowded along the road, and in the gray light we could see the vehicles, all traveling in one direction. They were trucks and ambulances, they were full of wounded men, and they were Marines.

    The walking wounded were bandaged, their clothes dirty and torn; they were unshaven and unkempt, and they were angry. When they spotted us for brother Marines, they began yelling, "Kill the dirty sons-of-bitches! Kill them for us. Don't show them any mercy. Kill them!" and so on.

    As the ambulances and trucks rumbled by, there was a rising cheer of our men echoing the cheers of the wounded. As the last vehicle passed by, daylight gripped the world, and we were shocked at what we had seen; the Marines up front had run into trouble, and we, the light-hearted ones, now knew why we were being rushed to the front: it was our turn now.

    Before chow, I went down to a chateau about a quarter of a mile away and there made my toilet with a bunch of others, in a circular, open, horse trough. We spent some time there, discussing what we had just seen, and wondered if the many men that we knew in the 5th and 6th Marines had survived the slaughter; and whether the Marines had won the battle.

    After breakfast, a long line of trucks appeared, heading the opposite way. They closed and lined up beneath the trees, and we were quickly assembled and loaded on; 50 men to the truck, with only room enough to stand.

We started out at a fast pace and turned northward, but soon the trucks were forced to a crawl, as the road was congested with refugees, stragglers, and broken-down artillery outfits, all French, fleeing the Germans.

Filing slowly by on our left, they stopped to watch us pass; the peasants, with a hopeless look on their faces, and the French soldiers, stoically lamenting, "La guerre—finis; beaucoup Boche." They were licked and had given up.

The peasants were carrying bundles of clothing, trinkets, and other valuables; and an occasional cart rolled by, drawn by a cow or a blind horse, filled with personal property, and atop the load an old French woman or old man. It was heart-rending to see, and as far as I knew the Marines said nothing.

Things ahead must be bad. First, the countless trucks and ambulances, filled with wounded Marines; and also, the people of the country-side, fleeing, and mixed into the column units of French artillery and stragglers from the infantry.

We entered Montreuil aux Lions and alighted in front of the Mairie, now headquarters of the 4th Brigade of the Second Division. The 4th Brigade was made up of the 5th and 6th Marine regiments. The din from the front was continuous, and the war had come to have definite meaning to us.

We were directed into an old orchard on the edge of town. There were several new shell holes in the orchard, and as we gazed at them, Marines from brigade headquarters tried to get our goat by telling us how many had "got it," by *this* shell, and Jack, Ernie, or Fred had lost his life by *that* shell. It didn't work; we were ready for them; and they began telling the story a little bit bigger and better.

We were finally left to ourselves, and it became extremely quiet around there. About that time Nellie found me, and we talked over the war in our own way. And I was glad for his company; as it would be the last I would see of him for some time to come.

Nellie stayed with me until the companies moved out. We marched in two columns up the right side of the road under the shelter of tall trees. No vehicles were on the road, and we were getting close to the front; and in vantages high in the trees, French soldiers were observing the enemy's lines.

At the command to form to the right and left of the road, Nellie's company took the left; and mine, the right; and at some point the left-hand column turned off the road, and we continued alone.

At La Ferme Paris, which was a cluster of masonry buildings, and a regimental headquarters, we turned to the left onto a side road, and soon filed into a draw where the stench was terrific. Some buck in ranks remarked, "There must be dead horses around here."

The guide, a sergeant, who had been up for some time, growled, "Them's not dead horses; they are dead men." To say the least, that quieted the talking in ranks.

About a mile farther, we came to another group of masonry buildings, La Voie du Châtel, and stopped in the lea of a wall to make combat packs; that is, we shed everything but necessities (though I managed to carry a blanket and poncho in mine). Then suddenly there was a shriek; followed by a burst; followed by two others in quick succession: a German battery had opened up and was trying to reach us. We all hit the dirt and stayed down for some time. They were "longs," that is, they went over us. We were veterans of fire now—and we didn't like it.

We lay until dusk set in before going on. And we were all eyes. A short way from us was an aeroplane message station in a field, and occasionally a plane with a ribbon or marker on the wing would fly over it and drop observations. The drop was a cylinder with ribbon trailers to mark its descent, and a ground crew would then retrieve the message and relay it to a nearby battery. And also, now and then, we would see a French artillery unit come riding by from the direction of the front, and in a cloud of churning dust gallop out of sight beyond the buildings of La Voie du Châtel.

At dusk, we began to advance, taking the road to Champillon. It was a sunken road with high banks, cut several feet deep by centuries of travel. At one point there was a cluster of trees at the side of the road—when suddenly, without warning, there was a flash of fire across our path, followed by a terrific concussion.

We hit the dirt again; only to be derided by loud laughter of artillerymen. The friendly battery had held their fire until a group of us were in front of the guns—then fired a salvo over our heads. To cover our greenness, we laughed, too. But I am sure none of us felt like laughing.

We stayed on the road about a mile and passed through Champillon, the stench growing worse—and they weren't "horses," either: the front was mighty close now.

After our section cleared the town, shell after shell burst in the town behind us and there were numerous cries of "First-aid!" We learned later that there were a number of casualties then. Miller, a friend of a short time, was killed there. And it was the end of the war for many that night.

Word was passed to make no noise now, as we were within hearing distance of the Germans. Then we were stopped and the officer in charge told us to take ten pace intervals and run for it. When my turn came, I took a good look; it appeared to be about 200 yards across a slope between two wooded tracts. And I cut and ran for the other side.

When I was about half way across I heard what seemed like the buzzing of bees, and the two men in front of me dropped and rolled. I was wrong; they were machine-gun bullets; and the two men were killed. I reached the trees on the other side, and my legs gave out, and I dropped in among the fellows that went before, breathless.

A nameless fear got hold of us; and while we lay there we snuffed a new smell, and the screams and groans of wounded men filled the air. The officer in charge walked throughout the group and explained that we had been under fire, and the screams were from a first aid station just above in the trees: and the smell was blood.

We were up and on our way again and led to a clearing. Here were piles of supplies; food, ammunition, and grenades, and we were told to take all we could carry. While gathering up the supplies, another terror came upon us. Over our heads came a burst, followed by three or four more. A few of the men dashed for shelter in the woods; others hit the dirt, while the most of us were still standing when it was over. But for some reason no one was hurt. The officer, after ascertaining there was no damage, then hurried us away.

We ascended the hill on our right; this was hill 142, taken from the Germans in the terrific fight of June 6. And starting on a wagon trail leading through the trees, I tripped over something that gave way as I stepped on it. And looking down, made out the form of a dead Marine. I had stepped on his arm. I was chewing my heart for air: then another dead Marine lay in my pathway. I jumped, and warned the man behind me. And for the rest of the march was prepared.

When we came to the end of our journey, someone said, "These men are for the 49th."

And a sergeant then said, "Four men in this hole." I needed no second invitation, and jumped in. The "hole" was about six feet long, two feet wide, and about two-and-a-half to three feet deep. We immediately sat in the bottom and stooped down.

After a while, we were rudely prodded with a bayonet by an angry sergeant—and he didn't mean maybe; and he bellowed angrily, "Fix bayonets, and stand to." I thought I would be helpful and told him that they had said to us that we were going into third line trenches.

"Third line, hell! this is the only line! Load your pieces, and stand to!"

There was terrific fire concentrated at a point of the hill 80 to 100 feet on our left, and we could hear men yelling for first aid and for help. The woods fairly leapt and flamed with the bursts; it was hell at its worst, and occasionally a bandaged man would go past us to the rear.

There also was terrific rifle and machine-gun fire on our left rear; although the parapet of our trench was in the opposite direction, all very confusing to the four of us. We finally decided the "front" was to the rear of the trench, and we stood facing the rear till dawn.

A few shells lit in our vicinity, and finally one came screaming in—and we hit the bottom of the fire trench, showered with gravel, dirt, and stones. We lay a long time waiting for the burst; but it never came.

When we got our nerve back and ventured a look, we found the butt end of the shell protruding a few inches out of the parapet. Any one of us could touch it with our hands. I gave a silent prayer; but felt very futile in my effort. We decided to hold our trench till morning, and try to get along with our unwelcome guest.

Self-Inflicted Wound

During the shelling, we heard the word passed: "Pass the word—Sergeant Gilligan has shot himself." He was the "hard guy," the tough sergeant from Nellie's company, the one who had given them such a bad time; he couldn't take it and shot himself in the hand to get out of this hell.

Shortly, he came by on his way to the rear. He was as straight and regular as ever, only he held his left hand before him, his right hand holding his wrist. No one said anything to him; the first-aid man had more honorable wounds to dress. So he was alone in his misery.

June 8

The dawn of a new day approached, and we looked about us. A visible row of helmeted heads extended to our right and to our left—only they were all facing the opposite direction. We silently about-faced and took the dawn watch with them.

We later learned that there was a sharp bend backwards on our left and that there had been an attack on the French; thence, the rifle and machine-gun fire on our rear. An officer came walking by, and we hailed him and pointed to the "dud." He shook his head, looked at us for a moment; and he silently pointed to a new hole. And we crawled to the new hole, much relieved.

That morning, we saw what war really was. Men who before had no mutual grievances now were pitted the one against the other. The one, an unfortunate, who was armed by his master; the other, an unfortunate, who volunteered to fight this aggression by that same master: and the senseless butchery that ensued.

For hours in the early morning the stretcher-bearers labored by, removing the victims. They lay in all positions on the stretchers, in grotesque positions; some died in agony, others, in peace. One—whose body I will always remember—lay on the stretcher on his knees, his head propped up by his right arm, his tunic and clothing pulled up to the shoulder, and his left hand groping for the wound in his back. The skin was mottled, gray and white, and his face, turned to the left, was grimaced in pain. That was war.

The captain soon wandered by, and not knowing us sat on the end of the firing trench and chatted in a pleasant and friendly manner. He was Captain George Hamilton,[1] the highly respected commanding officer. As I lit a tailor-made cigarette, he fairly drawled for one; and I removed my gas mask from its container, took out a couple of packages, and offered them to him. He objected to more that one cigarette, and at the same time proceeded to bawl me out. He did so in a positive manner, and in a way that I got the message: the gas mask was our means of preserving life, and anything in the bag would likely shut off the chance of air getting to the breather at the bottom of the canister. I got the point, and reddened up for not thinking. I gave him the packages of cigarettes, and told him that I'd had them quite a long while and that I didn't smoke much, anyway. He grinned, and said he would share them with the other officers. I enjoyed myself afterward for an hour, or so, passing out cigarettes to the men in the vicinity, who had been up for quite some time.

Burial Detail

There wasn't much to do during the day but keep a look out, and duck when the Heinies began shelling. Nights were our busy time, and we got little sleep; and my first night at the front was no exception.

About 9:00 p.m., Lt. Thomason came around and selected eight of us; all were veterans, except two of us, and we went out in single file from the line. We were a burial party to "dig in" the German dead. They were "ripe," and for the welfare of our own men, must be interred.

We were divided into parties of three, and coming to the first group of dead, our party was assigned the job, the rest moving down the slope toward the German lines. It was unpleasant work, and disintegrated rock near the surface forced us to use picks. We dug the first hole about two feet deep, and by means of a Maxim machine-gun belt tied to this ankle, a shovel under his buttock, and a pick hooked under his neck, we dragged him in and covered him up: three days dead in the terrific heat had accelerated decomposition, and the stench made the job highly unpleasant.

2. Fire and Smoke and Screams and Blood

The second body lay near a shell hole, and we enlarged the hole, slid him into it, and covered the body. We had to work quickly and quietly, and had to stop and listen often; if a flare went off, we halted in place and held our pose as long as the light glowed; and that occurred often.

We moved up the slope to take care of another body, and I received a shock that was to last throughout the war. The body was a big Prussian infantryman, about 6 feet 4 inches tall, and rigor mortis had set in. He lay as he had fallen, on his right side, his body in the last position he was in before he died. He had died praying: he was on his knees, his hands folded in an attitude of supplication, and his head thrown back. On the ground beside him were pictures, a letter, and a string of beads; and on his face a serious, stern look. We enlarged a nearby shell hole, but the rock limited our digging efforts; and when we put him in, and covered him, his knees and forearms were above ground, giving the grave a grotesque appearance.

I then took the letter out of the envelope. It was in German script, and hard to make out. The letter was from his wife, and told about the children and of their worry about him. I picked up the pictures, and found them to be of his wife and three children. I was tempted to keep them, with the idea of trying to deliver them to his wife after the war; but knew that would be improbable. I placed the letter, the pictures, and the beads at the head of the grave, and put a stone on them, hoping the next party would take care of them properly. Never again would I hate the German "monster"; he was such a man as I, and with all the normal characteristics of a home-loving individual. In war, he was to be feared; and as an enemy, to be killed; but the propaganda fed us was bunk, and I knew it for what it was worth.

We crept farther along the slope hunting for the next body, but a noise disturbed us. We stopped and listened, and made out the shuffling of feet and the occasional breaking of a branch. After a hurried conference, we sent one man to locate the lieutenant and the other men. Then we two lay flat on the ground and waited.

Before leaving the lines, we had put our bayonets in their scabbards to avoid any betraying glint. Now we slipped them on the pieces and unlocked the safety on our rifles. The metallic click sounded foreboding in the dark. I felt terribly naked and wished that we had found heavier cover. But we were better off than we realized in the darkness.

The shuffling of feet was unmistakable, and about forty to sixty Germans came out from the trees about fifty feet from us. I knew that if we fired, it would be all over with us; and as the other fellow didn't fire, I knew he had sized it up as I had.

Four or five Germans broke off of the column and advanced toward us.

They stooped and peered hard into the darkness. I held my breath till I nearly burst, and I listened to the discussion—"Was hören sie?" (What do your hear?) "Wie viele?" (How many?), etc. At last they were satisfied, and quietly reversing their column, turned down the slope and were swallowed back in the trees.

I expelled my breath—and then heard a twig snap several feet to our right. There couldn't be Germans there, so I quietly gave the command to "halt!" and got ready to fire. Lieutenant Thomason answered and approached, soon followed by the other six men. Our group had made their approach much more quietly than had the Germans; too quietly for comfort.

The lieutenant questioned us carefully for several minutes, and I believe was disgusted with us for not making a fight out of it; and secondly, thought we had the dander up and had seen nothing. At any rate, he formed us into a semi-circle and wandered to one side and whistled and hummed a tune or two. Nothing happened. And I got a new picture of the American Marine: he had nerve, and thought nothing of odds of six or eight to one against.

He then said, "Let's go."

We thought that was enough for one night, but he thought differently: we went looking for them. We wandered all over in No Man's Land into the vicinity of the German lines. We would move in, listen, then stealthily advance another short distance, then listen some more. We must have covered a mile, or more, of the German lines, and heard nothing. Then, to our relief, he said—"It's getting towards dawn; we had better go in." And he led us off.

We went down the slope, across the drainage system of the valley, up the opposite slope towards our own lines. Suddenly, we heard the charging handle of a machine gun slide back. And we froze: I'll swear my helmet stood high by my hair and froze with two feet in the air.

I noticed the lieutenant and the rest of the party were in frozen positions, too—French?—Germans?—Americans? Which? And then a weak, scared voice—"H-a-a-lt—wh-o-o-s th-e-er-e?"

The lieutenant answered, "A lieutenant of Marines with a party—take it easy."

The lieutenant, arms akimbo, waited for the signal to advance. "A-a-dvance lieu-u-te-e-nant of Ma-ri-i-nes; party, st-ay the-r-e." The lieutenant advanced arms above his head.

We heard the low mumbling talk; then—"Advance, party."

We were still jumpy, realizing that a misstep would bring us down, and we weren't at ease till we passed the gun.

As we passed, the gunner said, "D-ooo-n't yooo-u kn-ooow any b-e-tt-er than to aaad-v-a-nce o-on a ma-chi-ne gun a-at n-igh-igh-t?"

Believe me, we did; but who was there to tell us a gun was planted there?

I looked in as I walked by, and saw a white-faced kid hunched over his gun, and three or four others hunched beside him; and we all mentally thanked a kid who had nerve enough to hold his fire. Our hold on life was slim that night.

3

Such Was Belleau Wood

The environs of Belleau Wood were scenic and pleasing to the eye. It was a rolling country, with most of the hills capped with trees. And the open fields and side hills were crop land, covered with grain.

There were numerous little villages in the valleys. They were not like the barren villages at home, with their solitary buildings dotting the surrounding countryside; but they were in clusters, built along the main road and also a side road, or two. The masonry homes, barns, and other buildings appeared tied together by high masonry walls, and there were no front and back yards, as at home, but the buildings abutted the street. And each home had a court yard, in which were kept chickens, the work animals, and an accumulation of junk.

There did not appear to be any stores, where clothing, hardware, or groceries could be bought; only a shop, or two, liquors and wines the customary goods dispensed. There were no movie houses, no pool halls, or other places of amusement; there were no phones, or other developments one would see in modern America. There was a church, not modern, usually with the high-hipped roof and a spire, and a clock in the tower, built in the 1600s. And there were shrines at various places in the town, where the people knelt and prayed as they passed to and fro. This, then, was the setting of war.

Vicious, modern war had come and disrupted life in these villages. The town may, or may not, be completely ruined. The church steeple had been holed, the walls and roofs had gaping holes and the homes and other buildings had been hit countless times by both light and heavy artillery; the masonry walls were tumbled down, and the roads were cratered by shell-bursts.

The inhabitants of the villages were gone, except, perhaps, for a few old men and women, who chose to take their chance on life and with the enemy. For the most part, they were just ghostly habitations, and the inhabitants were the soldiers who occupied the remains.

The grain fields were lush with growth, but were crisscrossed with paths, a line of trenches, and acres of barbed-wire entanglements. The farmers were gone, and during the day not a soul was seen—but night was alive with hurrying soldiers carrying out their various details. In the woods only, in the daylight hours, was there life; for the soldiers were to be seen moving about.

There were trenches cutting the border of the trees, and wire entanglements strung about and through them. There were the isolated locations of batteries, the guns erupting in fire and smoke, as they fired on unseen targets, a kilometer, or so, away. And in the underbrush you would find the huddled bodies of the slain, and their equipment, letters, and personal belongings strewn about. In the more cleared areas, the living, huddled in fire trenches, and others walking about.

But of bird life and small animals there was nothing, except a hare or two. And over all there hung a cloudy emanation, the acrid smoke of big guns and little, the smoke and debris of bursting shells, and perhaps the acrid or pungent odor of gas. And over the area, and for miles around, hung the air of death; the sweetish, sickening odor of the dead, the unburied, and the wounded. Such was Belleau Wood.

June 11

One evening, near dusk, several of us were placed on the line. It was an area clear of trees, and our detail was to do "panel" work for the air force. It was explained that at a certain time a plane marked with a trailer or streamer halfway out on the right wing would fire a three star rocket, and then swoop low over the position to take pictures. At the signal, we were to display our panel, a strip of white cloth, perhaps two feet wide by six feet long, leaving it exposed while the plane flew over. This was necessary for the artillerymen to determine by the pictures the front line, or point of advance, and save us from "shorts" from the guns. The fighting was fluid, that is, the points of advancement or retirements varied each day, and calls for artillery support were many; and the battery could not know where it was safe to lay down their fire.

On this night, we were spread out and waiting, and then a plane appeared. The plane had the streamer positioned exactly; the plane did fire a rocket as prescribed; and we spread out the panels. As the plane swooped down to get the pictures, we perceived the German cross on its wings—and most of us hurried to gather in our panels. We were too late, in most cases, and, as a result, we were treated to an unusual bombardment from the enemy that night.

As for our plane, it never appeared; and we wondered at that. It seemed strange, but the old bug-a-boo persisted. Somehow, and in some way, the

Germans had the information correct and we paid for their knowledge in casualties.

The next few days held nothing too serious for us. One day, another Marine and I were detailed to carry out a dead Marine that lay in the tangled brush, not far from our position. He was from our company, killed on the 6th of June, and decomposition was far advanced, and the job was not nice.

I reached the body first, and at first glance took the lead position of the stretcher. He had died on the stretcher, his wounds in the groin, and maggots were busily at work in the wounds and about the nostril and mouth.

We picked up the stretcher with the gruesome remains, and started to the rear area. We had not gone far, when the rear of the stretcher dropped and I heard the retching of my companion: it was too gruesome for him. So we changed places, and once more went on.

We had been told to cross no cleared areas and to keep to the woods; but bucks will take the easiest way out. We crossed a large cleared area on the run—they were right; for we were targeted by machine gun and rifle fire. The insistent hissing of machine gun bullets and the sharp crack of rifle fire spurred us on, until we were under cover once again.

The swaying stretcher with its load was hard to carry, and we collided with the brush and swerved around the many trees, until we finally came to the trail, and the collecting station; where we turned over our burden to the burial detail.

The day-time hours were generally uneventful. We did take several spells of fire, and lost a few men, but they were often passed either visiting or observing the German lines for movement. But the nights were spent watching and waiting for German attacks. On our particular point, though, the Marines had made their objective, and we waited quietly for the rest of the line to gain theirs.

Every day at some particular place along the lines there was a raging of rifle and machine-gun fire. The fight was severe, and we were glad that we didn't have to go up against them. The 49th Company on the 6th of June had lost over 60 percent of enlisted men and 90 percent of officers, and the replacements had not yet brought us up to strength.

We were arranged along the line of battle in groups of three; one night on watch, and two, sleeping. During watch, we would pass the word at intervals, "On the alert," whispering it to the man on the right or left, as the case may be. And beware the man who failed to pass it on. It happened, though rarely, when someone did sleep, and didn't get the word. And at the hours of dawn and twilight, all the men were on alert.

Our company formed the left flank of the Second Division,[1] adjacent to the French forces; and the Germans attacked them one night with a small force. There was quite a flurry of firing of pieces[2] and the yelling of French and Germans as they clashed. And it was over about as soon as it started. Then the night's sky was filled with flares for hours after.

The next night, a platoon from our company was moved over in support of the French; again the Germans attacked, and again were driven back. On the third night, a platoon from our company took over that portion of the line, and when the Germans attacked, they gave them the works; and there were no more German attacks at that point.

One night, while I was on alert, and all was quiet, except for the machine guns, which kept up a continuous chatter; a Sho-Sho[3] gunner on my left started firing. This gun fires at a rate of about 250 shots per minute, which is relatively slow. It was soon joined by a Hotchkiss, firing at about 400 shots per minute. Then the riflemen adjacent became involved. The fire steadily grew and gradually worked to my position. Though dark, and not seeing anything to fire at, and not knowing what it was all about; yet I also joined in the shooting. And so it went down the line for about a mile; until all were firing into the darkened void ahead. It was possible to tell every twist and turn of the line from the blaze of weaponry, and the air above us was lighted with flares, both German and American: and the German rifles and machine guns also could be heard.

Then company officers and noncoms went running along the line yelling, "Cease firing," until they got the Sho-Sho and the Hotchkiss stopped; then the men adjacent; and finally the whole line.

All was quiet on our side, but the Germans were unremitting, and filled the sky with flares. We were still on edge, when the Sho-Sho started again, the Hotchkiss resumed fire, and gradually the fire again extended the length of the line.

At the height of fire we heard a voice directly ahead of us crying out, "Cease fire, for ---- sake; cease fire, and let me in!"

We immediately stopped; and an outpost crept in. He slid down into our hole, and was near paralyzed with fear. He said the bullets tore up the ground all about him. He didn't know what had started it, but was glad he had made it back to the lines. We were, too.

The shooting on the left was finally stopped, and the guns gradually grew silent all along the line. The Germans kept the sky well lit with flares the rest of the night, and rifle and machine gun fire was spasmodic from then till daylight.

Just before dawn, Captain Hamilton and a group left the lines to investigate what had caused the fire. They returned after day-break, grinning, each man carrying the spoils of German equipment, and also a light Maxim gun. The captain proudly displayed an officer's No. 9 Lugar pistol and holster.

Not all the fire went astray; some Germans were dead to the man; but they also found one of our outposts dead, bayoneted in the back. That was what started the show. The Sho-Sho gunner heard the muffled scream of the outpost, as he was bayoneted, and then cut loose with a burst of fire. It was a real fire hysteria that swept the lines that night, and it affected both Germans and Americans, alike.

Sometime the next day, I was in the fire trench below ground level and had just completed cleaning my piece and was balancing it in my hands, when I heard somebody coming toward me. I looked up just in time to see 2nd Lt. Johnson staring down at me and my gun. He turned white, about-faced, and went rapidly back to where he had come from. I looked at my piece; it couldn't have been pointed more accurately, if I had intended using it. I was plenty disgusted to think that he would be sent to the same company. As far as I was concerned, he was just a bad dream, and I was sorry to see him.

For a week we held this spot on the top of the hill, overlooking "No Man's Land." We could not see a soul, except for the few men of our own outfit. All life had disappeared from our vista, and only the roofs of the village of Torcy were visible. We could see a huge clock in a tower, which had stopped at 4:20. A shell had vented the tower, and we wondered whether it had stopped in the small hours of the morning, or had died in late afternoon.

The only completely visible building was a large, red barn on the outskirts of town, near our line. This place only showed any sign of life. And as we watched, we saw a tile or two slither down from the roof. And then gradually there appeared a hole. And we knew German eyes now looked back over to our lines.

We set our leaf sights and carefully aimed a few shots at the hole, but we did not know whether they were effective, or not; only a new hole would appear at some other part of the roof. Officers, who watched, finally sent word to our artillery, and in a shortly while the red barn was the scene of action, as our shells put new holes in the roof and through the walls of the barn, and tore up the ground around it. The red barn itself remained a point of high casualties thereafter.

The only other sign of life was when German stretcher-bearers appeared on the slope before us. They were seen apparently to bear a body, and so not a shot was fired. As they came near cover, the wind lifted the blanket and revealed their burden: a Maxim gun. And from that time on, no German was immune from our fire, and all niceties of warfare were at an end.

4

Friendly Fire

We were relieved by an outfit of the 6th, and moved to the woods northeast of Champillon, as counter-attack troops. There was no line ahead of us, but we were in a valley, with Belleau Wood on our right, and our old position of Hill 142 on the left; the line making a big U-turn here, our battalion in the depth of the "U."

The day was lazily spent in sleep. Later, I became bored with things in general, and started prowling the woods. I noticed bandoliers of ammunition throughout the area, so to kill time I piled the bandoliers in a neat pile.

I busily worked at this and had a pile over two feet deep by about four feet long, and there was much more in sight. I forgot everything, engaged as I was deeply in thought—when a hard voice interrupted me, demanding, "What are you doing?" I whirled about and saw the battalion major and three or four captains.

Saluting, I remarked, "Sir, I was just gathering the ammunition into a pile." He glared around, pried into a few bushes, and then took a bandolier and looked over the ammunition. He glared at the captains and ordered them to turn out the men and gather it all in piles, then stalked away.

I felt as though I had been caught sucking eggs. Then one of the captains came over, and said, "That's all right; take it easy now, and we will get it all up—I wonder how it got thrown around like this?"

I had been over all that part of the woods, so I told him that it looked as if there had been a big fight there, as equipment was scattered throughout. He walked with me through a part of the woods and we looked at the equipment; combat packs, blouses, caps, helmets, letters, and other personal stuff; but the rifles and bodies had all been cleared out.

Later in the afternoon, Cpl. Gavin and I took a cup of warm coffee to a sentry on gas watch. Gibson, the sentry, greeted us with a smile, and rested the muzzle of his piece on his foot, and held the butt end with his left hand. He stood drinking the coffee and talking to us, and, when he finished, he handed the cup back to Gavin and picked up the piece with his right hand:

and there was the sudden roar of his gun. He looked at us in a silly manner, and said he had shot his foot.

A group of officers and men immediately crowded around and took our statements; but I'm afraid the opinion of the officers differed from ours, and Gibson was marked an S.I.W. (Self Inflicted Wound), and sent to the rear.

Later, just after dusk, I saw a member of the 20th Company sitting on the ground with his back to a tree, twirling his .45: when flames spurted from the gun—and another S.I.W. was on his way back.

That night, the Germans bombed, as well as shelled us, but very little damage was done. One bomb landed very near the hole I was in, but didn't burst.

At daylight, another fellow and I searched for the live bomb and found it after going a short distance; we were thankful it hadn't gone off, for it was quite large. We put a barricade around it and called an officer.

After he looked at it, he went to consult with the demolition officer. He returned with a crew and after warning the men and ordering them to seek fox holes, they set it off. We were lucky that the bomb was a dud; for the blast that resulted shook the area, and for minutes afterward there was a rain of shrapnel throughout the forest for a radius of a hundred yards or more.

After the shrapnel quit falling, the other fellow and I went to the scene of the explosion and found a nice large hole in the ground; but more to the point, a column of smoke was issuing up. The bomb was an incendiary, too, and the resulting smoke locates the position for enemy observers. So we covered the debris with about two feet of dirt. But still the smoke poured up.

We worked fast to try and smother it, but German artillery opened up on our corner of the wood, and we had to quickly seek cover. The fire was accurate, and kept us in our holes. All you could hear were the many bursts and the cries of wounded men as they were hit. We were glad when the Germans decided to let up, and, relieved, we went wandering about the area again.

That night, our captain, who was the acting officer-in-charge of the battalion, was replaced by a new company commander, Quigley by name. Captain Quigley then ordered the company to fall in. It was an asinine thing to do. While waiting in ranks, I was talking to Joyce, and he was telling me about his home, his widowed mother, and his two brothers; the older was at home and had lost a leg in an accident, and the younger was in the Marines. Just then there was a scream—and I hit the dirt. The shell exploded immediately and there was much confusion in ranks. The shell burst just overhead in the center of our squad; and when I scrambled to ascertain the damage, I observed three forms on the ground. Joyce was writhing with a terrible hole in his head. He was on my right. Rusinow was on my left, a corpse at my feet. And Whiting, the one who stood in the rear ranks behind Rusinow, also was dead.

We were a much shaken group of men. The captain was yelling, trying to get our attention, when a second shell hit and burst immediately behind us. And as the company was dispersing and trying to get into the woods, a third shell burst in the vicinity of the second. Fortunately, no damage was done by the second and third shells.

We were in holes again, and now nothing could get us out. The captain stood in the clearing, and yelled, "Fall in, damn you; come out of there, and fall in."

But all hell couldn't budge us. The men had lost faith in the captain. Even the noncoms crawled into holes, and spoke their minds of a captain who would use parade ground tactics in the front lines.

The shelling did not stop; the Germans pounded the woods: and a few men were killed that night, and several were wounded. The yelling of the wounded was incessant—"First aid! Help; help—first aid!"

Their frantic cries were enough to drive us crazy. And to make matters worse, several men had eaten spoiled canned tomatoes, and they howled in misery with ptomaine poisoning. It is strange to say, but a lot of the men insisted that the Germans had spies in the area, who gave information to German artillery, causing that night's disaster.

After a night of horrors, the men filed out of the woods in the early morning light and wended their way to the east, and we took up positions in the western part of Belleau Wood proper. We made it without incident, except for me. I got tangled up in phone wires, and mentally had a bad time of it for a few seconds.

The only thing of note this day is that three of us were detailed to gather canteens and go back to Lucy le Bocage for water. We started out, keeping to the woods, and as we neared the crest of the hill, we reached an open field. It is said that Germans won't fire on individuals with artillery; but that is bunk; they did. They opened with one gun, and the first burst was to our left. We moved to the right, the burst of a battery alighting where we had been. We worked down the slope, the shells trailing us, always too late.

When we reached the outskirts of Lucy, the Germans concentrated on the road, and their bursts were ahead of us, knocking gaping holes in a stone wall. We drifted along behind the bursts and arrived in the town square without being hurt.

The town was filled with troops of the Third Division. The 7th Regular Army Regiment was on the job, and as they said, to relieve the Marines. We

Lucy le Bocage, where Everard and his fellows went for water. June 12, 1918. The spring still runs today, and is in a washroom which villagers use (courtesy Gilles Lagin).

found the well we sought guarded by doughboys, who said the well was polluted and that we could get no water. Several shells hit the buildings in the square while we were there, so we decided that we had better return.

The things that I remember pertaining to the polluted well were, first, that it lay at the junction of the road we came in on and a road running through Lucy to Torcy; secondly, the surly 7th Infantry men (they hate Marines); thirdly, in the center of the square and leaning against a column or monument was the wrecked Ford that Sgt. Major John H. Quirk had used when he ran ammunition into Bouresches and won the Navy Cross for the dead.

We returned by a different route, and as we passed a food dump, we gathered all the "monkey meat" (Madagascar canned horsemeat) we could carry, and made our way back, sans water.

That night, Smith and I had a nerve-wracking job. Lieutenant Corbett routed us out and took us to the edge of the woods, where a mule skinner had dumped a load of hand grenades. They had been dumped in a hurry, and the French offensive grenades were scattered all around out of their containers.

4. Friendly Fire 35

The French offensive grenade has a light metal bulbous shell, which carries a concentrated high-explosive charge. It is detonated with a pin, and this pin is covered when not in use by a thimble of light metal attached by beeswax to the grenade. The grenade when detonated has about six seconds before the burst. The caps were all off of the grenades, making this a very touchy job.

Corbett warned us to be careful; any sudden movement would start the pile rolling, and would probably detonate the grenades. Smith and I had been working some time, when suddenly the pile shifted and began to roll. We yelled a warning and ran a safe distance and waited a reasonable count—without the expected explosion; and then returned to our task.

Again the pile shifted, and grenades tumbled down. Again we went through the motions of safety, and all was well.

We worked at this about three hours, carefully picking up grenades, finding a cap, capping the grenade, and placing it in its box. We had several good scares during the process, and finally had a neat pile of grenades, all capped and in their boxes; and sought our holes for some rest.

I had not been in my hole very long when I hear the lieutenant yelling, "Bullis—front and center." Bullis was conveniently "sleeping"; but repeated calls kept his rest uneasy. Then, as Bullis feared, the lieutenant came; he was angry, and a prodding foot brought Bullis to an upright position.

"Isn't there anybody in the company, but a guy named Bullis?" was my response. The lieutenant laughed, and asked how many times I had been on assignment that night.

"Three," I replied.

And he said he would find others, and that I should get some sleep: "I am sending a detail for ammunition."

"I'll go," I answered; but he was off, and sent another man.

The famous French *grenade citron* Foug model 1916, used abundantly by the Marines. With the caps off, as in the account, the duty was a dangerous one (courtesy Gilles Lagin).

The next morning, I learned that the detail had all been wounded; and one, Claude Garvey, had been killed. I didn't know whether I was lucky, or not, when I heard that.

That day, half of our company was sent forward to connect with the 17th and cover a gap in the northern part of Belleau Wood. Our half of the company still held a front line position, though the line bulged inwardly at that point, and we were in a relatively quiet zone.

But the other half of the company came under our own artillery fire, as well as the Germans.' It was hell where they were, and star shell and other means of signaling failed to get our batteries to change their firing point. Runners went back with messages; then officers went back; but the artillery still pounded them.

In the late afternoon, the firing ceased, and we heard rumors about an American officer that was a German spy, who frequently changed the firing point and juggled the setting of the guns; but managed to keep on target. The rumors further stated that a sergeant finally checked and caught onto what he was doing, and shot the lieutenant. Whether it is true, or not, the story was well received by us.

5

The Inevitable Question

During the daylight hours, we lay in our holes or on the ground and had "gab-fests" with those nearby. The topics were varied, but they eventually turned to religion. The sum and substance of it was, "If you didn't have religion before the war, you had it now."

It seems strange that in a living hell, the furthest from a God-like atmosphere, those men should turn to God. A group of us, Frank Schroeder (killed), Guy Potter (wounded), John Casey (wounded), Cpl. Bill Gavin, Tim Keville, Robert Brock, and a few others, debated and argued the question.

Potter, who claimed to be a school principal in civilian life but who in no way resembled such, would stand up and gruffly question our professed religion, all the while pulling and scratching his right ear. He had just finished a scathing rebuke at Schroeder, when he spoke up stating that he was a deacon in his church back home: "---- ----, my ear itches," was Potter's next remark; only to have one of the others say, "You ---- ---- fool; let it alone, you've got a hole through it." And sure enough, he did; a Heinie bullet had just missed his head and punctured the ear in the fighting on June 6, several days before.

Potter lapsed into a brooding silence, and soon afterward was evacuated to the hospital; for the ear became infected.

Then Tim Keville began a tale of his early years and boasted of "wild and wooly" times. He stated that several times he and his brother had been in jail for fighting and carousing: "And who do you think put us there?" he questioned the guys, with an impudent grin on his face: "Bill Gavin, there."

And we looked at Bill for confirmation. Big Bill Gavin just sat with a good-natured grin on his mug, and nodded his head. Bill, in civilian life, had been a sergeant on the Medford, Massachusetts, Police Force; but here in Belleau Wood, Tim was a special friend; all things past were forgiven and forgotten; they were pals now, and fighting a common cause.

Sergeant John Casey, a large man, just stood and grinned at these exchanges and said little; but even so, the men all looked at him with respect, for in the fighting of June 6, he had rushed a group of Germans, killed several, and had with his .45 automatic taken the rest prisoner. For this he was awarded the D.S.C., the N.C., and had received a SS citation.

I never took part in these arguments, for the simple reason that I didn't know where I stood. But when Potter pointed his big finger at me one time, I said, "I'm a Sunday School Boy—I went to church and Sunday school all my life, before joining the Marines."

The group laughed, but nobody kidded me for my admission. And I went on reading my pocket Testament and finished the New Testament three times before I was taken out of the fighting.

At times, we would make coffee to pass the time, a spoonful of coarse coffee in an aluminum canteen cup filled with water. Then lighting the "stove," we would sit and hold the cup tediously over the flame until we had a blackish brew. Never did the maker get more than a sip; for the men in the surrounding holes knew when it was ready, and begged for a drink.

My "stove" consisted of a Sterno tin filled with melted candles and an old sock for a wick. The candles were stubs left by the Germans, and I had no knowledge who had worn the sock; nevertheless, it did the job, slowly but surely.

Later, when my stove was burned out, one of the fellows, who had been foraging, handed me a new fuel, which was faster—but not safer. He had raided an artillery site and came back with a bunch of lyddite explosives, the stuff that propels the shells. It was in sticks approximately 6 to 8 inches long, by ¾ of an inch wide, and about ¹⁄₁₆ of an inch thick.

All that was necessary now was to light an end of a stick, which burned rapidly, and by feeding a second stick—and another—and yet another, under the cup, the coffee was done in a hurry. The only difficulty with it was to keep from burning your fingers and trying to dodge the fume, which was sure to bring tears to your eyes.

This lyddite was used for several days, until a 2nd lieutenant, with nothing to do, and with the world on his shoulders, saw fit to stop its use.

Cigarettes and smoking tobacco gave out; chewing tobacco was unheard of, and the men growled for want of them. But one day, a supply of "Horseshoe" plug tobacco was issued. To the old-timers, this was heaven; but to the new model Marine, it was hell.

We tried the chew, but at best we drooled and hiccupped, and not a few retched: might as well die one way, as another. Finally, we gave up and held on to our plug, thinking to exchange it later with the old-timers for cigarettes when issued.

To kill time, I spent hours looking over the German lines. I had picked up a sniper glass in the woods and viewed the scene with that until an officer appeared one day and took it, saying, "All field glasses and sniper scopes are to be turned in."

So I went back to my hole and cleaned my piece, again and again. I checked my bayonet, and cursed, because it was dull as issued; and wondered if and when I would be able to sharpen it to my liking.

And so passed my first assignment at the front, the rumor being passed; "We are going to be relieved."

June 15

We were scheduled to be relieved by units of the Third Division tonight. We waited in the rain, and the Germans poured into the woods a heavy bombardment of gas and high explosives, and the relieving troops had a high percentage of casualties and were scattered. No relief.

Trucks from the 2nd Ammunition train of the 2nd Division, taking the Marines to the Marne valley. According to French historian Gilles Lagin, the photograph was taken the same day of Everard's account (courtesy of Gilles Lagin).

June 16

Word had it the 7th Infantry was shot up by artillery fire last night and the relieving units were badly scattered and "lost." In the dark, amidst the shelling and gas, they had taken the sensible way out: they had taken cover; and then when it became too light to travel, they laid in their positions.

We who had expected relief suffered in resentment and were forced to stand another day of that hell in misery: I think all of us felt that we would be killed or wounded, before we ever got that relief. However, tonight they came, and so we were relieved from the front line—and we lost no time in leaving. On the 16th, the 2nd Battalion of the 6th Regiment, 2nd Battalion of the 5th, and the 17th and 49th Companies of the 1st Battalion were relieved by the 7th Regiment, 3rd Division; and we started out to the rear.

We hiked back until we came up to a line of trucks, and were loaded for the ride to the rest area. I was lucky and rode with the driver and a lieutenant in the foremost truck, out of the dust of the convoy.

We finally crossed the Marne River, unloaded, and were billeted in the village of Saâcy sur Marne.

6

Idling on the Marne

We are idling in a little town on the Marne. It is not much of a place, but it is nice and quiet. It seems strange to be where it is dangerous and din one day, and quiet and peaceful, the next. The river Marne flows softly by, and it is hard to picture the carnage that exists but a few miles upstream at Château Thierry and Belleau Wood.

Today, they were giving instruction on the Sho-Sho automatic rifle. An officer dismantled and assembled the gun, then asked who would try it. I kept quiet, as I didn't want to be a Sho-Sho gunner; but when he couldn't get a volunteer, I stepped forward, and said that I could.

The officer seemed surprised, but grinned, and said it wasn't hard. I looked the gun over, and then began. As I took it apart, I named the piece and its function, then put it together again, and stepped back into ranks.

The officer looked rather funny at me, and asked where I had learned the gun. I told him that was the first time I had handled it, but also said, that I had been to the Lewis Machine Gun School,[1] and knew the operation of machine guns.

Formation being dismissed, I crawled into the hay at the billet to sleep, but was roused by a runner from company headquarters, who said that I was wanted. I brushed the hay from my tunic, straightened my clothes, and reported in.

As I stood, three or four of the company officers came out, grinned, and presented me with a new Sho-Sho. I told them I didn't want the gun, as I preferred the rifle—but that didn't work; the officers said they didn't have gunners, and I was elected. One thing I gained, though, was relief from all petty details.

The billet we were assigned was a hay loft over cows and horses. It had that peculiar ammoniac odor of a stable that was not kept clean. The hay door, the only means of access or exit, was located immediately over an enormous, well-ordered pile of manure.

The courtyard of the French farm had the home on the right, a high

41

masonry wall in front, and the barns on the left. The back of the court was a maze of fences, farm vehicles, chicken yards, and the accumulation of several hundred years of effort.

The manure pile held the place of honor, and was about 15 feet in width, 40 feet in length, and 5 to 6 feet in height. It constituted the measure of wealth by the French peasants—the larger the pile, the more successful the farmer. We were honored in that our "pile" was the largest in the village.

We made use of the manure pile as a means of exit from our sleeping quarters. A jump from the door landed us in the pile, and a slide down completed the descent, much to the annoyance of our French host. He usually appeared and in a huff waved his arms, and yelled, "*Vous cochon! Vous vache!*"

This seemed to be about the peak of French oaths, for we heard it often: "You pigs! You cows!" It was well that he didn't understand English, for our oaths were more to the point, as we hurled back some choice American cuss words at him, with a definite reference to his ancestry.

At night, the odors nearly overcame us, but worse still were the slimy, cold feet of "Ye old barn rats"; as they ran all over us, trying to get into our iron rations. After the first night, we had to jab our bayonets or trench knives into the rafters and tie the hard tack to them. The rats would stand on our faces, chest, or stomachs, and paw at the food. The next night, and thereafter, we were careful to fasten the food to one side; for when the rats were after the food, a sudden movement by us caused the rats to nip at us.

The Marines are good providers when the regular "slum" doesn't provide either taste or satisfying flavor. Our billet adjoined a chicken coop, and the boys waited in the hay until a hen cackled—then there was a stampede—the race was on—first one there got the egg. A bunch of hungry Marines against an old man—he always lost. He would come stamping out of his kitchen with an old 1870[2] war musket and bellow, "Vous cochon! Vous vache!" But he always lost. He would bring the rifle to his shoulder, but it never blazed, because the egg, Marines, and all evidence of the crime were gone.

The French grindstones were busy from early till late, always a line of Marines waiting in turn; they were putting an edge and point on their bayonet for the work ahead. I have seen German and French bayonets; but of them all, the Marines' bayonets were the sharpest for the job they had to do.

June 24

The company did not drill much at this place; it consisted, instead, of troop or inspection. On the Monday afternoon following a day spent in peace, the bugles frantically sounded, and, as we hurried to fall in, we got the order, "Fall in with heavy marching order in ten minutes."

The bugles were right: we were "going in" again; something was wrong, and there was no time to waste.

As we fell in, the next order was given, "Forward—march!" and we faced an all night march back to the front.

The men didn't say much on that hike; the rests were shorter; we were on a "forced march."

Toward daylight, we were back in support lines in the Bois de Belleau. The men were quiet and wrapped in thought; we were back in that hell again, and for many it was the last time.

7

Belleau Wood Is Ours

June 25

Belleau Wood was no longer the hell I knew when we first came in. The dog-fight for possession had been in our favor, and only a small portion of the northern end of the woods remained in German hands. The shelling had dropped to a spasmodic fire, and we were not too active. Our company was in support during the first part of this stint, and little happened to us. On the 24th and 25th, the 3rd Battalion of the 5th attacked in the northern part of Belleau and drove out, killed, or captured the Germans there. Belleau Wood was ours now, and the Germans were to look at it for the last time.

Late one afternoon, I had a detail in charge of chow supply and gas watch. An old-time Marine colonel came up to battalion P.C. and in a stentorian voice demanded a half-dozen men. The battalion commander answered in like voice, that all his men were busy. Whereupon the colonel roared back that he would get his own men then, and stalked away. As these squabbles were always interesting, I decided to be conveniently occupied with the chow guard when he returned.

Some time after dark he came in with about a dozen men, stopped at battalion P.C., and reported the party was going out in front to gather information. After arrangements were made, and all was cleared, he and the party left at 10 p.m.—and in his stentorian voice announced that they would return with prisoners at 11 p.m.; and he would be "blankety-blanked" if he wanted our outposts to shoot them up.

He was a colonel of Marines about whom there were many tales; the first being, how and where he gained his nickname, "Hiking Hiram."[1] He earned this after hiking a detachment of Marines across one of the Philippine Islands during the Insurrection, through hostile territory.

At eleven o'clock, my sentry on the chow pile yelled, "Put out the smoking lamp!" And when the glow still showed, he said, "---- ----, put that damned smoking lamp out, or I'll put it out for you!" And there was a shower of sparks on the ground, and the lamp was extinguished as the party came up.

"---- ---- good sentry that you have got there," said Hiking Hiram, back with his party—and two prisoners.

The party had gone up to the German lines to the red barn that stood on the hill in front of Torcy, where they jumped a German machine-gun crew on outpost duty. They shot and bayoneted all the crew except two, whom they made prisoners; and then made their way back. The prisoners were the worst scared men I ever saw, and could scarce talk as they were interrogated.

Colonel Hiram soon left with the party and their prisoners. He was commanding a regiment of the 26th Division, the "Yankee," a National Guard outfit from the New England States, which was shortly to relieve us.

One story about Hiking Hiram that was going about tells of the time he took a battalion of Marines on a hike in France. The "hike" was a good one, too; and toward the end when the men were about "done in," two men stepped out of ranks and took pot shots at him. The colonel whirled about and spotted them as they got back into rank. Pulling into their billeting area, he halted the battalion and ordered a sergeant to "get those guys," as he pointed them out. When they were brought before him, he glared at them, looked them over from head to foot, then in turn ripped off their Expert Rifleman's badges, threw them to the ground, stamped on them, and then roared, "Any guys who can't shoot better than that don't deserve those medals. Fall in!—Captains! Dismiss your companies!"

And with that he was off. It was rumored that he wasn't allowed command of Marines at the front because too many of the old-timers had sworn to "get him."

Sergeant Bowness joined our company about this time, a friendly, thoughtful man, who was always trying to help the men. Earlier in the war, he had been a member of the Canadian Army and was a sapper, undermining German positions. He had seen plenty of action, had been wounded, invalided home, and discharged. Now he was back in the mess with the U.S. Marines. He talked freely of his experiences, and a group of us many times lay on the ground and listened to him talk. He gave us many valuable hints on how to make life easier at the front, and we were the better for it.

He got in the habit of awakening me about 3 a.m. to help him make coffee for the men. We managed to find enough charcoal for fires, and soon had a big can of coffee steaming hot by the time the men were aroused. The coffee was a hit with the men, and, by the second day, we also had visitors from other companies in the woods. On the third day, some officer got an inspiration and secured a can of beef, but on opening the can we found that it had spoiled, so we stuck to the coffee.

Throughout these days, we had the usual "good morning" and "good night" rounds of shell-fire from the Germans. They laid it on heavy and tore up things around us but were not too successful on personnel.

We had only German aviators over us during our time in Belleau Wood. It seemed that they had complete coverage of the air. But on this morning, a new note sounded. About 4:00 a.m., three German aircraft appeared, cruising high overhead, when we heard a roar as a buzz saw ripping through a knot, and we dashed to the woods to watch.

From above and behind, two planes in nosedives roared down with bursting machine guns, firing at the three German planes. Two of them burst into flames, and the third streaked for home. We sent up a rousing cheer, as it heralded a new era in the skies, and we could expect some protection from the air. They said it was the "Hat in the Ring" Squadron, an American outfit that had appeared in our vicinity.

One night, three squads of us, under a gunnery sergeant, were loaded down with canteens of water and large condiment cans of beef, and detailed to carry them to that half of our company which was holding the line far to the right flank of the division. I was given the third squad, and told that I was accountable for them.

We had a guide from headquarters, and started out, hiking quickly and quietly through Belleau Wood, south to the Paris-Metz highway. We hiked parallel to the German lines, just behind our outposts, and had to be extra careful not to make any noise, as the Germans were still very nervous and would fire at any sound.

We made this portion of the trip in safety, however, crossed the Paris-Metz highway, and found the rest of the company in a deep trench in the side of a hill. They told us we were lucky in getting to them, as the Germans were only about 100 yards away, were nervous, and would fire at any noise.

We exchanged canteens and issued the meat; and as it was nearly dawn, we needed to return quickly: and with the empty cans, it would be a noisy trip back. We re-crossed the highway, and went on our way.

But the gunnery sergeant was nervous and so took the lead, the guide dropping back with me to the tail end of the column. The guide was angry, because, technically, he was in charge and responsible for the detail; but the "gunny" had pulled rank on him.

Soon the guide became agitated and said the sergeant was going in the wrong direction, and hurried forward to warn him. But the sergeant stubbornly pulled rank again, and disregarded the guide's warning.

We were in an open place cleared of all timber and moving fast, when an outpost stuck his head above ground and whispered a warning that we were almost on the German lines. And the sergeant stampeded, starting on a fast run, the men close on his heels, to the attending clatter of cans and canteens. I remained with the guide and three or four others to let the main bunch get well ahead of us. Then the guide and I picked one of the boots that had fallen in fatigue and carried him between us, following the noisy, stampeding gang ahead.

The Germans opened up on the main bunch with light artillery and pounded the area just behind them. We could hear them and the clanking of cans long after they entered Belleau Wood, the shelling pinpointing their trail through the woods.

We drifted along well to the rear of the holocaust in a safe zone, and finally reached the company area after daylight. The guide and I were plenty sore at the sergeant and both "spouted off" to the lieutenant, who was waiting for us. His reply didn't cool us off any, as all he said was—"Yes, I know all about it; you had better get some sleep."

So I turned in and slept.

8

Shell-Shock

We lived in holes in the ground at the front, just long enough to lie in and wide enough for the body, and from two to three feet in depth. We used these holes to sleep in and in time of artillery fire.

We were fairly safe from most artillery fire, but when a shell burst overhead, the shell fragments rained down, and one was apt to get killed or receive a wound. The shells, for the most part, were high-explosive, and the shell-fragments could make a terrible wound. Shrapnel-filled shells were seldom used in Belleau Wood, as there was little penetrating power through the trees, and the pieces were uselessly "spent."

The Germans used three calibers of artillery on us, the light 77mm, the heavy 210mm, and the Austrian 88mm. Of the three pieces of artillery, the "88" was the worst, for its velocity was nearly equal to sound and the shell reached the target without warning. It was know as the "whiz-bang," and we seldom had time to seek cover from its fire.

Aside from the bursting shells themselves, the pieces or fragments of shell casings that "screamed" in direct from the burst were the worst, and the only protection was the hole in the ground. The pieces that traveled up returned to the ground as spent shell fragments, and these usually did small harm. There was not one of us who wasn't hit countless times by these spent pieces; they stung, were hot, but seldom did we get more than a scratch.

We feared the "210" the most, as the shell was filled with high explosives and had great penetrating power. Its shell would bear down and dig in deep before the explosion, and the effects were disastrous; both from the effect of the explosion, as well as from the pieces. Our holes, for the most part, gave us good protection, except for the direct hit, which usually ended the war for the unfortunate in the hole.

One day, three of us decided to make a real dugout, and dug a hole 7 feet long, by 4 feet wide, by about 2½ feet deep. We scoured the woods and found plenty of trees to cover the hole. As we worked, we noticed a group of officers watching us and a lot of the men, but thought nothing of it. On finishing the covered hole, we crept in, and proceeded to stretch out in comfort.

But our rest was rudely disturbed by the company commander, who immediately moved the company 200 to 300 yards deeper into the wood. We were very bothered by this, as the move seemed deliberate and senseless; and besides this, there was much kidding by the men in the company. They suggested we return and see for ourselves who the new tenants were. So, still smarting over the episode, we returned to the area and discovered that the battalion commander had moved in. With much cussing, we returned to our new location, and mutually agreed that it wasn't worthwhile. And we solemnly hoped that the major would have a "210" shell for a bedmate.

During the daytime, there was little we could do, except keep a sharp lookout for German movements. When in support, we were free to wander about, but we had to stay within the shelter of the woods, so that German eyes or aviators couldn't spot us.

At night, it was a different story. We had details of all kinds, from carrying out the dead killed by shell-fire, or the wounded back to dressing stations, or going to the rear for ammunition and chow; to special out-post duties, as watching for German movements, or to detect gas and give warnings. Toward daylight, we were finished and back in our holes, in readiness for the usual dawn shelling the Germans liked to give us.

Our ration for one day usually consisted of one can of "monkey meat," that is, Argentine or Madagascar horsemeat, and one loaf of French war bread, to be divided among a squad of eight men. The meat was stringy and put up with gristle; it was unpalatable and unsightly. The cans were approximately 4 inches in diameter, and about 2 to 3 inches in height; a fair ration for one man, but decidedly not enough for eight. It was always cold, and took a good bayonet to open the can. I don't know where the term "monkey meat" came from, but supposed the sight of a bunch of men hunched over a can eating the stuff while scratching cooties gave the general appearance of monkeys.

The French bread was tough, with about a one-quarter to one-half inch crust over it. The bottom of the loaf was over one-half inch thick and filled with sawdust and charcoal. The rounded loaf was about 8 inches in diameter and about 4 inches high at the center. It usually took good bayonet work to cut it into eight pieces, and I am sure a bayonet would work better than my teeth in chewing it. I suppose the French could eat the bread with relish, as they had red wine to soak it in, but we had only water—sometimes.

While we were with the French army, that was our meal at the front; while in reserve in French villages, they substituted a "hard-tack" in place of the bread. This was a hard, tough biscuit that defied teeth to bite or break it—again, the bayonet worked better.

The monkey meat and the hardtack were cooked into a slum, but it was even worse to eat, and much more unpalatable. Most of us would take this "mess" in our mess kit, and with our feet in the gutter of the road, look at it, then sadly get up and dump it into the slop pail, and watch the French women fight over it.

We had another daily task, and that was ridding ourselves of "cooties." They were unwelcome "pets," a body louse that plagued us night and day. It inhabited the seams of our underclothing and at the top of our wrapped leggings or puttees. They wrought in us and vexed us continuously, and often left raw lines in our skin. Most of us were hunting these when not engaged in duties

Sergeant Wagner and I found a short cut in this work. We would strip down, and lighting the French match, or "fumette," would pop the cooties by running the seam of our clothing through the flame. It was effective, and we kept them down to a minimum in this way. A word about the "fumette": it was somewhat shorter than a good old U.S.A. match, but it had a thick, heavy head, about three-quarters of an inch long, and the burning sulphur fumes would nearly gag us.

At the end of June our company was in the front lines on the east flank of the northern portion of Belleau Wood. We had little respite from the shelling, both light and heavy caliber, and there were also gas shells to vary the regularity; and they swept us with machine-gun fire low through the trees. Lying in our holes, we would count the duds among the live shells, and it seemed to us that the Germans were getting to the bottom of the pile, for the number of duds was exceedingly high. The gas shell was easy to detect, as the scream of the shell was different from the regular shells; it had a quavering sound, as though the liquid in the shell was continually shifting balance as they went over.

One night, Smith and I had outpost duty at the edge of the woods, with instructions to detect gas, give warning, and rouse the men in the vicinity. Our other assignment was to watch for infiltrating Germans and warn of attack.

Things were going smoothly, except for a high percentage of duds and gas shells. Without warning, Smith became sick, and I chased him from the hole. He alternately retched and relieved himself for some time; and I laughed at his discomfort. He finally crawled back in the hole with me, but had little to say. Then all at once, I, too, was hit with nausea and retching. I immediately jumped for the alarm, an old shell casing, and pounded on it until I had every man on alert around us. By that time, the cry of "Gas!" was being shouted in all sections of the woods. The Germans were pouring "puking gas" into the

8. Shell-Shock 51

woods first; and as men couldn't "puke" with the mask on, they poured in the real stuff.

I was in a bad way, crying my eyes out, and puking, and between-times holding the nose clip on and trying to use the gas mask. Besides all this, I was set up behind my Sho-Sho and ready to shoot any Germans that might appear.

The woods behind me grew very noisy as the men in masks were moved to the edge of the

The steel 75mm shell casing used as a gas alarm. French historian Gilles Lagin uncovered it in the same area Everard's outfit was in reserve. It was the only shell there. The hammer marks are still visible (courtesy Gilles Lagin).

woods, to resist an expected attacka. But it all quieted down, and the men lay with their masks on and rifles at the ready. In the meantime, officers and non-coms sought us out to get the lay of things, and soon left.

The Germans did not attack; the men in our portion of the woods were all right. But farther down the slopes there were a large number of casualties as the gas filtered to the lower areas.

The next night, about fifteen of us were detailed to go to the lower part of the woods to remove men wounded that day. We had just made it to the P.C., when we noticed a heavy machine-gun fire sweeping the woods. An officer crept out of the P.C. and dismissed us, telling us to get back to our holes. The fire was so intense that we had to crawl, and even then it didn't feel safe.

Getting back to our area, it became imperative that we secure cover, and we groped about in the inky blackness for an empty hole; but it seemed they all were filled. Finally, Smith called out that he had found one, and we made our way toward him. He tumbled in first, and as we began to crowd in, we were met by a frantic Smith scrambling back out. It was sometime before I could get the story of what happened, but after I found a hole for us, he told me that there was a dead man in the hole.

The third man with us had also discovered the dead man, and became shell-shocked. He was a raving maniac, and Smith and I spent the night trying to hold him down: the dead man was to be preferred.

At daylight, a lieutenant came to our hole, and wanted to know what the yelling was all about. We got off of the man, as we had him pinned down, and who was still a blubbering hulk, and explained to the lieutenant all that had transpired that night. He immediately called a couple of corpsmen, and we turned him over to them. The man had become quiet by then, and insisted he was all right; nevertheless, he was sent "out," as he would never be any good for front-line duties again.

This was no strange behavior at the front then, for many men broke under the strain of Belleau Wood. Some men would fall on their faces on the ground during heavy shelling, and quiver all over, only to resume their natural behavior after the shelling let up. Such a man was Green, a quiet fellow, likeable, and decent, who in odd moments gave us haircuts. One day, he was cutting my hair, when several large-caliber shells screamed in and burst in the vicinity. He had almost completed clipping my hair to the scalp at the time: he dropped to the ground and lay tense and quivering; only to get up after the shelling was done and continue clipping me. We tried to get him to go to the rear, but he insisted he was all right, and would get over it soon. But we weren't so sure.

Other men would sit and brood, become morose and glum, as though they knew that the next shell would wipe them out. Bob Smith began acting peculiar during heavy shelling, and would whine and complain, and would about drive me "nuts" during these periods. I would curse him and punch and abuse him at these times.

One night, during a particularly heavy shelling, when both light and heavy caliber shells were pouring in on us, I couldn't take it any more; and jumping up from the hole, I exclaimed, "I've had enough! I'd rather get hit, than lie here listening to you!" And I started off through the woods. As I left the hole, Bob scrambled up, too, and grabbing my hand walked with me. We tramped through that portion of Belleau Wood, and through the hell of the bombardment. We didn't talk; we walked, or stumbled, rather, through the woods, until we finally made our way back to our hole, and crawled in for the rest of the night. We had settled our nerves and had gotten a hold of ourselves. Both of us felt better, and were over our panic caused by the shelling.

On the Fourth of July, the Germans gave us an especially heavy shelling. But they soon let up and then dropped in only a few random shots, as though it were the final dying gesture of Belleau Wood.

That night, a new outfit came up, green in the ways of an active front, but welcome nevertheless. They were the 103rd Infantry of the 26th Division. They were National Guard troops from the New England States, who didn't know any better, or who didn't give a damn.

When they came into the woods, they were yelling back and forth, lights flashing, and having a glorious time. As they flashed a light into a hole they would yell, "Hey, down there, is this a latrine, or a dugout?"

General John J. Pershing, awarding the Distinguished Service Cross to officers of the 4th Marine Brigade for actions during the fighting in the Aisne Defense (Belleau Wood). Awardees, left to right: Lt. Col. Logan Feland, CO 5th Marines; Maj. Julius S. Turrill, CO 1st Bn. 5th Marines; 1st Lt. James F. Robertson, 96th Co. 6th Marines. Officer behind Pershing on far left of photograph (in French helmet) is BG James Harbord, USA, CO 4th Marines; officer in front of him with hand to cheek is MG Omar Bundy, USA, CG, 2nd Division, AEF. St. Aulde, France, July 10, 1918 (courtesy SSG Steven C. Girard [Ret.], WWI Marine Corps Archivist/Historian).

We hoped it was a latrine they jumped into; and we quickly got into a long, thin line, and hurried from the woods. We had just made the rear area, when all hell broke out behind us—the Germans had heard all the confusion, and were pounding Belleau Wood with every thing they had.

July 5

We hurried up the road anxious to get away from that place. We hiked till dawn, passing through Coupru to a wood, where, in a cut over a rough piece of land, we received our first hot meal in a long time. We rested there till late afternoon, and hiked farther into the rear area, where we pulled into another wooded area, and bedded down for the night.

July 6

We had not been asleep long, when there was a burst of auto-fire over our heads. Hugging the earth and startled, we grabbed our guns to sell our souls dearly. There was considerable shouting from the direction of a Sho-Sho that had "cut loose," and then there was silence. Soon officers and non-coms moved among us, and checked all guns to see that they were unloaded: it seems that one gunner didn't unload as he came out of the lines and dreamed the Germans were advancing, and so cut loose. Luckily, the bullets all went astray; and before he had a chance to reload, several men piled on him, and disarmed him.

Sleep for most of the men was over for the night. The next day, we moved down into the valley to the village of Crouttes sur Marne for a short stay and a well-deserved rest.

9

The Naked Battalion

Crouttes sur Marne was a quiet little village, nestled on the banks of the Marne River, with high hills beyond. The inhabitants consisted of womenfolk, young and fair, to the elderly, and but a few old men. War was no stranger to them, and the quartering of American Marines in their buildings and barns was accepted with the usual French pathos.

Our group was quartered in the loft of a barn. The one mark of luxury was the staircase and the low window through which they passed the hay. Outside the entrance was a huge wine barrel. It was perhaps 8 to 10 feet in diameter, and about 6 feet high, in which the girls of the village "tramped grapes" when making wine. While we were there, the barrel was empty and dry.

Beyond that was the customary masonry wall with the archway that led to the street. Inside the wall and to the right of our quarters was the house. Just inside the door, we could see the family dinner table. It was marked by numerous bottles of wine, that being the main drink of the peasants of France.

The first day, the battalion was marched to the Marne, where we were issued soap and told to clean up. Diving in, I was busily soaping and scrubbing when I looked up: the sight of a thousand stark-naked men didn't startle me: but the sight of the female population of the town did. I don't think one woman was left in town; they all had brought their laundry with them, and were scattered along the bank pounding clothes. There didn't seem to be anything we could do about it, for they were laughing and joking with the men, and didn't mind our nudeness; so I soaped on, and swam.

There were diving boards along the bank, and we who were more proficient in that art entertained them with many a fancy dive. Finally, coming out of the water, we joined the others on the river's edge in a grand "hunt" for cooties. We picked them from our clothes and squashed them between our thumb nails, until there were no more to be found. There was a re-issue of new underwear, which we donned, and then dressed in our uniforms, feeling clean again. It was the first change of clothes we had had since going to the front lines; and it was a wonderful feeling to us all.

Afterward, the men scattered to whatever fun they could find, some to fish with grenades, others to seek out wine and women, while others yet, to sit and chin.

The grenade fishermen interested me most, so I went to watch. Detonating the grenades in unison, they hurled them into the river, and after the burst beneath the water's surface the fish turned bellies up and lay stunned on the surface. Thereupon a group of swimmers swam out and retrieved them. This went on till some officers appeared and stopped the sport. The men with the fish disappeared, some to "chisel" grease from the galley force, and others to forage for vegetables in the French gardens; and then proceeded to prepare a grand feast.

I went back to town to learn that an empty chateau had been located where there was a well-supplied wine cellar. So I grabbed my canteen to get in on that "sport." As I hurried down the street, I met Wells, who told me that M.P.'s were corralling the men. Wells had a full canteen with him and invited me to share it, and, returning to his billet, we lay in the hay and drank it down.

I then returned to my billet, where I joined another group which was arguing with a sergeant. It seems that this sergeant was trying to impress the boots with his "years" of service; so I dared him to show us his dog tags, which gave his enlistment date and which we all wore about our necks. He was reluctant, but as the others backed me up, he showed the tag: enlisted September '17. I showed him mine: June '17. So after telling him to forget about calling anybody a boot in the future, we had a good laugh at ourselves: boots, yes, in period of service; but all were veterans of war and could rightly call ourselves Marines. And the sergeant became a good friend of mine after that.

The 5th Regiment came to France with two-thirds of its personnel having more than a year's service; and by the time Belleau Wood battle began, they had over two years service. Thus it was the most fortunate regiment in France. But by the time the battle was over, most of the old-timers were casualties, and the boot had taken over their duty of maintaining the reputation of the United States Marine Corps.

10

Hell's Angels

One fellow in our billet soon became the favorite; this was Jimmie Duke,[1] a young replacement, who was good-natured and full of fun. We had many a laugh with Jimmie, and he soon had us forgetting all about the hell of Belleau Wood.

We also had a gunnery sergeant, whom the men didn't like—the same which led us into trouble at Belleau Wood. And he appropriated the space in front of the hay door which shut off our much needed air. That night, ignoring the sarcastic remarks of the men in the hay, he sprawled in front of the door. But after he was asleep, two or three of the men, who had been "seeing the town," came stumbling up the stairs. One, who was somewhat drunker than the others, had to relive himself, and straddling the sergeant's body, proceeded to make water. The unfortunate sergeant received most of it, and woke up roaring; but by the time he got his bearings, others had grabbed the drunken man and hid him in the darkened loft. The sergeant, spluttering and muttering threats, was soon drowned out by the howling of the men, and quickly stamped out into the night. We were not troubled by the fact that he sought quarters elsewhere.

The next day was a repetition of the first. We loafed, swam, and idled, and most of us kept out of trouble. A few sought "wine and women," but mostly found wine. And they showed up for roll call the third morning, visibly showing the effects. They had ended their "binge" with a free-for-all brawl, and showed up with swollen noses, blackened eyes, and cut and swollen lips. One had two beautiful shiners, his eyes entirely swollen shut. The captain looked over the wrecked contingent, and showed them no mercy: they got all the "police" duties for the day.

That day, we were marched to the top of the hill, picks and shovels the weapons of the day, and put to work digging trenches in the brow of the hill. We didn't hurt ourselves digging; "soldiering" most of the time; but even so, the trenches gradually took form. As we dug, we covered the exposed areas with grass and weeds to "fool" the Boche aviators. They had us continue the trench the next day, but this was mainly to keep us out of trouble.

Then came the day when German artillery fired upon a nearby captive balloon[2] and tried to force it down. It floated serenely over our heads, and when fired upon would be quickly cabled down; only to reappear shortly after in a new position: although the Germans filled the sky with their bursting shells, they were unable to hit it.

That evening, before dark, when we were in town having a short arms inspection and checkup, a German plane appeared. It was paralleling the river and flying low. Directly behind it came four French planes, and we expected the "kill" to occur at any moment.

When the German was directly overhead, about 1,500 feet high, he fired a burst of bullets to warm his guns. Then, in a sharp Immelman turn, he headed straight for the balloon. All four of the French planes followed the maneuver, and shortly all five were bearing down on the balloon.

The balloon company was caught unawares. The first Boche plane fired into the balloon; the second continued and also fired into the balloon: and then we were aware of the Boche deception. All five of the aviators were Germans, four of them in captured French planes. They had fooled the Allied artillery all along the lines, and attacking the balloon had shown their true colors.

The men in the balloon were unaware of the trickery and had stayed at their post observing the German rear areas; but with the approach of the planes were seen frantically heaving their gear over the side of the basket.

The first observer scrambled out of the basket and his parachute immediately opened, and as he fell away from the balloon the third plane fired on him. We could see his body twisting and writhing, as though to ward off the bullets. As the third plane cleared from the scene, the fourth came up, and continued to fire on the hapless, drifting man.

All the while, we wondered what had happened to the second observer[3] in the balloon. Then at last he appeared, throwing things from the basket and tumbling out after them. The balloon was red throughout with flame, and we doubted that he would make it; surely the burning balloon would fall on him.

He twisted and turned, desperately trying to slip his parachute to one side and away from the fiery mass above him—only to meet the machinegun fire from the fifth plane. The plane dived low beneath the balloon, and whirling in space came back for another flying run at the parachutist.

By that time, the balloon was a falling, seething mass in the sky, and the German aviator poured his fire into the hapless chutist and then bore upward in the air, and in a great turn followed his comrades away and to safety.

By now, nothing remained of the balloon but a column of black smoke rising into the sky. The men about me were stunned at the senseless shooting of the observers, and they raved and cursed the Germans.

But they were soon to wreak their vengeance on them. We had two incidents now that foretold our future; the short-arms inspection, and the clearing of observers from the sky. We didn't want to believe the omen; we still wanted and wished for the aim of all "doughboys" in France: a liberty in Paris.

11

The Big Parade

July 15

That night, I awoke to a mighty explosion, and sitting up in the hay, another blast shook the building. And there were other explosions in the lower part of town and near the river.

Soon the street was filled with men, women, and children running to the shelter at the upper end of town. Most of the men in our billet also scrambled off to the retreat. But a few of us decided we could as well die in one place, as another, and so lay back down to sleep.

The Germans were apparently attempting to blow up the railroad bridge, and explosion after explosion thundered through the night and into the early morn. They were using 10-inch shells, and the shorts caught the town. One such shell tore out the corner of a billet behind ours, but that was the total amount of damage; not one of the men in the billet was hurt. All shells fell short of the target; but the sight of shells plunging into the river erupting in geysers of water was long remembered.

July 16

The next night, I had the eleven o'clock to one a.m. gas watch in the town. It was a dark night, quiet, and lonely. And then I heard the clattering clomp of boots running down the street toward me. I challenged the runner, and as he stopped he gasped, "We're pulling out! Rouse your officers and men; have them stand by for orders." And he turned and went back the way he had come.

I immediately rustled up the Sergeant of the Guard, who quickly went on the run for the officers. By the time I returned to my billet, the street was already filling with men. They were ready to move, with full packs and heavy marching orders.

11. The Big Parade

By one in the morning, we were assembled in the middle of the main street of town. The men were quiet, and the only noise, the shuffling of many feet. And we stood by at rest in ranks.

Finally, we were told to sleep in the streets: no one was to leave the area without permission. Most of us needed the rest, and we lay down to get what sleep we could. But the street is a hard bed.

About 3:30 a.m. the men were called to attention and told the galleys would feed us; that we should eat all we could, as they didn't know when or where we would see our galleys again. It sounded ominous, and the men quickly pulled out their mess gear and fell in line for chow.

It was monkey meat again and French hardtack. It was made into a stew, but that did not add to its flavor. We ate the mess silently, cleaned up our gear, and fell into ranks again. Soon the galleys and mess crew drew out, pulled by the mules: and we would not see them again until the evening of the 19th.

The sun rose and the town began another day: but we still stood in line. We remained in the center of the street until mid-morning, when we were marched out of town to the crossroad. But here we were given orders to fall out and stand by.

The entire Marine Brigade was assembling. The 2nd and 3rd Battalions of the 5th Regiment lay in the fields in adjacent towns; and the 6th Marines were forming downriver. The Brigade headquarters company filed by, followed by the wagon train of the brigade. The wagon train was unique, in that most of the wagons, in addition to their drivers, also had an animal, or mascot, on the seat. There was the famous anteater that had been captured in the Haitian jungles and tamed, and there were others of interest, too; but the scene of the Marine Brigade girding for battle was a memorable sight.

Late in the afternoon, we were formed in ranks and marched along the river, with the 2nd and 3rd Battalions following. Only then did we notice the continuous roar of artillery to the east. It seemed heavy, and it was concentrated. The Germans were making their last bid to finish the war: good bye to that leave in Paris: were we to go in and stop the Germans there, too? or, were we going to counter attack? And if so, where?

The men were silent as we marched, and all looked over their left shoulder; the battle for Rheims and the Champagne country was their only interest now.

We plodded on, and as we turned a corner in the road, there stretched out as far as we could see were camions lined up on the right of the road: we were needed somewhere fast.

Shortly we were loaded, 50 men to the truck, the seats so close we could just get our legs in, our knees interlaced. We held our rifles between our knees and our packs on our laps, back-to-back and face-to-face; we were surely packed in like sardines.

We started down river, and the men were all anxious as we approached Mary. If we kept on south or west, it surely was for our long-needed rest and leave; if to the east, then….

We turned east. We crossed the Marne and filed through Saâcy sur Marne. You could cut the silence as the men sunk into a stupor. We were going to help at Rheims, stop the Boche, and beat him back.

But now we turned to the right, away from Rheims and the fearful cannonade. And again we turned to the right—and to the *west*. There was no war in that direction, and the men took heart: that leave in Paris was a possibility yet. And the men broke into the tune of "Mademoiselle from Armentières" and its many apt verses.

Around mid-night, we pulled into Meaux, and the men were ordered to be quiet. The only sign of life in the town were two priests, and even they seemed foreboding. The new men remembered Meaux as the derailing place on our way to Belleau Wood. They likewise remembered that north meant trouble for us and west a sure rest and a leave in Paris.

The camions slowed to a walk, and we could see the trucks ahead turn *north*; and as we made the turn, all thoughts of that leave in Paris dissolved. The men became resigned to their fate; and, weary, we settled down to try and get some sleep.

But we slept little. The camions were seemingly without springs and the drivers missed no holes and drove hurriedly, and we in the back were crowded and jostled in bruising jerks. With no lights, and the dust remaining suspended over the road, some trucks crashed into one another, and others went into roadside ditches. But our driver got us through all right.

Our drivers were from the Malay Peninsula and spoke no English, which was just as well, especially for our driver, for the comments from his passengers were anything but complimentary. His ancestry and the ancestry of his ancestors, together with the remarks on his driving ability, seemed to be the main topic.

The men became surly and other remarks filled the air: "Get your damned elbows out of my ribs"; or, "---- ---- ---- keep your rifle out of my face, you ---- ---- ": "You son-of-a bitch, sit still and quit crowding; do you need the whole truck?" and many other vital remarks. It was well that we were jammed in as tightly as we were, for otherwise there surely would have been many fights.

At last, the gray of morning came, and soon it was light; still we plowed

11. The Big Parade 63

northward through the woods and hamlets which lay in our path. When we reached Crépy en Valois, the trucks were halted at road blocks. Parts of the town lay in heaps of smoking rubble. The windows, those that were intact, of some two and three-story buildings, were heavily crisscrossed with tape to preserve them from the heavy concussion of shell-fire. And near at hand we could see enormous craters, any of them large enough to swallow a fair-size house. Doughboys appeared and told us German aviators had just bombed the city, but fortunately most bursts had landed astray in the fields.

Then a trio of soldiers came along the line of trucks yelling, "Tim Keville—is Tim in there?" We hailed them, as Tim was in our truck. As they

Everard's honors and medals. Note bullet below Indian head that was removed from his body on October 10, 1918. The Campaign Clasps on the World War 1 Victory Medal are Aisne, Aisne-Marne, St. Mihiel, Meuse-Argonne, and Defensive Sector. The Marine Good Conduct Medal is award with the rifle motif. There is also a 2nd Division AEF Association Medal, VFW Association Medal, a full-size and miniature French Fourragère, World War I Marine Corps Marksmanship Medal (courtesy Robert G. Bullis).

hurried over, we searched for Tim; but as we looked we wondered when and where we had lost him.

The soldiers were disappointed on reaching us and about to turn away, when a struggle at our feet disturbed us and Tim's head appeared. He was in an ugly mood and cussing us all for disturbing him—when he looked over the side of the truck and straight into the face of his brother. With a yell, he was out of the truck and dancing with his arms about his brother's neck. It had been well over a year since he had seen him, but a chance occurrence had brought them face to face.

The trucks were beginning to move again, so we reached out and lifted Tim back into the truck, with Tim yelling out information at his fast-fading brother. We were all glad that one man had got to see someone who was close to him.

I kept thinking of Tim's prediction that he would last out the war, but expected a bale of hay would fall on him and break his neck when he landed at Hoboken: would he be on his feet at the end of the "show" we were going into?

We soon left Crépy en Valois far in our rear, and turning northeast, we rode toward the scene of our next battle.

Part II: Soissons

12

The Pick of French and U.S. Troops

Our road now was through the great Fôret de Villers Cotterêts, also known as the Fôret de Retz. Toward evening, we debussed in a clearing, for the camions could travel no farther, and the men were started hiking up the Paris-Maubeuge road. But Womack and I jumped the detail and sat down to eat a box of hardtack: a court martial looked better to us than hiking on an empty stomach.

After we finished, we climbed up onto a French forage cart going in our direction, and after passing by countless troops, we caught up with our own company and hallooed the men. Most of the guys waved back and made ribald remarks; but a few gave us resentful glances, angered at our traveling in ease.

To spite them, we decided to keep aboard, and rode on ahead. At a crossroad, we jumped off the cart, waved to the French driver, and sat down to await the company. When they arrived, we rejoined them, fresh and ready for whatever may come. One thing was apparent: the men were all-in, surly, and touchy: and that boded ill to anyone who crossed them.

We topped the grade in the road, and beyond could see the stretched-out lines of marching men. The road was crowded with war vehicles of all types, and light and heavy artillery, and light and heavy tanks were crashing through the brush and trees to the right of the road.

At another crossroads, most of the vehicles and troops turned to the right, and we were halted for the customary ten minutes rest. While resting, I noticed two of our men were having a mouth-fight, which ended in one knocking the other flat to the road. The winner, a sergeant, promptly turned on his heels, and stalked away.

The other lay briefly, then rose to his feet muttering and cursing, and picking up his rifle he turned to go into the woods. Several men nearby quickly yelled a warning at the sergeant, for Giles was going to kill him. The sergeant, a broad and powerful man, turned, drew out his .45, and, roaring, swaggered back up the road to Giles. And Giles, paralyzed with fear, just stood frozen in his tracks. The sergeant rammed the .45 into his guts, and we fully expected to hear the roar of the gun; but he shifted the .45 to his left hand, and hit him on the chin with his right: then, turning, he again stalked off down the road. Giles dropped face downwards, and lay still: he was out cold.

A minute later, the company was formed, and we resumed our march. Giles lay as he had fallen, no man having any sympathy for him. That was the last any of us saw him, or heard anything about him; he just disappeared.

We marched till late in the evening, and then we turned off the road to rest. Word was passed that men would be sent for water. Corporal McAulliff immediately called my name, and told me that now he would "get even" for my earlier ride in the wagon.

I told him to "go to hell," that I was exempt from those details.

He dispatched another for the water, and hung about muttering, and finally said, "I'll show you who is boss around here."

I jumped up and said, "All right, come on!" But he insisted on going deeper in the woods away from the men. I followed him, and stripped off my gear, blouse, and shirt. Now McAuliff wanted to talk it over; but I was eager to go.

Just then a couple of officers, noncoms, and a bunch of the fellows rushed in. We were ordered to put our blouses back on; and one of the officers asked me what it was all about. I told him what I had said, and why; whereon he read the riot act to McAuliff, and repeated that auto gunners were exempt from details on the march due to the load that they carried. McAuliff, red in the face, and still resentful, strode off, but the look he gave me in passing told me to watch my step.

A few minutes later, there was a check made on our iron rations; those with any missing would receive a court-martial: and I, of course, was short, along with several others. We were reissued more, but were put on the list to be court-martialed. But at that stage, before a battle, it was not of any worry to us.

At this stop, we were given information pertaining to the attack. But it was meager, and left us in doubt. All we knew, really, was that we were going to make a major attack. The Germans were making their bid on the eastern flank of the Château Thierry bulge, and we would hit them from the western end, drive south and east and close and cut off that bulge.

Three divisions had been selected, the pick of French and U.S. troops. The French First Moroccan Division had been selected to take the lead; the

12. The Pick of French and U.S. Troops

First U.S. Division was to flank them on their left; and the Second U.S. Division was to carry the right flank.

Of the First Moroccan's we had little information, other than they were from Africa. It included troops from the famous Foreign Legion, a tough, hard-fighting group, and the famous Manga's Butchers, an all-black unit of Senegalese. They were reputed to prefer the knife or bayonet to do their butchering; and who usually took a souvenir from their kill, either an ear, a finger, or in many cases, a testicle. And, too, there were the white troops, Algerians, with a reputation as famous as the others. We were to be in company with battle tried and tested units, and we knew that the battle would be tough.

Soon we were in ranks and marching ahead. The road was jammed with trucks, forage wagons, and light and heavy artillery. There were three separate lines of vehicles, all going in the one direction. Two single lines of men made their way forward on the right, one on the shoulder of the road, and the other, in the ditch; and there were similar lines on the left of the road.

As it became dark, each man had to hold on to the pack of the man in front, in order to maintain contact and to avoid separation. Both light and heavy tanks were wallowing in the woods to our right; they were invisible to us, but we could hear their clanking and the crash of heavy trees as they forced their way through.

While marching in the darkness, it began to rain; a regular cloud burst, with bright flashes of lightning, followed by rolling booms of thunder. We wished that the makers of the slickers we wore were there to suffer in our places, for the slickers absorbed the rain, rather than shed it, and the cold streams of water trickled down our necks and waists and miserably down our puttied legs.

The road became a quagmire of mud, and the boots I was wearing worked up and down and wore my heels into raw blisters. There was no getting away from the pull of the mud on our boots; or the misery.

Men continually bumped into the business end of mules, and the kick would send them crashing into the ditch, with broken legs and other injuries. Several trucks slid into the ditch, swiping their quota of marching men with them.

The lightning flashed incessantly, and several trees in the immediate area were shivered by the bolts, the tops cascading down on the men. Finally the rain let up, making it better hiking, although the mud still pulled on our feet.

In addition to the physical trials that the men endured, there was also the fear of a gas attack from the Hun. Over 70,000 men were wallowing through the forest on the few roads and tracks that night, wet and tired; and gas, especially mustard, would have been deadly. What would happen? Mustard would hang low in the air, and not disseminate readily; and the gas would attack and penetrate all wet areas of the body, as well as the lungs. Well, it was not nice to think of, and with that in mind, we plodded on.

13

Hesitant to Kill

July 18

We finally passed all vehicular traffic, as they had advanced as far as they dared, and the road opened up to us. There also was sufficient light now to maintain contact without holding on to the pack ahead, so making our march easier. And there was only a single file of men; the others had turned off into the woods and at various crossroads, to get to their jump off place.

We swung off the road to the left and made combat packs; that is, we jettisoned all except personal items, iron rations, and mess gear; and were on our way again.

We were marching on a down grade when a French outpost, his head sticking out of a hole in the road, stopped our advance. The German line was about a hundred yards ahead, and we were stumbling into them. We backtracked to find a trail leading to the left, and took it.

A Marine major rode up on horseback, and yelling at us to "double time," also ordered each man to grab two bandoliers of ammunition as we passed the "dump" ahead. We started running, grabbed the two bandoliers thrust at us, and slung them across our shoulders.

It was light enough to see now, and as I ran I looked over my shoulder, and I was astonished at what I saw: of the sixty or so men in our platoon, only about twenty were present. I turned toward Lt. Link running at my side, and asked what had happened to the others. And he told me that they had either been injured on the way up or had fallen out through fatigue; that the battalion was reduced to about 300 men. I remarked that it was hell to hit the Germans with so few men. And he grinned as he replied, "It sure is."

As we ran on, the barrage began. Thousands of shells split the air just overhead, and there was a tremendous roar. It sounded as if we were under a large viaduct and numerous trains were thundering overhead. It was so stupendous, that we could not think, and our heads felt as though they were in a vacuum. And the tops of many trees came crashing down, blasted by the shells.

It was 4:35 a.m., and we came to a cross-road, and our track ended. I was fourth man in line, and as we jumped up a bank, three feet, or so, and into the woods; I heard the lieutenant yell—"Get through the first line; let the rear troops mop up."

And we were met by a withering fire. Rifles ahead spat blue flame, and bullets whistled overhead. Then, advancing, we came upon a large trench, and as I jumped to clear it, I distinctly saw huddled forms in the bottom, their rifles spitting fire in our faces.

We were behind the front lines now, and as I turned to the left to form skirmishers, I heard my name called. It was Lieutenant Corbett, and he was calling others, as well. There were Sergeants Perkins and Gavin, Private Jimmie Duke, a rifleman, and Bob Smith and I; and we quickly gathered about the lieutenant. He told us that we would act as a liaison detail, and our mission was to make contact with the French forces, and to wipe out any infiltrating enemy group.

We turned left, and spread out, Sergeant Perkins guiding on the company, and Sergeant Gavin guiding on Perkins: then I came with my loader, Bob Smith, and Jimmie Duke, to protect me: and then Lieutenant Corbett to my left, guiding on me.

We were spread over about three hundred yards, and we proceeded forward, passing through a German area of dugouts. We saw shaving gear and mirrors hung on the trees, and uneaten food abandoned, and tunics and other gear lying about: we had gotten into their rear area in time to disrupt their morning chores.

Several bullets whistled by, coming from our rear. We turned to meet this threat and saw Gunnery Sergeant Nice blazing at us. We called Perkins and Gavin to disarm him, and went on.

Then I saw Jimmie Duke suddenly sit down; and before I could yell at him, the air about Smith and I was singing with bullets. Twigs and small stones showered us, but neither of us was hit. It was a Maxim gun, and close, and they had us within their cone of fire.

I yelled at Smith to take cover behind a large fallen tree about a dozen feet away, and dived to get down in its protection, too. I could hear the chattering of the gun, and the bullets still plowed all around us and into the tree.

It was dim in the forest, a dull grayish early morning light, and as I tried to locate the gun, another burst drove me to the ground. With my face in the dirt, I noticed the bullets were cutting in from above and that several had hit

13. Hesitant to Kill

the ground ahead of my helmet and was bouncing dirt into my face. I raised my head and looked up, and saw the flame of machine gun fire in the foliage of a large tree directly ahead, and about 80 to 100 feet away.

Quickly putting the Sho-Sho to my shoulder, I ripped out a clip of bullets directly into the tree top. Yelling at Smith for another clip, I took it and inserted it in the gun—when I heard a bullet whip into Smith.[1] By its sound and wicked thud, I knew he was hit hard: "Bullis, help me, I'm hit."

I yelled back at him, "I've got to get that gun," and stood up and fired from the shoulder directly into the tree. My gun spun me around, but I held the muzzle on the target. All fire from the tree ceased; I could see neither gun nor the men because of the foliage; but I knew that I had been the victor.

Gavin yelled at me to quit firing, thinking my gun would attract more fire. I yelled back that I was firing on a German machine gun. Turning back to help Smith, I found him gone, and that he had carried off all my ammunition.

I then ran over to help Jimmie. He was sitting, propped up by his right arm, and both Gavin and Perkins were with him. I quickly told them what had happened. Then, with Smith and Duke wounded, and that I was out of ammunition for the auto-rifle, I told them I would take Jimmie's rifle and bayonet and go on ahead. And saying "So long" to Jimmie, I grabbed his rifle, and was off.

After jumping from tree to tree, I hadn't moved far when I spotted a German officer a hundred feet ahead of me. He was aiming his Lugar, sheltered behind a tree. I took careful aim and squeezed off my shot at the light spot on the side of his face below his helmet. He jerked his head back and quickly jumped out of sight among the trees. I cursed and looked at the rifle sights: they were set four points right windage. I corrected the sight and wondered why Jimmie would go into battle without checking his weapon.

I moved ahead another twenty-five feet, or so, and a German jumped up ahead of me and ran to my left. I was startled but quickly brought the rifle to my shoulder. He was only twenty-five feet away, but for some reason I did not kill him. I ran after him, instead. He looked funny to me, hunched over running with the large square beaver pack on his back.

I closed to about ten feet, when he jumped into a covered dugout. I glanced around and took a position at the opening to the dugout, and yelled, "Komm her aus, händen hohe." I repeated these two or three times in my best German. And he appeared in the opening, a very scared German.

But I was too eager and I lunged half way down the ramp with the bayonet ready, and he scrambled back out of sight. I backed out of the hole quickly, and yelled again. And he reappeared, his hands over his head, visibly trembling. Without waiting, I lunged into the hole and thrust my bayonet at him. I hit him in the chest, held my bayonet there, and slowly backed out of the hole; and he compliantly followed.

I yelled again at him, asking, "Wie viele mehr auf da?"

"Nein," neun," or, "ein," I didn't know which he said.

Then another Marine appeared from the 2nd Battalion, which was just getting into action, and said, "I'll get them," and rushed down into the hole. He reappeared with a badly wounded German, grinned, and took off.

I immediately began to strip them of their equipment. I took a few souvenirs from the prisoner I had taken, and was about to take his watch, which was at the end of a chain in a large weatherproof case, when he said, "Nein, nein." So I dropped it, the watch swinging from the chain.

Then I noticed both Germans panic, and I whirled quickly, bringing my rifle to the ready: a huge Senegal soldier was rushing me, his bayonet thrust at my neck. I parried the blow to the right, and slammed him back into a tree with my bayonet at his chest. The Senegals are wicked fighters, and apparently some of them abandon their rifle, to fight with the bayonet. At any rate, this one did. And it would also seem that some did not care who they killed; for his bayonet was aimed at *my* back; and if I hadn't seen the prisoners panic, there would have been three more killed in this war.

The Senegal grinned and dropped his bayonet. And I stepped back and dropped my guard, with the French soldier on my left front, and the two Germans on my right front. While I was getting my bearings, the Senegal made a leap, jerked the watch and chain from off the German, turned, and darted away. I was angry, took a couple of steps, drew a bead on him, but decided not to fire, and let him go.

I prodded the Germans with my bayonet to get them started back. The wounded German objected and showed me his wound. I said that was "schrecklich," but we would have to get out of there.

Another Marine running past yelled, "Schrecklich, hell; kill the son-of-a-bitch." But I didn't follow his suggestion.

On the way back, I had to jab the un-wounded man three or four times in the seat to make him go in the right direction. We were near enough to the main German force that he apparently tried to circle back to where the situation would be reversed.

Soon we passed through about thirty Senegalese, who lay where they had been wounded, and their eyes followed us through. I am sure that if they were not as seriously wounded as they were, we would have been killed. A couple of first aid men were working on them, but as tense as I was, I was relieved to get past the group.

13. Hesitant to Kill

When we arrived at the "jump off" place, a group of French soldiers were standing there, and one of them came over and jabbered at me and looked as if he wanted to "kiss" me; but I brushed him off. I then noticed a Marine running back to get into the fight, his right leg bandaged from a wound; and as I thought it more fitting that he take the prisoners back than I, I turned them over to him and started back myself.

14

Sniper's Duel

I joined up with a grizzled old first sergeant and seven other men. On my first trip, we were outside and to the left of the 2nd Division. The main fight had been to the right, and all I heard of that was the roar of Maxim guns, the crack of Springfields, and the yells of the men. The yells were blood curdling, and there must have been many bayonet fights, all going on in our favor.

The sergeant led us through this area, but here we did no fighting. Then we entered an area that was heavily diffused with mustard gas. It was still dim in the forest and we felt at a disadvantage with the masks on. So, finally, fearing German bayonets, we pulled the masks off and hurried out of there.

When we emerged clear of the forest, we quickly jumped back behind the trees: a German battery was set beyond us in a wheat field about 150 yards away. We could not see any of the men, but after talking it over, we decided to rush them.

We spread out, and, stooping low, we dashed through the wheat for the position. We stormed into the gun emplacements ready to work with the bayonet, only to find them deserted, the guns and equipment abandoned.

Passing by a German trench, I noticed two belts with Lugar pistols, field glasses, and canteens. I grabbed one belt, and tossed the other to a comrade. I stuck the Lugar in my breast pocket, hooked the field glasses to my belt, and drank from the canteen. It was good; coffee mixed with rum, and the result probably made me over courageous for the next half hour.

As we struck off through the wheat, we were startled at seeing a German column descending the hill on our left, marching four abreast. We scrambled back to cover and wondered how eight men and a sergeant could stand off a column of the German army. We wondered, too, why they were in a column: why weren't they in skirmish formation? But as they neared, we observed a horseman off-side: he was French, and so other Frenchmen in escort: and now we knew; the Germans were prisoners, all with visible wounds, and were being led to the rear for aid.

14. Sniper's Duel

Going on and arriving at the crest of a hill, we observed a fight below, with the chatter of Maxim guns and the cracking of rifles. The enemy position was a walled farm on our right, across a highway, and we were on the flank.

We decided to join the attack, but at that moment were startled by a yell from behind; and, whirling, we found we were in the sights of a Senegalese machine gun battery sheltered in a copse of trees and brush, about to fire on the farm. We scrambled out of their way, and waited while they tore up the place.

Then we hear the gallop of horses, and a brigadier general and his staff ride up. The general was looking for some colonel or other, but I told him there were no officers here; that this was the front line, and that he should get back, before a machine gun opened up on them. He grinned, wheeled around, and was off to the rear area again: in luck, for the Germans had been busy at that moment and had failed to see them.

The German lines had ceased to exist. What remained were strong points, such as in farm houses or buildings, or scattered machine guns, here and there, employed in small patches of woods and throughout the wheat. The troops appeared to be a mixture of "old" men, forty to fifty, and young boys, fifteen to seventeen years of age; which certainly were not experienced. But in some places, however, we did encounter lines of dug-in troops, where we found the going tougher.

As we made a dash for the farm, we saw another detachment of Marines getting up from the wheat farther to our right, also closing in on the farm. They made it there first, and from the grenade bursts we knew that things were going all right. We arrived at the entrance to the farm, just as a couple of Marines with about a dozen German prisoners came out. The Marines grinned, and said the others were searching the building for more.

Since we knew by now that we were in the French zone of attack, we cut nearly 90 degrees to the right to get back into our own zone. We didn't know that there was a right bend in the division's line of attack, the attack had developed too fast to give us this information; with the result that it turned into many separate endeavors, each going in separate directions.

Part of our company had proceeded straight ahead into the French zone, and took Chaudon. This town was on the left of the French zone and in the path of the 1st U.S. Division. Other parts were scattered throughout units of the 9th Infantry, who likewise failed to make the turn, and were scattered in the wheat. What a grand mix-up; due in part to their failure to make attack-orders clear; to advise the men what was wanted; and also, the denseness of the forest, in which no one could keep liaison. In spite of all this, the attack was going ahead with success. Where we were, we didn't know; but what we did know was that we were too far to the left and north of the 2nd Division, and had to get out fast.

We didn't like that they were in too close a formation, and had a "goofy" sergeant in charge of the end platoon. He was striding up and down behind the men, waving his .45, and threatening them if they got out of position. He came to the left, and ordered us to get into line, but we all swung our rifles on him and told him to go to hell: and the first sergeant really told him off. He at once found more of interest to the right of his platoon. And we took a slant away from the crazy sergeant and his men.

Next, we observed a suicide artillery battery behind us: that was something new, artillery at the front line. And in the distance, a town, and espied a long line of slow-moving German trucks, too far for us to fire on. We quickly signaled the battery, and a lieutenant dashed up, and we pointed out the target. The lieutenant jumped from his horse, and took a minute's time looking them over with his binoculars; then turned and waved the battery up. With this, we stopped to watch.

The battery consisted of four guns drawn by horses, which galloped up, wheeled, and dropped their guns, all pointing at the enemy. While the artillerymen lined up their guns, the horsemen spurred their horses a short distance away, dropped the ammunition carts, and then dashed off to cover. This all happened very quickly and in systematic order.

The first shot blossomed out dead over the target: and then the guns cut loose as one, the shells bursting over the convoy, which caused pandemonium in the German column. We cheered the battery and their excellent work; and the 15th Field Artillery detail continued to pour in the shots.

Then up dashed the horses, the ammunition caissons hooked on again, and the guns, and as quickly as they came they vanished away, with a round of cheers. They disappeared into a woody clump far behind; and we, too, made away, to avoid the counter-fire, that would come too late.

We advanced down a ravine, and witnessed the doughboys on our right capture a battery of heavy howitzers. It was a short fight; and the Germans attempted to save their guns by hooking horses to two of them, but the doughboys swept over them.

Later, we came to the place and viewed the scene. There were four 210mm howitzers, and two of them had shells in the guns. I saw two dead, one, a doughboy, and the other, a German officer. There were plenty of supplies, including barrels of sauerkraut, and an ample supply of "kriegsbrot."

As we left the ravine, we ran into a Maxim gun. The gun was about a hundred yards away, at the head of a short draw gaping on the ravine. It opened fire on us as we crossed the draw; and although the gunner had us under direct fire, he failed to hit any of us. The bullets whined all around and the air was warmed by the bullets. It was so close, without hitting any of us, that we had to laugh. The only answer was that the Germans had a bad case of nerves, and that inexperienced men were manning the guns.

We dashed up the hill into the wheat again, and stumbled on a remnant of the 9th Infantry, about thirty men, who told us there was nothing ahead but Germans. We could see the tops of buildings in another ravine to our right, which was the town of Vierzy, and we had heard that mentioned as our objective; and that it was scheduled to be taken at 4:30. We argued with the doughboys for a while, that we should advance toward it; but they refused to move. Finally, the first sergeant said, "Let's go," and we started off in a nine man wave.

We soon emerged from the wheat onto a bare field, and we were immediately caught in a three-way cross-fire; and two of the men were wounded as we sprung for shelter. I looked for a shell-hole, found one a short distance away, and dove for it—with two of the fellows piling in on top of me, bullets kicking up the dirt all around us. It was my hole; at least I was on the bottom; and after some scurrying, the other two men found holes nearby, and every one was happy.

Our next move was to locate the rest of the men, and by calling back and forth we soon located them on our left, all in shell holes, and with only the two wounded.

We were pinned down, and every time we rose up a burst of rifle and machine-gun fire drove us back down. By trial, we found that we were safe with our heads protruding; but when we rose up, all hell broke out. We searched the fields ahead and on our left, but could find no signs of machine guns or riflemen. They were in good hiding; and nor could we detect the direction by the spurts of dust. It looked as if we would be held in our positions until dark.

On our right front at a range of 1,000 to 1,200 yards, we could see a trench filled with the beggars; they were digging in like men in a panic, and we had a straight view down the length of the trench. Every once in a while, a runner would leave the trench and run to the rear. We decided to make it interesting for the messengers; and calling back and forth, we set our sights from 900 to 1,200 yards, each man raising the sight 40 yards. We decided on two points to fire: one a field corner, the second a spot midway to the woods. We would all fire when he got to the first spot; and if he was on his feet, we would then fire at the second spot and then fire at will until he reached the woods.

Soon a runner left the trench, and, as planned, we waited till he reached the corner of the field: and then fired as one. The man fell, and lay still. We cheered: and then he arose, and ran hard for his goal.

When he arrived at the second point, we fired again, and saw him take evasive actions. He zigzagged, faltered, then ran ahead, and we continually popped away at him knowing that we couldn't hit him. At any rate, he would have a good story to tell. A man at a thousand yards is a hard target to hit. He appears about as tall as your little finger nail when held at arms length, and only a chance shot will drop him.

A second runner left the trench, and we treated him in like manner, but with the difference that he jumped, and then took off as though a swarm of bees were after him. He entered the woods unharmed.

A third runner started out, but we could tell he didn't like the assignment. We opened up on him, only to see him huddle in the trail; run a ways; fall down; and then start off again. He made a lot of work getting to his goal.

The Germans did not send another runner out, and we interested ourselves by firing directly into the trench full of men. We couldn't tell if our shots were effective, or not, but there was a good deal of activity as our shots struck. We wanted to disturb them plenty, for they would be in a fine position to repel an attack up the valley, and on Vierzy.

For some time now, I was conscious of an enemy taking pot shots at me. When I rose up in my hole—"crack," and a bullet would zing past overhead. I took the German glasses out that I had found in the morning and searched the fields ahead of me and to my left. The glasses were 8 Power and were hard to focus, making it difficult at first to make anything out. But I finally did get the knack of it.

I searched everywhere: I was certain a sniper lurked. I raised my head high, and "crack," another bullet went by: but I couldn't trace its path. The wheat to my rear absorbed the shot, so that I could get no direction by any puff of dust. All I could do was to draw his fire and search.

After about six or eight more bullets whizzed by, I did get somewhat oriented to the course of the bullet; that it was from a spot directly to my left. But on searching the area, I still could not find the point of origin. I had noticed a demolished house 300 to 400 yards away, that was high enough for a vantage point, and I then reasoned he must be in its chimney.

I wasn't much worried about him getting me, as the bullets all went about a foot or two above, and about as far to the left. And that there was no place for him to register his shots on me; I determined to gamble with him.

I examined the chimney, and found what I thought was the place of his concealment. It was in the darkened side of the chimney, about two thirds the ways up, as though bricks had been removed: that was my target.

I set the leaf of my sight for 350 yards, got into my sling: and all prepared to fire, I raised my head, and—"crack," his bullet went by: and I quickly drew a bead, and fired. I then grabbed my glasses, and studied the chimney. There was a light, round spot several inches to the right: I had got the elevation correct. I gave the rifle some left windage correction, and raised my head— c-r-a-a-ack: and I returned fire.

Again I looked for my bullet mark, and found it closer to the target. Again I corrected windage, drew his fire, and returned mine. My bullet marks showed through the glasses slightly to the right. I corrected windage again, and exchanged several more shots with him.

Finally, his rifle was quiet. I assumed that I had "got him," or at least made it too warm for him to continue. I then resumed a random fire on the trench, and hoped there, too, that I was doing some good.

(The "chimney," so called, was in reality an old stone tower, and possibly marked a vent to a chalk cave that extended into the hill north of Vierzy. Later I learned that a mess of machine guns located there had stopped units of the 9th Infantry, and we had fared no better. Some time after we were gone, a lone French tank was sent there to wipe out the nest. The tank crew approached the tower, and with a few shots demolished it and its defenders, thus wiping out a strong point, and clearing the way for the 9th.)

We remained in the holes for about two hours, and it still looked like we would not get out until dark. One of the men yelled a warning, and, behind, French cavalrymen were lining up for an attack. We were nervous with the Frenchmen in our midst. We wore the green uniforms of the Marines, unlike the doughboys; but rather much like the Germans; and anything could happen.

We started crawling back, and on reaching the wheat stood up to run. One of the cavalrymen saw us, and with his horse at a gallop bore down on us. He rode straight at me, and his lance looked villainous. He was hunched over the pommel of his saddle, and the horse looked as big as an elephant.

I threw my rifle to my shoulder. I planned on knocking him out of the saddle, but I quickly changed my mind. I threw up my arms, instead, and yelled, "American Marine." He pulled his horse to a sliding stop, and his lance hit me a resounding whack in the chest, and I was nearly bowled over. I was mad clear through, and with the sharply pointed lance at my chest, I convince him that I was an American. He was chagrinned at the turn of events, then grinned and jabbered a string of French at me. I returned a lot of Yankee Marine talk at him; and after clearing the feet of his horse of phone wires, he rode off to get back into line again.

With the sergeant and other five men we made our way down into the Vauxcastile ravine again. I thought, "I've had enough for one day, let somebody else do the fighting for a change."

15

The Cave of Blood

Sitting in the ravine, we watched a battalion of the 23rd Infantry advance to the attack on our left. They appeared on a knoll a quarter of a mile to our rear, advancing in three waves at a steady walk, with their rifles at high port.

When they reached the top of the knoll, the Germans opened up on them with artillery and machine gun fire. I thought they looked fine, but too fine for frontline tactics. Shells burst in among them, and we could see the pattern of machine gun fire in the dust. The bullets of machine guns cut an elongated figure 8 in the dirt, the ends and middle of the 8 being deadly. The troops maintained a straight line; and as they descended into the ravine and out of sight of the Germans; not a man was wounded in that advance. Unbelievable, but true. I couldn't believe my eyes, nor could the others.

Following the three waves, three men appeared on the crest and were instantly swallowed in a shell burst. When the smoke and dust cleared away, there was at first no sign of life. Shortly, one man got up and ran wobbling toward the battalion; then a second man arose; but he seemed to be in shock and ran dazed in a circle, his left arm jutting out in front of him. The third man did not get up.

The battalion ascended out of the ravine, their right flank about 100 yards from us. And then rang the clatter of Maxim guns, followed by rifle fire. The battalion passed on out of sight, and only the trailing sound of intermittent fire echoed back.

I ran out toward the crazed man, and yelled for him to come down. Then a shell came screaming in, and by the sound I knew it would be close. There was no shelter nearby, so I just scrunched down. The shell burst in the air above me, and my helmet was jammed down on my head; and I was all but knocked out. A piece of shell casing had glanced off my helmet and jolted me. But the only evidence to show was a badly dented helmet: and I took time to thank the Lord that it was not worse.

The man had heard my yells and now was close enough for me to see blood spurting from his left arm. The gore covered his entire front and the wound was

15. The Cave of Blood

in the arm just below the shoulder. I ran out and grabbed him, and I quickly cut and ripped away his sleeve and tried to stop the hemorrhaging artery. The man was frantic and near panic, and I knew time was running out for him. A French first aid man came running up to help me; and between us, we stopped the bleeding and got first aid on his arm. We put his arm in a sling, and then took him down into the ravine, where other wounded men were collecting.

For the next half hour, or so, several of us were kept busy doing first aid work. Most of the wounded were appreciative of our efforts, and joked with us over their wounds. But one fellow we couldn't do anything for; he just sat and bled, his head propped in his hands. He had a bad head wound, and the blood ran from his nose, mouth, and ears. He didn't look as if he would last until he could get to the rear and help.

By that time the sun had about set and the shadows were lengthening, and the tanks began arriving in the ravine; and we were all interested. We had lost them back in the forest in the march, miles behind, and they were just now getting into action.

Soon German heavies began pouring their shells into the ravine, trying to get the tanks. They made it pretty rough on well and wounded alike. The tanks sought shelter in the deepest part of the ravine, and so drew fire away from us. We lay for some time in the shelter of the bank of the ravine, until it was dark enough to cover our movements.

Then we remembered the wounded lying in the wheat, and thought they might be crushed by the tanks as they advanced into those fields. So we went out searching for them, and the dead, and helped any wounded we could find. We marked both dead and wounded alike, by jabbing their bayoneted rifles in the dirt.

After that, we met several of the arriving tanks. They were all led by a man wearing a square of white cloth on his back, the driver of the tank getting his direction from a third man lying on the outside of the tank. Several of these stopped and their crews talked with us; and although the men were French, they understood what we were doing, and were appreciative of our efforts.

We found one boy that had closed on a machine gun, but who didn't quite make it, for the gun had shattered both legs below the knees and through the feet. He was conscious and smoking. And notwithstanding the great pain he was in, he had formed tourniquets from ammunition bandoliers, and used his spare magazines from his .45 to tighten them. He had remained conscious since being hit, several hours earlier, and had intermittently loosened the tourniquets, from time to time, to avoid the onset of gangrene.

We needed a stretcher to move him, so I started back to the ravine where I had seen the cave the doctors were setting up as a regimental first aid station.

On the way, I caught up with four French soldiers who were carrying a dead comrade on a barn door; but they refused to dump the dead man and give me the door: "Mon pauvre camarade," they said, (ja da de la, and etc.); I didn't wait and went on.

I found the first aid station by the smell that emanated from it. Fresh blood in quantities is not a soon forgotten odor, and I had smelled lots of it. Coming to the entrance, I was momentarily stopped by the sight of a pile of limbs; legs and arms that were piled at the entrance. I had to fight back the nausea that swept over me, and then I went in. A group of doctors were amputating on yet another victim, but one took time to hear me out: "Sorry, we have no stretchers," he said, "and can't get them; but bring him in anyway"; and he went back to his grisly work.

I left the first aid station and returned back through the fields, when I heard the sharp command—"Halt!" And I halted pronto, with my hands in the air. Cautiously looking over my right shoulder, I saw a squad of soldiers, all with their rifles bearing on me, and also to one side a man with his .45 pointed at me: "Turn slowly; approach with your hands up." And fearing some eager beaver would shoot, I readily obeyed.

It was an infantry patrol, under the charge of a sergeant. He quizzed me as to my outfit, the name of the regimental commander, and wanted to know what I was doing running through the wheat, and where I was going. I gave them the answers; and when I said I was a Marine, they all grinned and became friendly.

When I left, the sergeant told me to keep to the trail, as there were other patrols searching the wheat. Some shot first, he said, and asked questions later, if needed. I told them of the other Marines up ahead in those fields, and warned them to watch for them; we were helping men from their regiment.

Returning back to the wounded man, I found the other three improvising a stretcher, using a blanket, two saplings, and a couple of boards. And with this, we were finally ready, and the ordeal of lifting him on it began.

It was excruciating for the man, so we had him bite on a .45 bullet; then spreading our fingers under each mutilated leg in turn, we gingerly lifted him onto the stretcher. The feeling of the pulverized bones and their grinding was pretty near as bad on us, as it was on the victim; then each taking a corner, we carried him to the dressing station.

When we arrived, a doctor came out to look at his wounds. He looked at us, and motioned that they would amputate. And we silently returned. As it was nearly 3:00 a.m., we then laid down to get some sleep. It was the first I had had in well over forty-eight hours.

16

Lieutenant Max Is Killed

July 19

We were awakened at 5:00 a.m. and started on our way again. Going forward, we passed the ruined tower, and then we followed a field-road that led down into Vierzy.

Arriving in the main street of town, I observed a German aviator approaching, flying low, and in the street, three sedans, a National and two Dodges. The vehicles hurriedly stopped and a group of officers scrambled for shelter. A second later, the aviator dumped his bombs, and the three cars were wrecked and three of the officers were slain.

I was one of the first to run up to the scene; one of the officers was a Major Berry, who was sprawled on his back covered with gore. There was nothing we could do. A Marine said Major General Harbord, the division commander, had just escaped the bombing. It was efficient bombing; but what a time and place for the divisional commander to arrive.

We lost no time in getting under way again, and in Vierzy we got word where we could find our outfits. Proceeding on, we came to the village cemetery, which was nestled in a ravine. And as we passed it by, several men called out my name, and I rejoined the remnants of the First Battalion.

I started up the hill, but suddenly found myself in the midst of bursting shells, though I somehow got through without a wound, and rejoined my company—or rather, what was left of it. They were dug in just under the crest of the hill, protected from direct artillery fire, but still subject to the spent pieces of the bursts in the ravine below.

The Germans kept firing intermittently at this spot, apparently to close the road to traffic. We were struck by countless fragments, but only a few received anything more than a bruise. Several of the men gathered pieces that either hit them or hit in the hole with them. I had a double handful myself, both shrapnel and high explosive fragments, that I had gathered during the day.

Davidian[1] had a bag full of the stuff, gathered both in Belleau Wood and also here. I tried to get him to jettison it, as it was heavy enough to be bothersome and a nuisance, but he remained obdurate. He said he was going to cart it home to show the folks, and explain to them that the fragments represented what he had gone through.

Several funny things happened that day, which were comical to us but not so comical to those experiencing them. The shells sometimes grazed the crest and exploded in the ravine, or ricocheted up the farther slope and burst. One such funny incident happened here. There were two men coming down the ravine, which had made a seat with their hands and were carrying a third. He had wounds in both legs and was heavily bandaged—when a shell zoomed in. The shell hit the road immediately in front of them and ricocheted up the slope and burst. When the shell hit the road it kicked up a great cloud of dust that engulfed the men; and when the cloud of dust cleared away, there were the three men running, with the bandaged hero leading the way. The men on the hillside had a good laugh at them. There is humor in war, though grim.

Humor sometimes is of the kind that finds the individual in an embarrassing position, though not necessarily harmful or fatal to him. For instance, the men, when they needed to seek relief, went down the hill to get behind the wall of the cemetery; there to avoid the shells. The wall had a nice arch in it, newly placed by an in-coming shell, and which the men used to gain entrance to the cemetery. One man, descending to the cemetery, went through this arch and sheltered himself behind the wall. A moment or two later a shell exploded to one side of the arch throwing skyward a great cloud of debris; stones, smoke, and dust. When the debris cleared, we see the man emerging through the dust frantically clambering up the hill on all fours. That was not amusing. But what raised the howl of laughter on the hillside was the fact that the man's pants were dragging about his ankles. A shell in war is no respecter of time or place.

The cemetery was well filled with graves. There were a good many new graves at the east end and outside the wall; some were back-filled, and others were still open, containing one or two bodies of newly-killed Germans; while still others awaited a consignment: perhaps they would be temporarily filled with French or Americans killed in the drive. What interested us was the effect the shells had that landed in the graveyard. Some had penetrated deeply into the soil, and in the explosion that followed upended the caskets of the deceased: the deceased did not interest us; but the caskets did. They were of odd designs, ornate and grotesque, and looked like the deceased's place in heaven depended on the fitness of the casket. They were ancient, like the

16. Lieutenant Max Is Killed

cemetery, but before our eyes profaned by the heedless weapons of modern man, which did not at all let the dead rest in peace.

Of the men lying in shallow pits below the crest of the hill, many were hit by small pieces, a few received slight wounds, hardly worth the trip back, and one was killed. That one lay about twenty feet on my left when a shell crashed into the hole with him and burst. I was looking in his direction at the time and saw parts of his body sail through the air and roll to the bottom of the hill: "Pass the word to those in command, Lt. Max is killed." That was all. Words are useless at such a time; just the words, "Pass the word, Lt. Max is killed."

In the late afternoon, we saw tanks coming up behind us. It was pitiful, a tank in the open fields. One long shot by the Germans, then a short on the opposite side of the tank; and the next would be on target: and smoke and flames would envelop it, and it was out of action. There were five or six such tanks all burning within our vision, and we could see smoke from others. In all, thirteen tanks were put out of action within our view, and not a single one got as far as our position.

Not all the fighting was on the ground. The Germans, though, had command of the air, and their aviators forced down, or shot down, all the Allied planes. This did not cheer us, but filled the men with contempt for the Allied flyers. We resented their carefree life and special favors, and could not see the reason, if any, for their poor showing in the air.

While on the hillside we witnessed a German flyer that we could respect. He repeatedly drove or shot down French aviators. There was one French flyer that did challenge him; but, again, to no avail. The German would time and again work above and behind him, and always gain the upper hand; he didn't shoot, but dove repeatedly on the Frenchman. The French flyer attempted all the maneuvers to get the best of the German, but the German always ended above and behind him; until, finally, he forced the Frenchman down. The Frenchman landed his plane across the ravine from us, and as the machine was rolling to a stop we saw his long, blue-clad legs hit the ground, and we cheered as he raced into the woods.

Then the German spotted us, and swooped down to harass us. He flew low over our lines, his guns spitting, and after he turned and came back, he repeated the maneuver. He did this a number of times until finally a few of us stood up and peppered at him with our rifles—but without effect. At his last trip over, we notice that he is not firing but leaning from the cockpit and saluting us. We could see a big grin on his face as he did so, and most of our men jumped up, waved, and cheered him. He then made his departure, and flew back to the German lines. A decent foe, one we could appreciate.

Thus the day passed, lying in partial shelter on the hillside, hoping we would not be called upon to resume the attack, and hoping the 6th Marines would hold the front: that is what support is like.

All the while, we were taking up the slack in our belts: we were hungry; we hadn't seen our galleys since the early morning of the 16th, and we didn't know when we would eat.

Toward evening, a cheer went up. One man spotted our mess crew coming up the ravine, but they went past us at a gallop. We called to them, but the cry was lost in their own commotion. They never stopped, but went up the ravine and out of sight. The men were sore, and many unpleasant things were wished upon the mess crew.

That the ravine ended up on a plateau in plain sight of the Germans we knew what would happen next. As expected, German artillery welcomed them in fine style, with explosives and gas shells; and it wasn't long before we see them coming back down again at a breakneck gallop, with the mess crew stretched out and hanging on. We cheered the galley on as it disappeared around the bend; and we took up another notch in our belts, and settled down to brooding.

Then the French cavalry began forming at the crossroads below the cemetery. Groups of horsemen assembled from different directions to our rear, and then huddled around their leader for instructions. Just then, a shell screamed in and burst in the center of the closely-packed group. And one of those things happened that is hard to explain. After the dust and smoke cleared away, we saw that not a man or horse was wounded.

They quickly reformed and attacked the Germans. And it was quite dark before they returned. I saw the remnants as they came in, with many empty saddles, men leading six to eight horses, the horses bleeding badly, cut and punctured by bullets. The men were grim, and all they said with their Gaulic gestures was, "Bon, bon; très bon": they had ridden down the Germans in the wheat fields, corralled a number of them; bolstered up their strength, re-horsed, then rode "hell for leather" again.

After dark, we were moved down from the hill and led to a clearing in the woods, where we were fed. The same old mess, horse meat and hard tack, stewed and warm: but it tasted like turkey to us. Four days without food, and anything tastes good.

We were then hiked into Vierzy and led into a chalk cave, where all noises ceased. I found a flea-filled German overcoat and a stretcher, and soon fell into a deep sleep amid the crawling fleas.

17

Gas!

July 20

We were aroused at 3:00 a.m., and quietly filed out into a world gone crazy. The Germans were pouring everything they had into Vierzy; it was one continuous burst, and the street was fogged with the acrid smoke of bursting shells.

We turned right, and went quickly down the Vierzy ravine, the smoke getting heavier, and in the smoke, the definite odor of gas. As we descended deeper in the ravine, we yelled, "Gas!" and put on our masks. The phosgene and chlorine odors were too strong.

An officious boot officer, though, who was marching on our right, gave us orders to take the masks off. He said importantly, "There's no gas here."

I attempted to explain that I knew the various odors of the gasses and that the haze was most certainly filled with gas. He became angry and yammered profusely about insubordination and a general court martial and that I'd get one when we came out. That didn't bother me, as I was already in the book for one; so a second didn't seem any worse.

"Gas!—gas!—gas!" the yells were frantic now, and then silence as the men got into their masks. And at that the officer thought it advisable to go somewhere else. Then, "Double-time—march!" and they led us quickly off the road.

I felt suddenly weak, and breathing became difficult, and I dropped out of the column. Men like me were sitting huddled along the trail; all were gassed. But one by one, we struggled on. I cursed the officer and wished I could get my hands on him: a damned boot officer, who had no business commanding battle-wise troops.

By nightfall, I came to the Viller de Cotterêts woods, the starting place of the drive, and found my company. They were lined up, calling roll, and accounting for our losses. When my name was called, I answered, "Here," and reported what had happened to Duke and Smith.

We had ten or so killed, and about forty-five definitely wounded: and that was out of a strength of about eighty to a hundred men that started the attack with us. We had lost the bulk of the men in these woods at the start of the drive. Killed: Jimmie Duke, Sergeant Harry Bowness, Corporal Snair, Sergeant St. Louis, Private Tritt; Giles was missing, and others that I did not know.

After we fell out, I made a wickiup out of branches, and I crawled in to die, or get well, I didn't care which. My lungs burned as from fire; it hurt to breathe, and it seemed to get worse, not better, and quiet was what I needed.

I was aroused in the night by the yells of the men. It seems a branch of the tree we were sleeping under, which had been cracked by artillery fire, was about to fall. It did; destroying my wickiup, bending and breaking several stacked rifles, and pinning down and hurting a couple of the men who failed to heed the warning-cry.

Afterward, I lay down again, first making sure there were no fractured branches above me, and attempted to sleep. I sat huddled up against a tree, cold, sick, and miserable. I tossed fretfully; but sleep was out of the question.

A while later, I became aware that our galley force was working and so walked over and told them I was sick and wanted the heat of the galley. It was warm, yes, hot, but I lay down beside it and slept until daybreak when the men were wakened.

I couldn't eat; I had no stomach for food, so I sought a nice, soft place under a tree to sit, and remained there hunched up till noon, when I was aroused again by the cry of "sick bay."

I fell in line, and when my turn came they pronounced it "Influenza." Influenza, hell! Gas was what it was. You have to have a bloody hole through you to get diagnosed correctly: however, I was headed for the hospital; I was too sick to argue, and nor did I care.

Chow call blew and the men were scrambling to get in line. I remembered my pistol, which I had given to one of the sergeants, and went to warn him that the gun had an extra shell in the chamber. He had already discovered it, and with that off my mind, I grabbed something to eat and made my way back to the hospital detail.

But I found them gone. Captain Hamilton and another officer were sitting on the ground, and seeing me with a tag on gruffly asked where I had been. I told him I had just gotten some chow. He blew up, and roared that any man who could think of food wasn't very sick and didn't deserve to go to the hospital.

I didn't say anything, but I tore off the tag and turned to go back to the company. Sure, officers and men were worn out from the attack and the conditions leading up to it, but I thought it strange he would make so much fuss about it.

As I walked away, Captain Hamilton rose up and followed after me. He apologized for his words and explained that he was very tired and that everything irritated him. He picked up the tag and handed it to me and led me through the woods to where the men were loading. Then saying, "Good luck," he turned, and went back to his place.

18

The Ladies from Hell

There were three trucks with thirty to forty men aboard, all gassed and going to the hospital. It was an uncomfortable ride, but welcome to the men.

On the way, we came into a village where a "cockney" regiment from England was quartered, and briefly stopped. The cockney's, in their obnoxious manner, started making uncomplimentary remarks about us. One that was particularly odious was the reference to our late entry into the war, and now that it was going in their favor, we got in it only to share in the "glory"; this despite the fact that the English had just successfully beaten a fifty-mile retreat. They would be going still, if the Americans hadn't arrived on the scene. And, besides, Americans were not there to fight England's battles, but we had a war of our own against the Germans.

After several of these remarks had been made, many of the men, as sick as they were, piled off the trucks and started for them. But cooler-headed men were there and quickly herded the cockneys away from the scene. We climbed back on the trucks, but the incident had made the Marines belligerent, and, as we rode on, we expressed our feeling to every British soldier, or soldiers, we saw.

At one place on our route, we crossed a viaduct and saw on the railroad track below the big 14-inch naval guns in operation. The guns were manned by U.S. sailors and had been remounted on great railway cars, which rolled backward on a semi-circular track to absorb the concussion at the mighty explosion of the guns. These were the same naval guns we had done sentry duty over while in the 1st Regiment: and here they now were blasting the Heinies. The trucks stopped on the bridge, so all of us had an excellent view of the firing of the big naval guns.

Toward evening, we were unloaded at a field hospital. We were herded into a long tent and told to wait. Not a cot, chair, or blanket was there, and nor did we see a doctor or nurses. It was sometime after dark when a buck entered and said that there was a hospital train on the siding and that any of us who felt like it should pile on board. Anything was better than this, so I climbed aboard.

The car was empty of regular seats, but a bench extended the length of the car on each side and we were told to take seats on one side only. We wondered who would take the opposite seat. Finally, a long line of Scottish soldiers filed in. They were big men, they were silent, and they looked tough.

We sat in silence, sizing them up, noting that most of them by their hash marks had been in service four years; most of them had been wounded several times, and one had eight wound-stripes on his tunic. They were all dressed in khaki kilties: so these were the famous "Ladies from Hell," the troops the Germans feared; the troops that we had heard so much about.

We silently eyed one another, until one Marine couldn't contain his curiosity any longer, and asked, "Hey, youse guys—what you got on under dem skoits?" And immediately five or six of the Scotties raised their skirts—and we saw; our curiosity was satisfied; not a one of the famous "Ladies from Hell" wore a damned thing under their kilts. Then the Scotties and the Marines roared with laughter. The ice was shattered; and with bars down, a great deal of ribald kidding went on during the remainder of the trip.

The Scotties had been caught in column on the march in, and German aviators had swooped down and dumped countless small personnel bombs on them. The fragments cause small, irritating wounds; and they had their "blighty."

The bombs used were about one inch in diameter, and probably an inch and a half long. They were painted shiny black, and were apparently detonated on contact. They were more of a nuisance, than a threat; and although creating a wound, it was rarely serious. I had seen a few in Belleau Wood, and again in our last drive; but aside from giving them a wide berth, they didn't amount to much.

We liked the Scotch soldiers, they were our kind; and the feeling was mutual: as regards the cockney soldiers, they, too, were loud in their disapproval of them.

The train pulled into Paris, and we were unloaded and taken by ambulance to Red Cross Hospital No. 5. This was situated in the center of the famous horse-racing track in Autueil, a suburb of Paris. We were told to strip down in the yards, were furnished with pajamas, and then assigned to a tent, which, in my case, was the gas ward.

While putting on the pajamas, we were surrounded by a group of hospital corpsmen, and one of them told me to watch my things, as "they would steal everything" I had. I was wearing a German machine gun belt with a "Gott Mit Uns" buckle, had a Lugar pistol, and had several other souvenirs of the fighting which I wanted to save.

The Lugar, which was hard to conceal, was quickly grabbed out of my hands by a captain. In deference to his rank, I didn't yell "thief," but politely implied it. Then he asked me how much I would take for it. I answered that it was not for sale. But he insisted on haggling for a price. I held out my hand; but he maintained possession of it.

The group of men was all eyes and ears, and watched hungrily to see what I would do. I finally said I would take 200 francs for it. He took out a 500 franc note, but as I had not been paid since leaving the States, and had no change, there wasn't anything I could do. He then said he'd pay me later, and walked off with the pistol.

I was pretty angry about it, but then a private hasn't much recourse against the actions of a captain. I became surly; I told the others to go to hell, and finished disrobing in peace. I was then shown to my tent; and having taken a shower, I got into bed and went to sleep. It was bright and early when I awakened: I had slept the day and night through, and I felt better.

During my stay in the hospital, I saw the doctor once a day. The ward nurse took data as to my name, age, and outfit, and took my pulse and temperature, both morning and night. Aside from the quiet rest we had, we were considered "morons," and treated as such.

The doctors did attend several in the ward which had received frightful burns from mustard gas. Several of these men were blinded, and were unable to talk; and two of them were burned about the body in a terrible manner. They didn't look as though they had a square inch of skin left. Their scrotums were blistered to the size of an indoor baseball, and their penises were swollen to a great size, too. As I witnessed them receive their medical treatment daily, I thanked God that I hadn't also been burned; and I didn't feel too badly at not receiving more attention. Also, I cursed the Germans for starting gas warfare, and their diabolical methods to win the war by any means.

One other incident occurred in the ward that cured me of any feeling of heroics, and showed me what we could expect on our return from the war. That was the nuisance created by "well-meaning" non-combatants that were in Paris. A certain American woman came into the ward one day, and in a "bubbly" manner said she was writing a book and wanted "our experiences" for material. She sat down on my cot to do her writing, but she was met with a silent ward. Some of the men rolled over and gave her their backs; others found something else to do, and busied themselves over it; while others still lay silent with their thoughts. I, finally, out of sympathy for her, gave her some German paper money and told her it was straight from Germany, as I had taken it off a prisoner. She "gushed and gurgled" over that; but aside from the money, she got no material from me. Finally, she got the point, and made her way from the ward.

France, the Home of the World

Weyburn, Saskatchewan
July 22, 1918

Dearest Everard,

    I have just received a card from Aunt Gertrude, telling us you are in France. And I suppose that you are enjoying the beautiful, as well as witnessing the destroyed. It is too bad to think that so much grandeur is being laid in ruin; but time will right that again. And possibly, if we could live to see it renewed, and then look back on it, we would say, "After all the trials, it is grander than ever." I think France will ever be looked upon as the home of the world, so many of our boys lie there....

19

The Doughboy's Dream

I felt much better in a few days and wandered about the grounds, though my breathing was difficult. I was determined to find the captain who had my gun, and I luckily ran into him at one of the hospital tents.

On my inquiry for the gun, he attempted to ignore me, and would have gone on, but I stepped in front of him and repeated my demands. He then denied having seen me or my Lugar, and attempted to pass again: but I stood firm in his path. I was plenty angry at his methods and told him that there were several men who witnessed the incident and were ready to testify against him. He changed tactics then and said he would get the gun, and we went together to his tent.

He shortly returned with the gun in one hand and a 100 franc note in the other. I took the gun, and started back to my tent: but he called after me, offering 150 francs. I told him 200 francs, or nothing. Thinking that was the last of the deal, I turned to go. He then drew out 200 in bank notes from his wallet, which I took, and left him with the gun and a good idea of what I thought of him.

We who were able loafed and wandered about the grounds. And then, several of the men, pajama-clad, took off on a sight-seeing tour of Paris. This, of course, offended the finer senses of the military, especially the upper bracket, which henceforth put a stop to it. Probably the ranking officers felt that any man able to walk was able also to go back to his outfit. At any rate, we were corralled and started on our way.

About fifteen of us Marines were taken into Paris and dumped off at the headquarters of the Paris military police. The M.P.'s also were Marines, at least they wore the uniform and emblem of the Marines; but there the comparison stopped. They were "heels" of the worst order; they not only refused us food and lodging, but they also refused to talk to us.

Well, we could at least pay them the latter honors: so, we talked of them, and about them—but not to them. Finally, one of them came over and told us we could get lodging in a hotel, and gave us directions as how to get there.

19. The Doughboy's Dream

We forthwith departed, and managed to get two rooms for the fifteen of us; two beds to divide up among us. I had noticed a bathtub when I first came in; it was ornamental, with fixtures dating from probably 1880, or so; it was deep, narrow, and stood on four fantastic paws. And I grabbed the tub for my bed. So I slept that night in comfort.

The men were without money for food and no place to get it if we could. Still, I had the money from selling the gun, so six of us found a French-American restaurant and had a real feed. The people who ran the restaurant were very nice and gave us a good price on the meal. I paid the bill; and it was worth it, but I knew from the way the francs shrunk that they wouldn't last for long.

We were the first American combat troops to dine there, and were recognized as Marines. A horde of people gathered around our table while we ate and had many questions about Belleau Wood and the Soissons engagement; and were quite frank about the way the French people praised the Marines. Their praise of the Marines' fight against the Germans at Belleau Wood gave us a great deal of satisfaction, and made us proud to have had a part in it.

The next day, Sunday, was a quiet one, and three of us started out to see Paris. We walked down one street and up another. We saw few people, and it seemed like a dead city. We hadn't eaten any food since the evening before, so we watched for some place to get a meal. All shops, though, were closed, and little life was showing.

Finally, we saw two Frenchmen, one sweeping the walk, and the other, which had stopped, and was talking with him. They were gesticulating in the best French manner, and we decided to ask them where we could get something to eat.

We crossed the street, and in our best French-American, all talking as one, we asked the man with the broom. An American would scarcely have understood us, and I know that it would have been impossible for a Frenchman. And while we were jabbering, attempting our version of French, he stood and heard us out, his feet apart, arms akimbo, and nodding his head with a massive grin on his face.

Then the surprise came, and in perfect English he said, "Well, Boys, I take it you want something to eat." We looked at one another, and then back at him; and he said further, "Come on in, Boys, I'll see what my wife can scare up for you."

We entered a shop in the front of the building, and met his wife, a plump, jolly, French woman. Smiling, she made us a chocolate drink, put a piece "des oeufs" on the stove to fry, and cooked a goodly pile of "pomme de terre frit," all the while keeping up a continual chatter in English. Both the man and his wife had spent a good many years in the States, each as a chef; she in the homes of rich New Yorkers, and he in various hotels and high-class restaurants. They had saved a modest fortune, and then returned to Paris, where they obtained this little restaurant, in which to spend their latter years.

They had a good laugh at our French, and when in the course of conversation we divulged that we were Marines, that through wounds we were taken out of action and were just out of the hospital; nothing was too good for us.

We spent a happy hour or so with them, and when I dug down in my money belt to pay them, they threw up their hands, shook their heads, and refused it. We thanked them for their kindness and made our departure. We were quiet on the return to the hotel, thinking of the kindness showed us by the Frenchman and his wife; the fried eggs, the French fried potatoes, and the hot chocolate drink they had served us.

At the hotel again, we stood for a long time watching the barges as they emerged from the long tunnel under the city. The Frenchmen operating them were of a different breed; they looked rough and tough; no smiling faces on this bunch, only a sullen stare. And somehow I was glad they were separated from us by a steep bank and the parapet wall. They were the notorious and infamous Apaches.

That night our rooms were taken by other Americans, and with no place to go, we slept on the floor. The next morning, we found that we were scheduled to leave at 10:00 a.m.; why or where we didn't know, or care. But first, I was going to the Marine Paymaster's office and try and get some money.

On finding the office, I went in and told my story to a smiling lieutenant. No pay since March; this was the first of August; all I had done was "sign the pay roll." He made a quick check, and then asked me how much I wanted. I took 450 francs, thanked him, saluted, and hurried to make the train. We were fortunate, six in a First-Class coach compartment, and we settled down to a good ride in style.

On arriving in Tours, the train made a stop of about 40 minutes, so I and the five traveling with me decided to get our first meal of the day. When we came to the concourse of the depot, an M.P. planted himself in front of us and told us to get back on the train. I, as usual, became angry, and told him, "We are going to eat—M.P., or not." He made a remark about Marines in general, so I shoved him aside and went into the restaurant, the others following.

In the restaurant, we took seats at the counter, and ordered "der oerf, pomme de terre freit, and chocolate"; our encounter with the Frenchman the day before came in handy here. The M.P. had followed us in and took a stand behind me, glaring and mumbling something about privates not allowed in there. Again, I stood up, and shoved him back a dozen feet, and warned him to "stay there." I returned to my place and enjoyed my meal.

Finishing eating, I paid the bill; and with the M.P. on our trail, we started back to the train. At the gate, I whirled, grabbed the M.P. by the tunic, told the others to scatter, and set myself to "cold cock" him. When all the bluster went out of him, and he whined and said he was sorry, etc., I told him to "shove off" and leave us alone. And I turned and made my way to the car with my retinue. I was uneasy till the train started and we were on our way again. But the M.P. was a good boy, and no one bothered us.

Soon we pulled into Châtillon sur Seine, our destination. But evidently a Marine was unwanted there, and they soon shoved us on to Celle sur Seine, where we joined up with other Marine casualties.

We were quartered in "pup" tents, had no formations, and had to hike five kilometers to get some chow; it wasn't very pleasant or comfortable, so we were up to some mischief most of the time.

It was raining hard one night, and we had to lie in mud and water to sleep. I was restless and uncomfortable, when I heard in the adjoining tent an argument going on where it shouldn't: Minneapolis versus St. Paul: the old argument debated in that pest hole in France; and I had to investigate.

I nearly tore down the pup tent in getting to the controversy: and sticking my head in, I said, "Now, St. Paul"—then blinked my eyes; for there squatted was Frank Tupa, whom I had last seen at the University of Minnesota, and a fellow named Johnson, who also was in my classes there: "Hi, Bullis, when did you get over?" And they introduced me to a third man, Zing, who lived on the same block that I had years before.

We sat in the water running through the tent and talked until the small hours of the morning, telling stories about the U. of M., and home. They were in a detail to leave at daybreak; so when I got up, they were gone.

That day, I wandered to a nearby town and shopped around for toilet articles. While there, I was hailed, and turning to see who called to me was surprised to find it was Joe Erwin. He was one of the boys whom I had last seen when the four of us stood on the deck of the *Henderson* the last night out. He was from home, and an acquaintance of years, and I was glad to see him.

We went into a restaurant and in our Americanized French ordered up a swell meal. He gave me much information about home, which was the first news I had of the Park and the fellows we had known. He had suffered a bad head wound, receiving a piece of shell fragment in the base of the skull. He seemed all right, but due to the nature of the wound I thought he was through with front-line action. I was to learn differently. We had a good chat, and then I bid him so long, as I had to go back to the town I was quartered in.

There was little, or nothing, to do except keep out of sight of the sergeants to avoid work details. One afternoon, a bunch of us went down to the railroad yard where there was a train loaded with troops. And we immediately began to inquire if there was anyone aboard from home. We found out that they had just landed, and, what was worse, most of them had been drafted only a month or so previously. What a crime; no training, no conditioning of the men, and nor had they been issued rifles.

That started it. We were all front-line veterans, so we began to feed them stories about the front. We told them epic tales, and our stories grew better and larger as time went on. And to cap them, we told them their train was consigned to the front and that they were going to fill the ranks, replacing the wounded and the dead.

They listened with their mouths agape; but the part where they were going in as front-line replacements did the trick. Soon there was a noticeable reduction in the number of men aboard. And we decided there was more important work elsewhere to be done, and we gradually dispersed. The train was delayed long into the night, the locomotive engineer frantically "tooting" his whistle, while the search parties scoured the countryside for the missing members of the train's compliment.

While there, I decided I needed a new uniform, due to an increase in growth, so I "finagled" a trip to the Quartermaster's Department. Arriving, I was not so sure that it was the American Army Quartermaster, but thought by mistake I had found a prison supply depot. The men in the Q.M. department were "heels," and you couldn't talk them out of anything. Everything "fit," according to them. A size 2 Large blouse was perfect on a 4 medium-sized man. As for shoes, anything you could get your foot into was perfect, no matter if you could place both feet in one shoe. Their answer was, "Look around, you can change with someone." As far as the quartermasters were concerned, they were along for the ride, and "to hell" with the soldier seeking their help.

I waxed loud and clear as to what I thought of them, and I finally was rewarded. A lieutenant came to investigate the disturbance, but he sided with his men: I was clothed, and that was that. But when one of the men asked me where I was from, and when I replied, "St. Paul"; the lieutenant nearly jumped over the counter: "Minneapolis," he cried, and the Minneapolis vs. St. Paul controversy was on again.

He invited me back of the counter, and in the course of our conversation

19. The Doughboy's Dream

I exchanged everything I had on; new stockings, new underwear, pants that fit, a blouse that was made for me, a new shirt, shoes that fit perfectly; and to cap the matter, I wrangled a pistol-belt from him, instead of the enlisted-man's cartridge belt. As an extra bonus, he gave me a spare pair of shoes and several socks for my pack. When I left, I was all for the age-old argument—but felt perhaps it should be Minneapolis, not St. Paul.

Arriving back at camp, the men made much ado of my outfit. And on asking how and where I had got it, I answered truthfully, the Army Q.M. But I neglected to state, you would have to be from St. Paul or Minneapolis to get it. For a while, there was an epidemic of men going to the Q.M.'s, but I noticed they all returned wearing their stained, wrinkled, deloused uniforms—and with a questioning glance in my direction.

I had a few teeth that needed attention, so I obtained a pass to attend dental inspection. On arriving, I fell in at the end of the one hundred yard line of men. After a long, tiresome wait, the line worked ahead until I was next.

I was greeted by a smiling lieutenant with, "How much will you take for the belt?"

I glanced down, and gleaming up at me were the words "GOTT MIT UNS" on the German buckle to my machine gun belt. I looked at him, and said, "I came to have my teeth examined, and I won't sell the belt."

All traffic in the line stopped while he argued with me, and getting sore, he yelled, "No examination for you, unless you sell the belt—step aside."

I ground my teeth; a buck private hasn't a chance against an officer.

I fell out and tried the end of the line again. Pulling my shirt down over the belt buckle, I thought I might get by. After a long time, and slowly creeping up to the examining section, I was again greeted by the lieutenant: "You ready to sell that buckle?"

After a moment, I answered, "Yes, for 35 francs."

He grinned and handed me the 35 francs. I was mad enough to kill the s.o.b., but aching teeth are no fun, either.

After the examination they handed me a slip: several fillings necessary—but no place to have the work done. I sure felt in a good mood; all that time to get an answer, when I already knew the condition existed: and no chance of getting the work done. I went back to the casual company sans belt, and my teeth still aching.

20

Sergeant Dan Daly

The next morning, 180 of us were called out and orders for our transportation handed to a first sergeant. He was a traditional character in the Marines, grizzled, who had won the Medal of Honor in the Boxer Uprising in China in 1900; and at Belleau Wood, in 1918, the Navy Cross, the Distinguished Service Cross, the French Médaille Militaire, and Croix de Guerre with Palm; and had received the Silver Star Citation: quite a collection of medals won in over eighteen years' fighting.

He was a typical old-time Marine. He growled in his throat, was blunt of speech (when inclined to talk), and who could chew a man out and be sympathetic at the same time. In Belleau Wood, he was reputed to have scattered a burning ammunition dump after it was hit by shell-fire, thus saving the lives of the men in the vicinity. Then when things looked darkest during the fight, he calmly visited all his machine gun crews on the line, adjusting fire, calming his men by his composure. He was all Marine; and even though it was to be but a short time, I felt it an honor to serve under his command.

About 10:00 a.m., we were marched into Châtillon sur Seine and halted in the road about 200 yards from the train depot. We Marines were not popular with the army, as they resented us for our "cockiness," and because our publicity department waxed loud and clear about our achievements in Belleau Wood. So, where Marines gather in a group, as expected there was an antagonistic army group gathered around us. They out-numbered us fifteen to twenty men to a Marine, and, as usual, the hazing began: "The army does the fighting, and the Marines take the glory"; or, "What's a Marine?" and gave their version of the answer: "A sea-going bell hop," and many other remarks less complimentary.

At first, we stood at ease and took it; but their baiting grew personal, and we angrily countered. Words led to blows, and the men on the outside of the column were taking quite a beating.

Sergeant Daly yelled for attention; and as we assumed the position, followed it with, "Fix bayonets! Form Company square—harsh!" It was a maneuver that the army wasn't used to; nor were they prepared. We formed the square smartly, with bayonets out, jabbing any doughboy that got in our way: "Forward—harsh!" and we moved out from among the mob of doughboys.

The sergeant led us to the depot yard, where were given orders, "At ease." Army followed us but remained at a respectful distance from our ranks.

It was a different crowd that came to watch. We stood at ease in the "square," all noncoms in the center. There were 180 men silently watching their enemy. And more army men and their officers came to watch. Finally, they broke into a cheer for the Marines, and the cheers accompanied us as we climbed aboard the train. As the train started to bear us on our way, we answered their cheer, and many waved their hands in farewell: quick-thinking Sergeant Dan Daly had saved the day.

We were now going back to our companies, regiments, and front-line duty; but at the same time, we were looking for trouble, anywhere and anyhow; and we didn't care who, what, or why.

Near noon, the train stopped for a short spell at a fair-sized town. The men disregarded the M.P.'s and swarmed into the depot. Those that had money immediately bought everything eatable at the counter. By the time I got there, the place was nearly cleaned out, except for about a half dozen small filthy cheese cakes. So I emptied the counter.

One group from the next car, for want of anything better to do, picked up the stove, fire and all, and retreated back to their car. When I returned to mine, I found a crowd of French soldiers there, which were selling bottles of wine for anything they could get. I had an extra pair of hob-nailed shoes, part of my haul from the Q.M. Depot at Châtillon that went for a bottle of rouge. A bunch of us were happy about that.

Of course the M.P.'s become interested, and soon broke up that brisk trade and otherwise made themselves obnoxious: particularly ordering us to the confinement of our cars. Later, the train was stopped and searched; but the stove was junked in the ditch, and they found nothing to incriminate us.

After dark, the train jerked to a stop in Is sur Tille, a large American rail center and supply depot. We had five cars, the 40/8 kind, also containing army troops. At the yards, the doughboys were allowed to visit the adjoining camp, while a cavalry detail stood guard over us, and we were not allowed out of our cars.

We sat in resentful silence, but a cavalry sentry, wanting to make something of it, kept making nasty remarks about the Marines in general; until finally, he made a remark we couldn't take. He yelled at us that we were "yellow" and had retreated at Belleau Wood; that the 7th Infantry had to save our necks: those were fighting words.

We piled off our cars and surrounded the sentry, and the smallest Marine in the group challenged him to fight. The sentry blanched and all but fell, and was shaking so that he couldn't talk.

In the meantime, a guard was rushed to the scene with a number of ranking officers. The guard stood silently back of us, while the officers, led by a major general, proceeded to rave at the marines. But the general hadn't met a man like Sergeant Daly.

Daly in no uncertain terms demanded to know why they had felt it necessary to put a guard on the Marines; why their sentry didn't know enough to keep silent; and why the Marines were singled out by the army to vent their spleen wherever they went.

The sergeant roared, the major general roared, until, finally, the general, apparently noticing the ribbons on Daly's chest, denoting the Medal of Honor, in a tone of respect turned to the captain of the guard and ordered all sentries removed. Then turning to Daly, they shook hands, returned salutes, and the general left with his party.

Daly turned to his men, and we waited to hear the verdict. We could wander about, but we weren't allowed in the camp, and we had to remain within calling distance. We wouldn't be fed, either. We had left without rations: we had had breakfast, but no lunch or supper, (except for the snack food at the depot near noon :) and this was not at all to our liking.

We eyed the adjoining boxcars, as though they were the solution to our wants. They were quickly opened and food was quickly passed out. Corned Willie, gold fish, jams, and canned tomato juice. The cans were stacked high in our cars, and we retired to eat—wondering why we hadn't been receiving such rations, instead of French iron rations and monkey meat. Perhaps the damned army felt we would all be killed soon and were not worth the cost of feeding good food.

The army men soon returned and loaded, and the train gave a couple of toots on its whistle, and with many jerks was on its way again.

The next day, we were unloaded at Liffol le Grand and marched five kilometers to the town of Freeville, where we were billeted in a National Army camp. Why, we didn't know, but again we were shunted to one side and not delivered to our regiments. Well: "Ours is not to cry; ours is but to do and die." At any rate, we could take anything and everything they gave us, and still ask for more.

The second morning, the 180 with the sergeant hiked to the drill field and did our stuff. It was noticeable that the army contingents stood around most of the day.

The third morning, we formed for drill. The army colonel and staff were present to look over their charges; but Sergeant Daly stepped up to the colonel, saluted, and growled that in the Marine Corps, "Top kickers don't drill," and stalked off.

The colonel looked as though he wasn't hearing right; but by the time he recovered, Daly was entering his bunk house. There was a quick shuffling of feet, and about 170 men left the ranks, leaving but a "corporal's guard" to drill.

We went up the hill back of camp and lay in the sun all day, returning at meal times for a bite. This was the pattern for several days; we answered roll call, then disappeared for the day.

One day, several of us were posted on the guard roster, and we fell in for guard, the rest taking to the hill—all but the corporal's guard of faint hearts. Soon "Flat Tire," one of the army lieutenants, who hated our guts, and Officer of the Day, assembled us in front of the guard house and instructed us in the action to follow. Flat Tire, who it was said had gotten his straddling stride from indiscretions with a French Madam, was short and to the point. We were to take the Marines on the hillside into custody and bring them back under arrest.

Well, an order is an order, and he armed us with loaded pistols, formed a skirmish line, and heroically waving his .45 ordered us to advance. We proceeded slowly abreast up the hill, stopping when we come upon one of our men, and explained to him that our orders were to capture him and put him in the brig: would he please go on up the hill to avoid capture. The Marine, grinning, would accommodate us, only to be disturbed again further up the hill. Flat Tire was in a rage, and worked back and forth behind the line waving his hat and shouting further orders.

Finally, we made the top of the hill and stopped to count our prisoners. We had eight or ten *army* guys, who had followed the pattern set down by the Marines; and only three Marines, who had gotten tired of being chased. Flat Tire was ready for the straight jacket, and raved about what he would do to us; raved about our not using the guns; and raved about the army men captured, and only three Marines.

The next day, I was on guard again in the early morning tour. I was assigned the duty of rousing the mess sergeant, cooks, and K.P.'s, and getting them on the job.

I awoke the men and went to the mess hall, as they were beginning to get breakfast for the camp. The men were all glad to see a Marine on duty, and I was treated to a fine breakfast, accompanied by much good-natured kidding. They said the men in camp got a big kick out of our maneuver the day before, especially how we got the best of Flat Tire. It seems as though they hated him as much as we did.

On completing my watch, I returned to the guard house, only to have the guard start out the same as the day before. As soon as the men of the camp had gone out to drill, we formed a skirmish line at the foot of the hill, and proceeded up. The only difference was, the men we were after went over the hill and disappeared. We managed, however, to grab some army men for the brig. The O.D.—Flat Tire—and two other army lieutenants that were assigned to the job did some high-class cussing and roaring. They didn't know it, but the Marines had planned it that way the night before.

That afternoon, I was put on watch in one of the peasant's prune orchards, to prevent its being stripped by the men. It was quiet there, too quiet, so I selected a tree and climbed up to feast on the fruit.

While up in the tree, I heard a noise and discovered three lieutenants coming through the orchard. I didn't have a chance, so I remained quiet, hoping they wouldn't see me, and pass on.

But to my surprise, they, too, had the same idea as I. Each one selected a tree, and climbed up. They were chatting, laughing, and having a feast; so I swung down under a low branch, stood, and gave them an exaggerated salute. All was quiet for a moment; they were caught, and so was I: then they burst into laughter, dropped to the ground, made a crack about being caught, and left the orchard.

And so did I. With the completion of my sentry work, I reported back to the guard house, and Flat Tire relented and dismissed me from guard for the rest of the day.

That night, I teamed up by chance with the shortest man in our outfit. And feeling somewhat at odds with the world in general, we visited a wine establishment. The place was full of army personnel, and, as we entered, all eyes turned toward us and amused grins swept over their faces.

The little Marine bet me that I couldn't drink down a bottle of wine without stopping. So we each ordered a bottle of vin blanc, stood, and upending the bottles guzzled them down. We both won. We straightened our overseas caps, smoothed our tunics, and stepped out into the street accompanied by the howls and laughter of the men.

We started up the street cold sober at first. Then the wine hit us. And we went staggering on our way: 6 foot 2 inches of me, and 5 foot 4 inches of him; the big Marine and the little Marine: and plenty drunk.

All I remember of the hike back to camp was he trying to convince me that he wasn't drunk: and I trying to convince him that I wasn't drunk. A mob of soldiers followed us, all laughing, and betting on which one of us would go down first.

We soon approached a group of officers, including the camp commander, and we gravely saluted, they returning the salute in turn; and we passed on. The little Marine staggered into his bunk house, and I staggered up the hill back of camp.

Nearing the top, I lay down supine and looked up at a wavering field of stars, and waited for them to cease. Then long after the camp had darkened and the men were asleep, I rose to my feet and returned to camp and to my bed. It was the first time in my life that I ever was drunk; and the last time that I ever got drunk in uniform.

The next morning, all the Marines were buzzing with the news. A bulletin had been placed on the board signed by the camp commander ordering all Marines to fall out for drill. We fell out and were in ranks, Sergeant Daly included, when the camp commander approached with a paper in his hand.

After the sergeant saluted the colonel and reported us all present and accounted for, the colonel stepped forward and read us a "call" from the 2nd Division—but added, that, as punishment, one half of the men were being detained and the other half would start that evening. We would find the names of those to go on the board when we returned from drill. He further stated that we would *all* go to drill: we *went* to drill; an order is an order, and we had been trained to obey orders; but, still, we wondered why the army had taken so long in getting an order out concerning our activities.

At the drill grounds, we found all the army units standing at ease on three sides of the field, and all officers gathered in a group in the center of the fourth side, waiting our arrival. Under Sergeant Daly, we marched up and took a company front position facing the officers; the sergeant saluted, turned the company over to them, and then retired.

We wondered what was in the cards for us. We soon found out. One lieutenant stepped forward and took command; but he was incoherent in his commands: he ordered one movement, but headed in the opposite direction. Soon we were enjoying this to the fullest, each man executing a different command, until we were all doubled up. The poor lieutenant, not knowing how to reform the company, gave up in disgust, and retired; and another took his place.

Again we fouled up the company, and flustered another lieutenant. By this, we wore out five lieutenants, much to the amusement of the army troops present. Even the lieutenants gave a sickly smile, or two, when another stepped forward to take command.

Then a final one approached. He looked capable, and as he neared us he smiled, and said, "Listen, you birds, I served eight years in the Marines. I served with Sergeant ---- at Guantanimo, Sergeants ---- and ---- in Haiti, and Sergeants ---- and ---- in San Domingo. Now, let's show them how Marines drill."

Under his commands, the company drilled as one. We executed right front into line; left about; right shoulder arms; counted cadence; and did squads right and left: and not a man made a mistake. He wheeled us into our former position, saluted, grinned, and gave us "at rest."

For a moment, not a sound was heard. Then from the troops lining the field a prolonged cheer went up. We had made our peace with the camp; all was forgiven; and we were in.

The lieutenant then thanked us, and explained the set up; that they were draftees, not long in service before being sent overseas; that the officers were new and needed experience in troop command: and they had counted on this bunch of front-line Marines to help them out.

For the balance of the day, we drilled as though for our own drill sergeants. Each officer had his chance at command; mistakes were overlooked, and good commands were executed smartly. In the middle of the afternoon, they marched us off the field and back to camp appreciative of a job well done.

At the camp bulletin board, I found I was on the list to be retained. No man was singled out, but they had gone through the roster keeping every other man. Well, that was that.

After supper, we were all gathered to bid the lucky—or unlucky—men farewell; and they were off again with the sergeant to their companies and regiments, to serve again in the 2nd Division

21

Bedlam in Freeville

The next morning, I answered sick call, as my teeth were acting up. I received a pass to go to the dentist, but I had to hike about ten kilometers to Bazoilles sur Meuse to find him. There was a large hospital and medical center there, and I thought my troubles would be over.

On my way, I passed the drill field and could see the remaining contingent of Marines drilling, and I was glad to pass them by. Then I came to a lovely chateau in the midst of a garden of trees with American nurses scattered about the grounds. They told me it was a rest home for nurses who needed it. I continued on, and finally came to Bazoilles, a pretty little French town nestled between the hills, and to the hospital that lay beyond.

I was unable to locate anybody at the hospital. I went through long, empty wardrooms, investigated offices, and tried several buildings, until at last I found a soldier to direct me. Following his directions, I found the dentist's office, but went in to find it empty. Soon a sergeant entered and asked me what I wanted. I waved the permit in his face and said I had some teeth I wanted to have fixed, and asked where the dentist was. He replied that the dentist was away that day, but added, "I'll take care of them; jump in the chair."

I blew up and told him I'd think several times before I had him look at a dog's teeth. We both got pretty warm in our talk—with the result that I stamped out of the room. What kind of an army is it, anyway—a "boot-licking" sergeant, who would attempt to fix teeth—a lieutenant, who insisted on buying your belt before he would look at your teeth: and then they tell you they don't do the work, but merely made a record of it?!

My return trip was in anger. A buck private didn't rate attention in this man's army. I fumed my way into Liffol le Grand and stamped into a Y.M.C.A. hut—and when I pushed my way through a crowd to the counter to get some cigarettes, I stopped in my tracks: there stood Gridley, the man who had been given a much needed bath by the men in boot camp: he was waiting on the counter.

I blistered him aplenty, going over his pedigree in my anger: a Marine waiting on customers in a Y hut! My contempt of him knew no limits. I remembered him in the company during the Belleau Wood scrap, always whining and playing sick to get out of it, until finally they discovered he had piles, (who didn't?) and sent him to the rear for an operation. That was in June, and now it was August: and here he was holed up in a Y hut!

After venting my anger, I put my money back in my belt and left. I went up the street, but soon heard voices exclaiming, "Ooh-la-la, le Marine," and two Mademoiselles grabbed my arms. The doughboys they had just left stood dumbfounded, their mouths agape, looking at the sight: a Marine who had just taken their girls away from them. I, however, told the girls, "Beaucoup malade," always a sure way to dismiss them, and went back to camp.

With Sergeant Daly gone, we had no noncom over us; we were just bucks with time on our hands. Time is bad for all concerned; however, we were now working to get out of the camp and Freeville. The only irregularities were caused by a few, and those after hours, so it was natural for the camp authorities to put a lid on the camp. Orders were given that no man could leave camp without a pass, and all would be in bed at taps.

The first night after that order, Flat Tire decided to get cute again, and made a bed check. Three were missing from our barracks. He posted a guard at each end of the building and took a position inside near the door.

We couldn't get any sleep, as the lieutenant kept up an incessant chatter with his guards. At first, our men kept yelling, "Quiet! Pipe down! Shut off the gab, and let us get some sleep!" which kept the lieutenant running back and forth to catch them.

After a while, it became a game, and we made the remarks more personal. We soon had the lieutenant crazy, and bedlam brewed in our bunkhouse. All this could have been stopped had the lieutenant any brains. I couldn't imagine anything like that occurring under Marine officers or noncoms. Besides, it would have been simple to ascertain the identities of the missing men and put them under arrest the following day: but Flat Tire always did it the hard way.

It was a long time after midnight when we heard the strays singing drunkenly on the road back to camp, and we knew we had to warn them. The lieutenant really "slipped his hatches" then, and he took out his pistol and rushed from one sentry to the other, yelling orders, and yelling at the men to be quiet.

As the drunks approached the barracks, they were warned by the noise that something was amiss, and they sobered up quickly and tried to sneak in. *Bang*! a sentry took a shot at one of them—and then things happened fast. Our men tripped the lieutenant, and milled around the sentries, knocking their rifles up to prevent more shooting. The whole camp jumped alive and suddenly was filled with scrambling men. Practically every Marine had his rifle with bared blade on, and the lieutenant and his men were crowded against a building and held there.

Two of the drunken Marines slipped in safely in the confusion, but the third—the one shot at—disappeared. The men put out search parties to ascertain if he was wounded or dead; but after searching the area well decided he had fled to more peaceful climes. Luckily for the lieutenant and sentries, no one was hurt.

The colonel came on the run and soon got the story from some of our men. He ordered us back to our beds and promptly read the riot act to the lieutenant. Then all was quiet. At day break, they caught the third Marine sneaking back into camp, and plunked him in the brig.

In the morning, the Marines went to drill and drilled well during the day. We had been hearing of communications from the 4th Brigade asking that we be sent back, and, also, one from 2nd Division Headquarters, with orders to send us back. That night, when we came in from drill, the colonel read us that order and told us to be packed and ready to leave after chow.

When we fell in to leave, they told us that the three wayward men were to be retained in the brig. But the men felt differently: they would go with us, or we wouldn't move.

The colonel and every officer in the camp down to Flat Tire was there, as were the men of the army units; and the three men still sat in the brig: and we stood in our place. We sang every verse of "Hinkey, Dinkey, Parlez Vous," and made up others more personal about Flat Tire and the colonel: but that didn't change their minds. We stood and sang for hours, until long past midnight, when we heard the train whistling for us down in the valley: and, finally, the colonel grinned, and ordered the Marines loosed from the brig, and turned them over to us.

We gave three rousing cheers for the colonel, for the camp, and, finally, we mustered up a cheer for old Flat Tire. The men of the camp returned the cheer as we swung down the road singing at the top of our voices, "Hinkey, Dinkey, Parlez Vous!" We "hinkey-dinked" straight to the train, scrambled aboard, and with two toots of the whistle, we were away.

Freeville and the National Guard men there will always remember that contingent of front-line Marines, every one a wounded or gassed veteran— and probably never wished to see another as long as they lived. The Marines were wrong in their actions, but, then, who wouldn't after being shoved around and discriminated against as we had. And why were the 180 of us shunted in Freeville at all? why weren't we sent directly to our units?

22

A Display of Might

We rode along enjoying the scenery with not a care in the world, when someone said we were approaching Chaumont, General Pershing's Headquarters. We were riding in French Third-Class coaches, and we all crowded to the windows on the right side of the train in hopes that we could see the headquarters as we pulled into the depot. We couldn't, as it was hidden from our view.

When the train stopped, some of the men got off to stretch their legs. But there was an angry snarl, "Get back on that train; you aren't allowed on the platform": an army sentry was pacing up and down the platform, and the remarks came from him. He was dressed in much finer clothes than we: apparently Headquarters' troops were for "show" and were something special.

He stopped his pacing and came to port arms, and said, "Take off your regimental insignia; you are not allowed to wear anything that will identify your regiment."

All of us piled out of the cars. This promised to be interesting, and we wanted in on it; for the "regimental insignia" that he referred to was our Marine emblem, a part of our uniform.

The men began to kid him, and he got real nasty about it, and said he would call the guard if we didn't remove them. We said, "Call your guard; we'd like to see them take them off."

He obliged us and called the guard and they shortly came on the run, accompanied by several officers. The guard hesitated taking on about ninety men, so remained still. Then the officer of the guard came over and repeated the order: we grinned and repeated our invitation to him, "Take the emblem off; we're waiting."

There was quite a hubbub and excitement among the guard, but we stood firm, grinning and waiting. Then a ranking officer dashed up, grinning at us but irked with the guard: "Those are Marines, and that is the Corps insignia: dismiss the guard."

22. A Display of Might

He came over and inquired what regiment we were from; and when he found out that we were wounded and gassed men returning to our outfits, he said it would be all right to stand on the platform but that we shouldn't leave the area. We all saluted, and he returned it as he left. So, another Army group was educated about the Marines.

The train started on its way again with many a jerk and frequent tooting of its "peanut" whistle, and, toward evening, we were detrained and met by trucks and continued our journey.

Just before dark, we were dropped according to our companies in various little villages. As I hopped off, I heard my name called and saw Lt. Corbett come running toward me. He was evidently glad to see me, and, after greetings were exchanged, he said he would check me in and gave me instructions on how to find the billet. He told me not to unpack, as we would be "hitting the road" at day light: and he further told me that they had a new Chauchat rifle for me.

I was near tears at the news and told him I wanted to be a plain rifleman, and that I had had enough of that gun. He grinned at me, and said, "It's hard to get a good gunner for the Sho-Sho and you are needed badly."

I felt somewhat better about it, but couldn't help feeling that it was a "suicide" gun and remembered the flanking assignment at Soissons and the death of Jimmie Duke: "O.K., I'm elected again; good bye to advancement, I am wedded to a Sho-Sho."

I went to the billet and renewed my friendship with my comrades. I was roused later when the company clerk showed up with a new Chauchat, six bags of clips, ammunition, and assigned me two new loaders.

After checking the gun and loading the clips, I turned in for the night. But I couldn't get to sleep; I was thinking of my loaders. Comfort was o.k., but Connolly I was not sure about; he was an irresponsible person, carefree, and not conformable to discipline. He was a "problem child," and I got him for a loader.

At daybreak, we were routed out and soon hit the road. It was not an easy hike, more like a "forced march." We ground out the kilos with about five minutes rest in sixty, and I soon found out how much out of condition I was. The gas I had taken in at Vierzy began to tell; I was short of wind, and my legs were buckling under me; I had no stamina: but I did not dare fall out. I was committed to the hike, and hike I would; for I was one of the largest men in the company and the little men were pushing us.

The men at first began kidding me, and the kidding made me sore—I'd be damned if I would give up. And, finally, the men began to be sorry for me, which was worse. I cursed and I raved, but on I kept, one foot before the other, no let up: left, right, left, right; and on I went, raving and cursing; left foot, right foot, left foot, right foot: on I went.

Men in my squad attempted to lighten my load, by carrying the gun and bags of clips; but no, I would carry my load and hike. Lieutenant Corbett began to hike beside me, and finally took my gun. It felt great. But soon I took it back, thanking him: I would carry my own load.

So it went, until after ascending a long grade up from the Moselle River, we came to a French training camp, and were billeted in a barracks. It was late in the evening, and we had been hiking since early in the morning. We had covered 25 to 30 miles.

Word was passed that we would have chow in an hour, so several of the men decided in the meanwhile to go swimming; and I went with them. It was a bad choice; for once started we found that the Moselle was about three kilometers away. But we hiked on anyway, until we came to the river.

We quickly shed our clothes and jumped in. The water was cold but invigorating, and we enjoyed it. The river was used as a canal, and large barges floated by. Some of the men swam out to one, and climbed aboard—but were surprised to find the skipper, the skipper's wife, and his daughter standing before them beholding and enjoying the show. There was one grand splash as they dove overboard to hide their nakedness. When they swam to shore, they received much kidding.

We dressed and returned to the camp; and although late for chow, we were fed by the cooks, and then bedded down for the night.

Our stay in this camp was short, but five days, each man engaged at his own assignment. For me, it was three days firing the auto rifle, the grenadiers throwing their grenades, and the rest at bayonet work.

There was a maze of practice trenches here, and the gunners and selected snipers went to these for firing practice. The targets were one foot square and were placed at various distances and over a wide front. They appeared for short intervals, and we had the job of spotting them as they appeared and firing on them.

Judges were in the trench with each gunner and these rated us on our perception and fire. I don't know how I rated, but assume it was good, as I spotted each target and put a shot or two through it as it appeared. They were hard to locate, and the range varied from 100 to 300 yards.

They released me on the third afternoon and sent me to the grenade pit, where I had opportunity to throw a few. The fourth day the regiment held field exercises. A simulated attack was made through wooded country and was designed to sharpen the eyes and wits of the soldier. Machine gun pits were positioned in the brush at various locations, and when targets appeared a red flag denoting the firing gun was continuously waved until the imaginary gun was flanked out. The flags were difficult to see, and I am afraid most of us were "killed" in the attack. Luckily, we weren't far from camp when the attack was over, and we had plenty to think about when we arrived. This was leading to something; but what?

Tueffel Hunden

On the fifth day, we were routed out early and the officers and men were told to "smarten up." We were in combat clothes and surely needed it. After straightening our tunics, brushing off the mud from our leggings and clothes, and setting our helmets on our heads, we were marched out to a long but relatively narrow field.

The 2nd Division was forming, and practically every unit was there; the 3rd Brigade, the 4th Brigade, the machine gun battalions, the 12th, 15th, and 17th Artillery Regiments, the 2nd Engineers, the tanks, and numerous truck companies were there: over 20,000 men in rank. It was a grand sight, and one most of us had never witnessed before.

Divisional staff officers were gathered on one side of the field and many visiting dignitaries of the French and American Armies; behind them stood the lesser officers, and ladies and gentlemen. There was another group of fifty or more men of the division who were singled out for honors due them.

In front of the 5th Marines were gathered the massed colors and standards of the units in parade, and to their right the grouped bands of the regiments, battalions, and other units. The Infantry and Marine regiments stood in columns of battalions, each regiment in three columns of four companies. It was to be a great show, and one in which we were proud to participate.

The 1st Battalion of the 5th Marines had acquired seven dogs, one bitch and six males, which were running around and through the companies. The stage was set. First was the decorating of the heroes. That took some time. Various French and American officers took turns pinning on medals and either kissing or shaking the hand of the recipient; then came the playing of "The Star-Spangled Banner" and the French "Marseillaise" by the massed bands. And they had just begun to play, standards lowered, and the men at present arms or at right hand salute: when as though a signal had been given the dogs: they romped out on the field and in between the "brass" and the grouped colors—and there began fighting.

Two of the color guards, forgetting they were at present arms, tore out onto the field swinging their rifles at the dogs—only to realize their error, and rigidly reform to stand at present arms, alone and conspicuous, with the dogs at their feet.

At the conclusion of the "Marseillaise," red-faced, the general of the division bawled out: "Second Division, pass in review." And the 2nd was on the march again. What I could see of the parade was long remembered. After a long wait, and while the 3rd Brigade was passing in review, we were given the command to march. We passed in review in front of the officers and dignitaries on our right and column after column of 2nd Division units on our left: then a German plane appeared high overhead: but anti-aircraft fire drove him away.

After passing in review, we formed into columns of squads, and each battalion took a different road to hike to the next billeting place. Toward dark, we were halted for a rest, and there were found by divisional motorcycle messengers with a direct order from the general to "shoot those damned dogs." While we waited, seven dogs were summarily shot, as per the general's orders.

On we went till after dark, and then pulled into the town of Selaincourt where we were billeted.

23

Something Big Is Coming

Selaincourt was a one-street town. Masonry buildings lined the street, and filth and the accumulation of the ages lay about. The town was populated mostly with women, a few old men, and a scattering of the young.

The first day, we had the distinction of giving the town what appeared to be its first bath. Men of the company were put to work cleaning its street; we swept, we shoveled, and we hauled away the filth. By late afternoon, we were finished and Selaincourt was cleaned.

As we sat with our feet in the gutters, admiring our work, a herd of dirty dairy cows lumbered past. The herd was followed by a mademoiselle, just as dirty as they. She was fat and stumpy, with unkempt hair, and her dirty dress swept the street.

Behind her followed a retinue of a dozen or more Marines. They were all smiling and singing, "The mademoiselle from Armentières, who hadn't been kissed for forty years, hinkey, dinkey, parlez vous…." The girl was laughing, too, but it was well she didn't understand English, for the words of the song were not nice nor polite.

As the cows wended their way up the street, the song drifted back to us, as we contemplated the scene, "Oh, the French they are a funny race, Parlez vous; they fight with their feet … hinkey, dinkey, parlez vous…."

The people of the town were of another age. They had no modern conveniences, no phones, no movie houses, and no place of amusement; all they knew was work, and once a week to go to church. The only excitement there was the drumming of the town crier, who, dressed in his ancient costume, paraded the streets of the town and cried out the latest news, or read edicts from the local or state government. I suppose the government allowed the people to keep enough to exist on, but all the rest went for taxes, to pay for wars, past, present, and future. It didn't matter to them who won, the Germans or the French; life went on as before, in either event. Well, we would furnish the amusements and the laughs while we were there.

One of the first projects done by us was to build a latrine. It was probably the first ever built in the town. It consisted of a long, deep trench, with a log split lengthwise. The log was something to lean on or sit against, and, with care, to help prevent one from falling in. It was located in a field about one hundred yards from the buildings, and it had no screen around or over it. It was a popular place in the morning, between drill sessions, and after drill, and, we thought, private.

The first time we came in from drill, there was a rush to our new latrine—and we found that we had no privacy: about every woman in town was there to watch. It must have been interesting to the French women to see fifteen to twenty men seated on the log, with trousers trailing, enjoying their rest; then being replaced by another contingent when they were through. The women were properly amused, but the Marines carried on as if they were in private. Like clock-work, the women were there at regular hours while we were in the town.

Something big was coming; all the indications were there, and we were going to have a part in it. As yet, no one knew when or where, but from the training we were getting, we knew it was big. From morning till night we were at it, close order drill, bayonet work by the hour, with gas masks on and without, and as skirmishers across the countryside. Long hikes were taken to condition us, and lectures were given on gas warfare, booby-traps, and on fortified positions. It was hard work, and when the day was done we were glad enough for the hay loft to sleep in.

The auto-rifle gunners were exempt from the sessions of bayonet work and close order drill, and time was spent in dismantling and assembling the gun, until we knew the gun perfectly. Shotguns were added to the armament, one sawed-off gun to the squad, and it was to be loaded with buckshot. It appeared as though we were going to mix it with the Germans on a hand-to-hand basis. Even the sergeants were armed with the Springfield rifle and bayonet, and were included in all exercises.

I had kidded Sergeant Wagner about having to go through the close order drills and bayonet work, like a buck private, while the gunners were comfortable, seated in the shade, taking life easy. But I kidded once too often; for he handed me his rifle and *I* went through the paces, while he lounged in the shade. From then on, it was a game; he hunted for me, and I hid out, with the result that *he* did the drills.

One morning, I got a break from company maneuvers, as I had been posted for guard duty. While cleaning my .45 and prior to going on guard, I

23. Something Big Is Coming

let the slide slip when putting the gun together and the recoil spring and cap went flying off into the hay. After searching, all I found was the spring; the cap to the spring container was gone. As there wasn't much time before guard. I was up against it.

While bemoaning my fate, I remembered a .45 cartridge was the same size; so, breaking a cartridge open, and discarding the bullet and powder, I inserted the empty cartridge in place of the cap. It worked perfectly; the gun was as good as ever, and I passed guard inspection with it.

Guard duty was simple at Selaincourt. It amounted to "chasing prisoners," that is, taking four to six "summary" prisoners out on work detail and standing by as they did their chore. At first my name wasn't called for this, so all I had to do was sit around the guard room and listen to the chatter of the guards. But at 11:30, my name was called, and they brought out eight general court martial prisoners, and instructed me to march them to the next town, Dolcourt, and feed them at the company mess. I was hesitant to take more than three, as Marine regulations specify that that is all that should be entrusted to one man: and further, it was rumored that any guard who lost his prisoners shall serve their sentence. Well, the sergeant of the guard must know what he is doing, so I marched them off to Dolcourt.

As we arrived, mess call was blown, and in an instant the streets were crowding with men—and among them my prisoners. They melted in among the throng: "Halt—halt—halt," I commanded, and tried to get a bead on one; but he was lost in the mob.

I received much kidding from the men—and a lot of advice. Even the officers were free with their advice; good-natured, but irritating to me. Apparently, the story got around, for they were unmerciful, and the cooks, too, and K.P.'s had their fun at my expense. And I told them that I would stay there until the prisoners showed up, or I would take the first eight men I could grab back to the guard house.

I found where the chow lines were forming, but on looking them over, I failed to find any of my prisoners. Discouraged, I climbed up a bank and sat down.

Chow was over, and the K.P.'s were cleaning up, but still I sat alone. Soon a Marine climbed up and sat down beside me; then another; and another: until eight were lined up with me. I then arose to my feet and ordered them to fall in and marched them away.

Just before we arrived in Selaincourt, I halted them, and said, "I had eight prisoners when I came to Dolcourt; I have eight prisoners now; I don't know whether you are the same eight, or not, but I want to thank you, if you are."

They all laughed, and one said, "Hell, where could we go?" Another remarked that maybe they wouldn't be too hard on them anyway; so why "shove off" and make the punishment worse? Well, they were a good bunch, and I hoped they wouldn't get too hard a punishment.

After I turned them in at the guard house, I told the sergeant what had happened. He laughed, and said, "It happens every time we send them to chow; besides, we will turn them loose shortly. We are going 'In' again."

On Sunday, there was little to do, police duty in the morning, and lay around the town during the day. I shed my underwear, socks, and shirt, and proceeded to the town washing center to do some laundry. On reaching the washing center, I found that I would have to wait, as all places were taken.

The washing spot seemed to be the one place in town where the people gathered to visit. It was a well, and it consisted of a circular masonry structure filled with dirty, soapy water, about a dozen feet in diameter. Outside of this was a second ring of sudsy water, around which the French women knelt and busily pounded their clothes. When a piece of clothing had been pounded enough, it was tossed into the inner circle where here it was supposedly rinsed.

Finally, there was a vacant spot, and I knelt down between two madams of ample proportions. As I began my wash, they started their jabber at me, accompanied by much laughter. From their remarks and laughter I gathered they did not think much of my efforts, which consisted only of soaping and rubbing. After some little effort in this, they insisted I take their paddles, which I did, and pounded the clothes with some healthy whacks.

"Ca—ca—comme ci! Comme ci!" they ejaculated, and grabbing my clothes, they proceeded to wash them for me. They were friendly and kind, and we talked, each in our own language, neither of which was understood by the other. When the wash was done, I gave my place to the next, and spread my clothes out to dry.

Lieutenant Galliford took the company out for a day and put us through our paces, but called it off early and gave us some competitive sports instead. One such concerned the Sho-Sho gunners. He offered five francs as prize money to the fastest gun crew. We were to dismantle the gun, put it together again, dash a specified distance, get down, simulate fire, then dash back to the starting point and have the gun checked.

About thirty gunners and their crews lined up for the start, and, at the signal, we were off. I tore down the gun, put it together again, we ran to the designated point, simulated fire, returned again to the starting point and had the gun checked. We were first; no one else was even close; we received the five francs.

But then the losers howled, "Give us another chance at the money." With this certain men of the company saw a chance to make some money and

23. Something Big Is Coming

selected their champion and bet on him. About six crews remained in the race, with good hard cash going to the winner.

We were off again, but Connolly got excited and attempted to help me, with the result that I lost time and came in a close second, Gowdy[1] winning the pot. I was content to leave it at that, but the men who had put their money on me matched the winning and demanded a third match. They told Connolly to keep his fingers out this time, and do only what I told him to do.

There was a good size pot for the winner this time, as the race was between Gowdy and me; all other gunners were out of it. I told each loader exactly what to do, and what not to do; and got set for the match: and we awaited the lieutenant's signal to go.

This time it was different; we worked like clock-work and finished before Gowdy had barely put his gun back together. There was a great deal of shouting and glee; we had won the money and the honor.

I brushed the money aside, and got out from the clamoring pack; I was content, and I went over to Gowdy to shake his hand. But he was sore, and wouldn't shake: "When we get out of this next drive, I'll beat you," he growled.

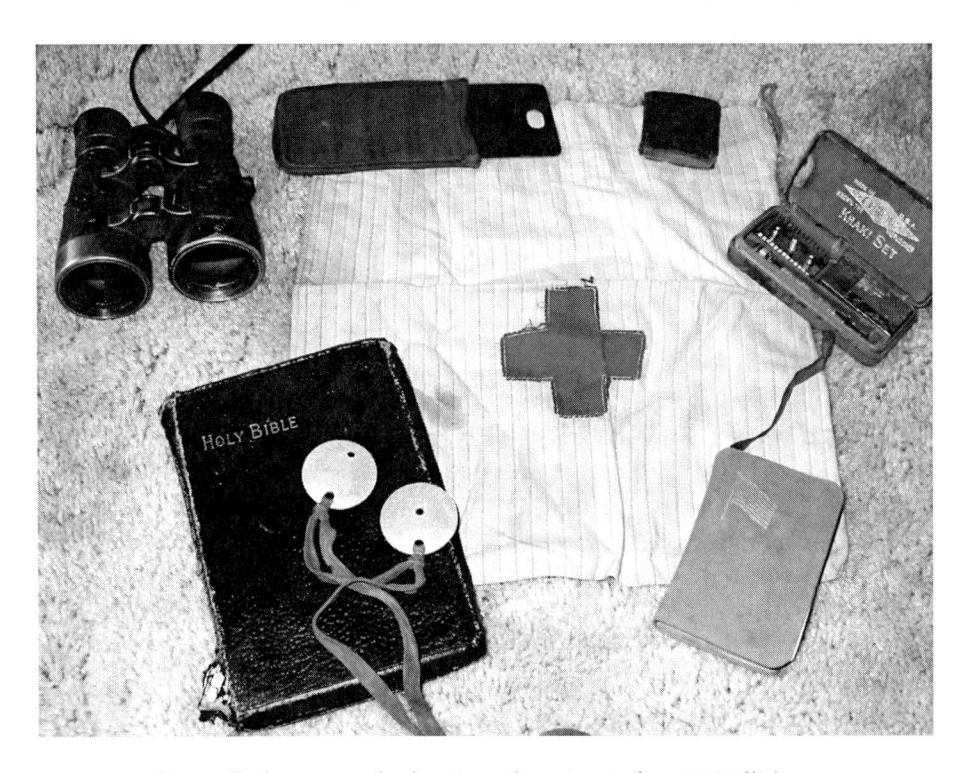

Everard's dog tags and other items (courtesy Robert G. Bullis).

Everard's dog tags (courtesy Robert G. Bullis).

And that ended the activities for the day, and we were marched back to our billets.

Our training was nearly completed. We were in good condition, but we had a field problem to go through, and we were hiked to Colombey les Belles. Here we joined the Brigade in field maneuvers in and about the Bois de Colombey. It was tough, hard work, and supposed to simulate our coming action.

We adopted a new attack formation here that was supposed to cut down on casualties, and give more control to our officers. The first wave of the attack was to be the same as before, a long, thin line of skirmishers, but with the second wave in section and platoon columns. It seemed all right, but I noticed there was difficulty in maintaining liaison when in the forest. However, it would do when in the open.

We were in the second line and formed in section columns, when we lined up for the mock attack in Colombey les Belles. We casually advanced, until we came to a dense forest. As it was impossible to get through in formation, we did the next best thing: each man for himself.

We forged ahead, until we came to a fire lane about ten feet wide running across our way; then took the easy way out. All the troops were there, and we followed the trail, until we came out on the other side. We reformed there, and shortly merged with the company, and set out on the return hike to Selaincourt. It was not according to instructions, but the officers could hash that out later among themselves. This would be our last night in Selaincourt, and we were not sorry to be on our way again.

Part III: St. Mihiel

24

A Private Speaks

We had the word to fall in at three o'clock in the afternoon. As the company formed, the first thing noticeable was the officers; they were decidedly irritable, and growled and snapped. The captain gave a short talk on what was ahead, gas, booby traps, concrete pillboxes, and well-registered artillery fire. He summed it up by ordering all gunners to check their guns, the others to check theirs, and then dismissed us.

I took my loaders aside and … dust, checking each clip to see that it was clean and checking the side of each clip to see that there was no undo pressure on the cartridges. It was enough to keep them busy for a while, and then I started cleaning the gun itself. The loaders worked well for a while, but there was a steady interruption by men who hadn't anything to do, so I told the loaders to beat it, and I would check the ammunition myself.

I was busily engaged at this, when Connolly returned—drunk; and tried to grab the Sho-Sho: he was going to "shoot up the town." There were five or six drunks with him, and I had quite a time fighting him and his cohorts off. When I finally convinced him that he wasn't going to get the gun, they shoved off, only to return and tried to take my .45, for the same purpose. I had my hands full; and it would have been tough, if a bunch from the company hadn't come to my help. So they shoved off again, looking for more trouble.

The captain appeared and roared, "Fall in!" and a sorry looking company lined up. There were three or four sober men in my squad, and not many more in the other squads. There was a concerted move underway to get drunk and have a last fling before getting killed in the coming action. The captain was roaring, the other officers were roaring, and the drunks were roaring. The sober men were grabbing the drunks, fastening their equipment on them, and pulling them into rank. At least we had them in rank; but it was impossible to keep them quiet, and difficult to keep them in their place.

I held on to two, Comfort and Connolly. Comfort behaved all right, but Connolly kept striking at me. So I let him have a good one in the belly. That doubled him up, but he began cursing and yelling, until finally the captain came over and ordered him to shut up. Connolly was beyond reason and cursed the captain, who became livid and pretty near lost control of himself, and shouted at him—"No man can call me that. If I had you at the front, I would kill you. You will get a general court martial for drunkenness, insubordination, cursing an officer, and being unfit for duty," and stalked back to the front of the company: "Squads left—harsh!" and we were off.

We hiked to a cross roads several hundred yards away and stopped. We were waiting for the rest of the battalion before resuming the march. For the sober men, it was another session of fighting the drunks. Connolly had become worse, and I had my hands full keeping his hands off my gun and keeping him in line.

Finally he had to relieve himself, so Womack and I, and another drunk, took him to the side of the road, removed his equipment, and tried to steady him; but then he passed out. We threw him to the ground and left him. We tossed his rifle and pack on the galley cart, and fell in ranks—only to find ourselves tending another drunk.

Soon the other companies arrived, and we resumed our march. We lost several more drunks in the roadside ditch throughout the next few miles. They all passed out cold. They had been drinking "White Mule," or prunella, a clear, hard liquor made from prune juice, which has a forty-mule kick.

From Selaincourt, we plodded northeast all night, until well after sun up, when we turned into a forest for eats and sleep. It was a terrible hike: between holding up drunks, carrying their packs and rifles, and trying to keep up with the company, I and the other sober men were all in. To make matters worse, the battalion was kept at a fast pace, to get to the woods where we would spend the day. But it did become much easier toward morning, for we had hiked the remaining drunks sober, and they were carrying their own load. At daylight, it was a relief to lay down in the woods and sleep.

After evening chow, we started out on another night march. The men were silent on this hike. Then in the early light of the approaching day, we passed through Pont St. Vincent, a mining center, in a deep valley along the Moselle River. This town was of particular interest to me due to the huge aerial tramways which crossed the river and the valley.

As we coursed through the outskirts of town, a German aviator began bombing the town and the bombs were exploding across the river from our line of march. The searchlights were busily trying to spot him, their fingers stretching high in the air and reflexively sweeping the sky. We had momentary glimpses of the avian as he twisted and turned to get out of the beams. We continued till dawn and entered a wood for the day's rest.

The next night, the hike continued at a fast pace. The only thing that broke the monotony was a large explosion miles ahead of us, followed by earth tremors and a brilliant light that flooded the night's sky. An enemy avian had dropped his bombs squarely on an ammunition truck. We were nearing the front.

My arches were bothering me, and it was hard to keep up. I hiked most of the way in the ditch at the side of the road where the soft dirt supported my arches. Men had been dropping out on this hike, so the captain ordered noncoms and officers to march alongside the column, with orders to keep the men in rank.

Womack had arch-trouble, too, so we got our heads together and decided that at the next dark patch of woods we would jump the detail. My old friend Sergeant Wagner was marching near us and either overheard our plotting or surmised our intentions, so we amended our plan. We would jump the detail as planned, except as we entered the woods we would split up, one to the right, and one to the left, halt, then collar the sergeant.

It worked perfectly. We dashed into the woods and the sergeant followed after; but before he knew what we were up to we had him by the front of the tunic. We told him to get back into rank, or take the consequences. The sergeant grinned and said he hadn't seen us and vanished after the column.

We went into the woods some distance, and taking a shelter-half we spread it on the ground and lay down to sleep. But an awful odor kept us awake. We got up and changed our position several times; but the odor remained. Finally, we abandoned the shelter-half and shifted farther away, and lay down in peace and quiet.

The shining of the sun awoke us sometime after daylight, and we opened our eyes, and there standing over us, grinning, was a couple of cute youngsters, a boy and a girl. They had their lunch pails and were on their way to school. We sat up and tried to talk to them, but again language was a stumbling block. At any rate, from their smiles and chatter, it was apparent they were happy to find two American "soldats" asleep in the woods.

We arose, and, arranging our equipment, we set out following the hobnail tracks to find our outfit. About 8:00 a.m., we came to the town of Fontenay, and found a store and purchased some jam, canned milk, and other confections. On rounding a corner, we came face to face with the captain. He read us the riot act and demanded to know what we were doing there. I told him I had fallen out due to falling arches, whereon he relented and told us to hurry and get up the hill back of town before roll call, as any not present for roll call would get a general court martial.

We hurried and fell in ranks just in time to answer, "Here!"—a stroke of luck, as many were not there. Sergeant Wagner came over to me and asked how we had found the company; and we both had a good laugh at our experience.

After roll call came sick call, and I apparently was not the only one whose arches gave way, for the hillside was covered with men whose shoes were off and first aid men attending them. Their remedy was simple, a rolled up bandage placed under the arches and the man marked "duty."

That night, the march was resumed. It rained, and we sloshed through the night in the water and the mud. We passed through four or five sleeping villages, and as we came into one of these the men heartily broke out into their latest verses of "Hinkey, Dinkey, Parlez Vous." Windows were hoisted and filled with old men and women in their sleeping hats, and, in a few cases, old men in their short night dresses and long sleeping caps in doorways to watch us march by.

Toward morning, we entered a wood to rest. Wherever we looked there was a pool of rain water. I finally picked the shallowest one that I could find and lay down to sleep, wet through and through and tired, but I soon found sleep.

We were awakened mid-morning and told chow was ready. I was deeply chilled; my fingers were swollen shut, and I had to work them for some time before they became normal again. My legs also were cramped, and took a lot of massaging before I could walk. But chow tasted good, and I ate enough to satisfy me.

After chow came the problem of drying out and finding a dry place to sleep. Later, I roused again, and, after working the circulation in my hands and legs, I roved about the vicinity. Throughout the forest men were huddled up sleeping; others sat disconsolately, their backs against trees; while others drifted as I was doing, alone in their thoughts. A small group worked about the galleys cooking up some concoction they called "stew"; while over there a group of officers sat in conference. They were probably planning how we were to be maimed or killed in the coming engagement.

I found a trail and followed it through the trees. More troops were scattered the length of the road, while at the upper end the road entered a walled chateau or farm. There was a lot of activity there, and it appeared to be used as a headquarters, regimental, brigade, or divisional, I didn't know which; and nor did I care. All I thought was, whoever they were they should be making some attempt at securing the men. Some needed comforts as warmer underwear, or raincoats that shed water and that did not blot it up as ours did, and to see to it that we were served some decent meals; at least once in a while. But, again, they only were planning the killing of men; and nor did it seem as though they cared which, the Boche or us.

24. A Private Speaks

The generals planned the campaign. They sat around the maps, drew a few lines, and delineated the sectors to be covered by each division, brigade, or regiment; they planned for the food, ammunition, supplies, access roads, and the time schedules. The colonels planned, fretted, and worried over the battalions: the majors planned, fretted, and worried over the companies: the captains planned, fretted, and worried over their sections: and the lieutenants sweated and worried over their details.

When the "day and hour" came and the men were committed to battle, the generals, colonels, and the majors were forgotten men. We had fleeting glimpses of the captains and lieutenants; they usually had rifles and were fighting like the men. But as the battle progressed, there were fewer officers to be seen. The noncoms had taken over the command, to become themselves scarcer and rarer; until the men were on their own.

We had a hazy idea of what the objectives were, and fought on in groups until only a handful remained and the place taken. Then a company or battalion would filter up and take over: your job was done. And you would look over the handful of your company that was left, and remember; remember the guy on your left or your right, remember how he went down; remember hazily the machine guns you had encountered and how the enemy had died; and remember the bursts of artillery fire that spasmodically ripped up the earth into a living hell.

The road back was a sickening nightmare; you were worried about "getting it" before you were in a safe position again, and you wondered what had become of the rest of the men. In a position far back, usually the spot you "jumped off" from, a day or two, before, you were reassembled. Men kept drifting back in small groups, by twos and threes, and a final check was made on the casualties. After the check had been made and you looked up and down the ranks you marveled: the casualties may not have been so bad; a few were escorting prisoners back to the rear areas; some had become lost in the tangle of undergrowth, and the battle had swept on; a large number had been scattered in groups and had moved forward with other commands; and a very few, known by their character, had just skulked in the first tangle or trench they came to.

You thought of those left behind forever—Duke, Bowness, Joyce, Rosinow, Tripe, Snare, and others—and you were stunned by the memories.

25

Privates, Jacks and Queens

It is time for noon chow now, so I went for my mess gear and joined the growing line of men. All was forgotten; the men were in a different mood, and hilarity was the keynote.

In the afternoon, the long awaited moment would arrive; the paymaster was coming. And, at last, I would receive my first pay in France. The last pay I had received was April 3 in the States; now it had caught up with me. September 8, five months of pay: aside from the money I had got from the Paris paymaster, I would get well over $100.

What to do with it? Money was no good here; it was a liability, and almost useless. I signed the pay roll and took the money; but I felt the weight of it as I tucked it away in my money belt.

As I turned away, I saw a crowd forming about the Y.M.C.A. secretary, a Mr. McKinley, who was shouting, "I will send your money home for you." So I again got in line. I gave the Y secretary $50 in francs, and received a scrap of paper for a receipt and consigned the money to Dad at home. I wrote a letter to the folks and mentioned paying the money to the Y secretary, and stated I was all right, well, and in good spirits.

The balance of the afternoon was quiet, except for the numerous poker games in progress. Every one seemed anxious to lose their money, and the money of the non-players, as well.

Toward night-fall, the number of games had diminished, as the money became centered in a few, and the inter-company games began. The stakes were high, and real gambling was more in evidence. On the other hand, a large number of losers were pestering the non-players for "stakes," to start anew.

I was a hopeful victim, as it was noted that I had received an exceptionally large pay from the paymaster. But I remained a poor prospect to the losers. In spite of numerous pleas and promises of riches, I clung to my money.

I had seen numerous poker games in the Marines, and had witnessed their dexterity in manipulation of the cards, and I didn't want any part of it.

That night, we resumed our march, ever northward and closer to trouble again. It was a miserable march, as it rained frequently during the night. We cursed the profiteering makers of our raincoats, for they were miserable affairs: we cursed the Germans for starting the war: we cursed our comrades for stumbling into us: and we cursed because we were miserable.

The men had forgotten "Hinkey, Dinkey, Parlez Vous" and the other marching songs we knew and settled down to the steady business of marching. Smoking was taboo, and the only noise was the constant shuffling of feet. Toward morning, we left the road and found haven under the shadowy wing of the trees, and sought rest where we could find it.

As we were to spend the next two days in this place, we pitched our shelter-half, or "pup" tents, as protection from the incessant rain, and lived in semi-comfort. The first day, they filled the ranks with boots straight from Parris Island and barely able to show three months as Marines. They were young and looked fresh and nice: "Oh, Lord, we once looked young and innocent, too; but long since."[1]

At first, we looked them over, hoping to find someone from home. Then we looked them over to single out a gullible victim and work him over. We showed them no mercy, and began to tell them the worst; the fighting they would have to do, and the terrors of the front. And when they were subdued, and in the proper mood, we urged them to show us what they had in their packs. Their packs held a gold mine for us, and we greedily plundered them: new socks, to replace the old; underwear that was clean, to replace our lousy, dirty ones; and in some cases, a new shirt, to replace the old, dirty, tattered ones.

After we changed into the new clothes, we thought of them, too, and cut their packs to a few essentials and tossed the remainder into a common pile. We were happy again and welcomed the new-comers into our ranks. They were spread throughout the company, so that each squad had two or three of these youngsters, and then we began to initiate them into the war as we found it.

During rainy sessions, we huddled in our pup tents, usually lying in a puddle. Corporal Davidian and I frequently played checkers on a pocket board that he carried, and I always came in second. Davidian, an Armenian, who had immigrated to California with his parents, had extreme hatred for the Turks, because of their cruel treatment of the Armenians. He carried a sack with him, in which he placed every slug that hit him or fell nearby. There was about ten pounds of shell fragments, shrapnel, and bullets in the bag;

and when I kidded him about carrying that stuff all over France, he became angry. He wanted that material to show his folks when he got home just how many times he had been near death.

On the night of September 11, we moved up. Before starting, we were again warned about the well-fortified positions we were going up against, the danger of mustard gas, and how we should protect ourselves from it with salve: how we would need grenades to take machine gun emplacements: and how we would need our iron rations. Then we were re-supplied with ammunition, iron rations were checked, and each man was given six grenades to carry: but no salve was issued for the mustard gas. Gas was more potent during wet weather and attacked the man in all damp areas, between the legs, underneath the arms, and the area around the neck being particularly vulnerable. We were wet clear through from the rain, and felt we needed it badly. However, it was not our lot to receive a tube of salve. We were furnished wire cutters for getting through the barbed wire entanglements, though, and various other gear.

As luck would have it, it poured hard on the way up. We sloshed through the wet grass and miry mud of the roads, and the rain was cold and chilled us to the bone.

At first, the cold rain, pouring off our slickers, hit us about the knees and trickled down our legs. To remedy this, most of us knelt down in the gutters of the road to wet ourselves thoroughly. It helped, but the sloshing of water between our toes and around our ankles was annoying, so many of the fellows cut slits in their boots to drain out the water. But that didn't help much.

We continued miserable in our hike, and so made up our minds to like it. Then the column halted; Sergeant Bill Gavin had passed out. He was ill when we started, and it proved too much for him: "Stretcher-bearers, up front!" was the word passed. And as soon as he was taken care of, the column started forward again.

We soon came to a road, the gutter of which was running full of water. We were to jump over it and Lieutenant Corbett would steady us as we landed. With the heavy load that I carried, I was cautious, and when it came my turn to jump, I walked up to the ditch to size it up. Then returning, I took a good run and leaped to clear the ditch. On landing, I hit the lieutenant and two other men and sent them sprawling, while I fell in a heap. I remembered the grenades as I went down, and in fear that they had detonated, I yelled, "Grenades—clear away."

Corbett and the men scrambled off to safety, and I was left alone in the mud. I had put them in the pockets of my slicker, three to a side, and fastened the web ammunition belt up over them. I couldn't get the fastening loose, and I didn't know whether they had detonated or not. As I struggled with the belt, I mentally counted off six, the number of seconds I had to live, cold sweat pouring off of me. I was near panic, until I realized the time interval was over and I was safe.

I carefully worked my way to my feet again and was unfastening the belt when Lieutenant Corbett gingerly approached and asked if I was all right. I replied that I was, but I would be damned if I would carry French offensive grenades any farther, and took the grenades of my pockets and heaved them off into the woods. Lieutenant Corbett grinned, and called, "Forward."

The protective caps of the grenades had come off in my tumble, but the grenades had failed to detonate. And with a sigh of relief, I shouldered my gun and took my place in file.

26

Over the Top

September 12

We came to the ruins of a town toward midnight. They said it was Limey, and according to the shambles, it looked as though it had stood four years of war. And we along with other American units were there to flatten it.

We were ordered into a trench, which was on a slope facing the Germans. At first, the water in the trench was ankle deep. But as we sloshed along, it became knee deep. Gradually it swelled, until it came up to my navel. God knows what the shorter men did: it must be up to their chin. It was cold and slimy, and along with the rain it all but drowned us.

We were halted in the "soup," and stood there from midnight until 5:00 a.m. There was a line of men in the trench when we arrived, replacements by their looks, and they were forlorn and shaken by the experience. And when I asked one of them whether they had any ammunition, the reply was, "No."

I immediately passed the word to company officers, and was rewarded after a time with, "Pass the new men without ammunition to the rear." Several hundred men thus were shunted to the rear and out of battle. But we wondered, who had blundered? Parris Island recruits, just over, and to be fed to the slaughter—sans ammunition.

We didn't know it—and soon were to find out—but a French 155 field artillery battalion was lined up thirty to forty feet behind us. The big guns began firing at 1:00 a.m. They made a steady roar, each gun firing a round every five minutes, until 4:30 a.m. With each burst of a gun, the flash of the explosion lit each man's face with an eerie light, and the fire and smoke swirled about us in the trench. It sounded as if the world was coming to an end. The continual roar and fire of thousands of guns was something new. You couldn't think, and the vacuum of each shell fired was terrific.

We cursed the gunners and the men who planned the set up; but there was nothing we could do but take it. Each explosion would start earth tumbling into the trench, and the water in it rocking: it surely was hell.

26. Over the Top

In spite of the din and confusion, I twice managed to fall asleep on my feet and slip under the water; recover myself, quickly clean up my gun, wipe my ammunition dry, and re-perch my musette bags of clips on my shoulders again. Some of the men scrambled up on the parapet of the trench, only to have officers and noncoms order them back into the trench.

Finally, at 4:30 a.m. the real barrage began, each gun firing at its limit, and this maintained until 5:00 a.m. What we thought of the artillery bombardment before was nothing compared to this: it was out of this world. We soon howled in ecstasy: we were on the sending end; the Germans were on the business end; and what a shelling they took.

At 5:00 a.m., the Infantry jumped off, the 9th on the left, and 23rd on the right. And we waited for the burst of fire expected from the Germans. But it didn't come. They had taken the German front line with hardly a shot being fired.

We climbed out of the trench and took up the attack in support. We first passed through what was said to be a village, Remenauville; not a wall stood, only piles of rubble, and we hurriedly advanced forward.

Our fingers were stiff from the night's experience, and our legs and feet were dead. Long into the morning we were stamping our feet and rubbing our fingers and hands to restore circulation.

Through the mist and smoke of the battle, we could see the famous Mont Sec on our left, looming high above the surrounding territory. The French were attacking at that spot, but the mount itself was being by-passed, due to the persistent use there of deadly gases.

As we advanced, our interest turned to the activities of the 2nd Engineers. They were bridging the trenches, almost with the first line troops. They had little gasoline locomotives and they laid preformed track to run on: on coming to a trench they would rush to get a bridge across, and then hurry on their way to the next. The Engineers are a "hairy" group; nothing stops them; and they are always ready to lay down the shovel, grab a rifle, and fight. The 2nd Engineers are the best of the lot: God bless them always.

Next, was the light artillery, the 15th. They were showing us war as the recruiting poster advertised. A battery would come on the dead gallop, and rush for the next cover, the caissons careening from wheel to wheel and the gun carriage bouncing merrily behind. The gunners sat straight and firm in their seats as the caisson bounced out of shell holes, and we wondered what made them stick in place.

As we went up a long slope and left the engineers and artillery behind us, the men began to feel hilarious; no machine gun bullets and no shell bursts. And they lightheartedly singled out the captain to form on; for his pockets were full of French chocolate bars: and also forming on every winner at poker and who was lousy with francs.

A wedge of men followed each. They were in a jocular mood, and they openly boasted of what they were after if one of them should become a casualty. It was gruesome, though no man meant anything by it. But the captain put a stop to it in a hurry, making some gruff remarks. So the men went back to the business of making war.

An American observation plane was flying fast and low over the lines on our left. Suddenly there was a puff of black smoke and a rain of debris. He was struck by a German shell, and little was left of the plane or of the men in it.

We had two or three German fliers directly overhead at about 1,000 feet elevation, and we could see by their flight that they were maneuvering into bombing position. And we anxiously watched them. We were spread out into a long, thin line, and when one plane dove and leveled off overhead, we watched and saw the bombs drop and fall, and so were successfully able to avoid them. Not a man was hit. The bombs buried themselves in the earth and burst with a great shower of dirt.

Our progress here was slow, as we occasionally had to stop in place until our artillery advanced the barrage and the infantry ahead cleaned out some stubborn machine gun nests. While waiting, we observed a real "dog fight," American and French aviators against the Germans. About twenty planes were engaged in this fight, and it was a hot one. We saw several planes tumble down, but it was hard to tell whether it was ours or the Germans'. But one plane I could tell was ours, which had its right wing torn off, the wing preceding the plane in its crash to the earth.

Another American plane was completing a loop when we saw the observer thrown out and come tumbling down. He was spread eagled and made perfect cartwheels as he plummeted. I watched him as he dropped, but averted my eyes before he struck the ground.

Several planes left the scene trailing smoke, and we wondered if they reached the ground safely. But one American plane received a fatal hit, and we observed the plane nose down in a very steep glide and then crash in a field of barbwire on our right.

Other German planes flew low over us, and Sho-Shos and rifles cracked away at them. Officers yelled to cease fire, but they rattled at them, anyway.

The Bois de Four stood dark and forbidding on our right; the Bois les Haie Leve'que on our left; and the infantry was momentarily slowed ahead as they came to some strong point. And a quick storm of machine guns and rifles, then silence, as they overwhelmed the enemy.

Trenches, concrete pill-boxes, and concrete dug-outs were all holed by

26. Over the Top

our artillery fire. They had done their job well and completely. There was little for the infantry to do but to take and hold. How far and how long would this last?

We jumped a trench at the upper part of Bois de Four and entered its dark, shadowy cover. Connolly lost a musette bag of clips in jumping the trench, but I ordered him forward to keep up with the company and gave him one of mine to carry. We filed up a fire lane in the woods, and we noted machine gun platforms in the trees covering the lane, and dead men, mostly Americans, scattered along the trail, and a great deal of German equipment strewn about. The Germans had been able to remove most of their dead and wounded as the attack progressed, leaving guns, machine guns, helmets, and other gear behind.

As we cleared the forest and burst into the open, we resumed attack formation of section files or columns. We hadn't seen any troops ahead of us; nor had we encountered any artillery or machine gun fire. Aside from the dead we had seen in the Bois du Four, we might have been on a practice hike. We had covered about five kilometers of captured territory, and except for the spasmodic fire ahead of us and the hundreds of men advancing, it didn't seem like war.

Passing a curve in the road where the Bois d'Heiche jutted on our right, we observed some refugees ahead. They were a group of women, some old men, and about a dozen wounded Germans. They were coming toward us, and we swung over to intercept them. The women were all smiles; but the Germans were sullen. They had evacuated Thiaucourt due to the heavy fighting in progress there.

We advanced about a kilometer farther, and stopped on the east bank of a ravine for the night. We sustained our first shelling here, and it was bad. Our own artillery got mixed up on range, and as a result we took a half hour's beating. Signals to lift their fire were to no avail, and, finally, an officer grabbed a horse and galloped back to their position. Following that episode, the same rumor floated about that a German spy was in the battery. It was the 15th Field Artillery, the same that gave us such a bad day in Belleau Wood.

I prowled a ravine just north of our position and found a German field hospital. It was filled with wounded, mostly German, and a few American and German doctors were in attendance. There was a team of horses rigged to a two-seated carriage there, numerous German band instruments, and many other items of war. It smelled as all field hospitals must; so I left.

I managed to find a half-bale of hay, which I thought would make my night's rest more comfortable, and I returned to the company to bed down. The hay felt fine, and I thought, what a pleasure if they would furnish each man with hay for the night. But, as usual, when a man is comfortable, something always happens; the company was roused, and we moved on.

It was dark and the troops walked slowly. The front line had run into trouble, and there was much rifle and machine gun fire, and considerable artillery as well, and it was close. The front line troops on our right fell back approximately a kilometer to protect our right flank, which was exposed. The 5th Division on our right had failed to keep abreast and was holding up our attack, and the Germans were counterattacking at that point. We were moved up in immediate support, and were finally halted for the night in a deep ravine of the Bois de Fey.

September 13

We were able to see our surroundings more clearly in the morning. It was a deep ravine filled with German concrete works. There were concrete pillboxes, numerous concrete miniature houses, and sidewalks, all the comforts of home. There were phonographs, and one place even had a piano. There was only one drawback: every building and pillbox was holed by our artillery, and it was a prime place to run into the booby traps they had been warning us about.

We advance slowly that day, a short distance at a time. In crossing one hill, we came upon a prisoners' stockade, newly built, and ready to house *us*: but we put it to better use, and put *German* prisoners there.

There was also a supply house, and the men ransacked it. And for the hour or so that we were there, the men arrayed themselves in German dress-parade uniforms. They "goose-stepped" up and down, waving German sabres, imitating the Prussians. West acquired an officer's cape; it was dark blue on the outside and a brilliant red lining the inside. He put on a spiked, patent-leather helmet with a "Gott Mit Uns" plate on the front, and he waved a German sabre as he did his version of the Prussian strut.

One thing we found that interested us most was the boots. We were all trying them on. They came well up on the shins, had slightly rounded soles, and were heavily hobnailed. They were comfortable and dry: but the thought of dying in German boots was too much for me, so I shed them.

And there was the German caretaker's garden which we raided: cabbages, potatoes, and rutabagas, which we ate raw with copious salt.

The company moved forwards a short distance, and we took up new positions and waited. We learned that the 9th Infantry had not only taken their objective, but had also taken ours, too. Real thoughtful of them. Thanks.

27

Outpost

After nightfall, we crossed a railroad trestle over a piddling creek, the Rupt de Mad, then re-crossed it on a bridge and entered Jaulny, a town the Infantry contended for and won. We removed to the southeast corner of the town and relieved the Infantry unit there, and took up front line positions.

We were in a cemetery, and the old and new graves made a somber picture to the scene. The new graves, some back-filled, some open, contained the victims of our attack, and many contained two bodies of Germans recently killed. There were many empty graves, too, and the men of our company took up position in these.

Sergeant Moneypenny posted the outposts for the night, and when he came to me, he noticed that I had only one musette bag, and in a huff demanded an explanation. My explanation wasn't good enough, so he promptly bawled me out and put me down for a general court martial.

After posting me, he jumped into a grave—and from the grave's mouth came an unearthly yell, and the sergeant scrambled back out in a panic. The men in the surrounding graves began to jeer him and laugh, but he was past the point of reason; for he had landed in the hole directly on top of two dead Germans. That was all we saw of Moneypenny; he apparently went to the rear, probably to be made into a shave tail.

My gun crew was posted in a loose pile of rock at a corner of the cemetery, and I was raging at the brainless ass for selecting the site. There was no protection or cover for us, as the Germans were on top of the hill about six hundred feet over us, on the north and east sides. I raved and fumed, and proceeded to erect a breastwork of rock about the point, although I knew it to be useless. Any fool would know that we were "sitting ducks" and apt to be picked off by the Germans at daylight.

After every one was in position, the C.O. immediately sent out a large detail of men into the hills ahead of us, to reconnoiter the Germans' position.

September 14

The patrol sent back one man with the information that there was an enemy commissary building with supplies abandoned in the woods. A large party was then selected, containing cooks with troops to protect them, and was sent forward to cook for the men.

We waited impatiently for the results, and, after about an hour, they returned with the concoction: a grand slum made up of chicken, rabbit, cabbages, potatoes, carrots, and other vegetables. We ate it with relish; it was good; the best we ever had; and there was enough for two mess tins apiece: but we warily eyed the heavy smoke rising from the cook spot, and waited German artillery to seek it out.

Sergeant Wagner came for my crew and said we were to go forward on outpost duty, but kindly waited for us to finish our meal. We went up the ravine, past the commissary building, past the burned wreckage of an Allied plane, and far in advance to the northeast corner of the Bois de Hailbat. It was over a kilometer ahead of the lines. We were on the right of the 2nd Division's zone, at the edge of a clearing, in a trench built during the war of 1870.

In case of attack, our orders were to send one man back with the information, giving the direction of the attack, and whether it was in force or a small enemy movement. The gunner and one loader were to remain behind and slow down the attack as much as possible; in other words, to stay and die fighting. We were a sacrifice squad.

We had some consolation, though, knowing that other Sho-Sho crews were thinly spread over the front in advance positions to our left. This was a tough assignment, as the Germans had counter-attacked twice over this ground the day before, and the 5th Division was two kilometers to our rear.

There was a wooded ridge extending to the northeast, and directly to our east a heavy clump of trees; they would come from either direction. We had a German barbed wire entanglement immediately in front of us, about 50 to 60 feet in width of knee-high wire, that made the position more secure from the south. There was a lot of evidence that the Germans had used this point, too, but the 2nd Division's attack had caught them from behind and forced them out.

The area was strewn with German grenades, and I had Comfort and Connolly gather them in a convenient pile for emergency use. The grenade was shaped like a potato masher, and had a long string attached for the purpose of detonation. The string ended with a button, which was held between the fingers, and after detonating the grenade, a very powerful explosion occurred in four seconds. I never fired one, but always wondered about the string. If it didn't loosen from the grenade, you might find the grenade about your neck—with unpleasant results.

We settled in to watch. The first day was uneventful until evening, when a detail of Marines cleared the enemy out of the woods lying east of us. By the rifle fire, we determined that the Boche would back out of the woods near us, so we got all set to "shoot them in the rear." But Connolly could always be expected to do the wrong thing. Unbeknownst to me, he had climbed up on a large wooden horse in back of our position, and was sitting swinging his legs, fully exposed, when suddenly there was a sharp "crack," and a bullet whirred by his ear—and Connolly came tumbling down from his perch, one scared boy. Thus our position was known, and the Germans changed their retreat and escaped out of the woods on the opposite side. I tongue-lashed Connolly good, but it didn't seem to faze him for long.

With night coming on, I arranged the watch at two hours to a man, one coming off watch every hour, thus giving each man two hours watch and one hour to rest. I took the watch in the hours 8 to 10 p.m., 11 to 1 a.m., and 2 to 4 a.m., intending to remain awake until morning.

All went well on the 8 to 10 watch, and I went to sleep, expecting to be awakened at 11:00 p.m. But at about 2:30 a.m. some noise awakened me. I looked around—and Comfort and Connolly were sound asleep. I heard a "ping" of wire and knew something was up.

I put my hand over Comfort's mouth and shook him. He came instantly awake. I motioned him to be quiet: and treated Connolly the same way. Again I heard the ping. I whispered to them to grab grenades and stand by; but under no condition to fire, unless I gave them the order.

I then crept down the trench twenty to thirty feet so we all wouldn't get it, and challenged, "Halt, who goes there?"

All became quiet. I could make out a group of men, but I couldn't detect any identifying marks. As I received no reply to my challenge, a second time: "Halt! Who's there? Answer, or I fire."

Soon the answer came, "Captain Quigley, and a party."

I sucked some air into my lungs: "Advance, Captain Quigley; come straight toward my voice to be recognized. Party, stand firm."

I was lying prone in the old trench keeping my eyes glued to the spot; I could hear someone making his way through the wire; there was no other sound. Soon the figure approached, and I waited until he all but stepped on me; then I arose, keeping him covered. I knew Captain Quigley by sight, and I peered at him to make identification. And, finally, discerning his features, I relaxed. Captain Quigley, an old-time Marine noncom, was a man with guts.

It takes plenty to come in, in answer to a challenge, when one doesn't know whether it's friend or foe.

After answering his questions as to the best way to get to battalion headquarters, I advanced his party. He told me that they had prowled the woods to the east and to the south of us, and had found no enemy troops; an occasional outpost was all, losing four or five men in the resulting fire. I directed him to Jaulny; and as the last of his party came through the wire, he said to me, "Thank God for an outpost that can hold his fire."

I went back to my post, and, to relieve some tension, I bawled out both of my loaders. I didn't report them, as they were both upset over the episode; but I henceforth determined that I would stand watch all night rather than take another chance like that. Death by court martial is the penalty if you are caught asleep on outpost. I wouldn't have been able to clear myself in that case, as there were two against one, and I was in charge.

September 15

When daylight came and bathed a troubled world in sunlight, we lay back and relaxed looking skyward. We lazily watched two American planes high above us returning from a reconnaissance flight. The reverie was soon disturbed, though, when three German fighters appeared. They were behind and below them, in a dead spot from the Americans. The Germans swept upward and opened fire on the trailing plane. He didn't have a chance; black smoke and fire issued from his plane and it lay over and headed earthward.

The second American now saw the danger and hurriedly climbed away from his attackers. The first plane was a falling ball of fire, as he tumbled toward us. But then we noticed that the pilot began side-slipping his plane, holding the fire off his wing, until finally the fire was extinguished. Now we could see the plane. It was still smoking but was a blackened wreck, and the pilot leveled off directly above us at 500 feet. He settled wounded to the earth south of Bois de Bonvaux, in the territory of the 5th Division. Comfort and Connolly started to the pilot's aid, but I stopped them and reminded them that they were on duty. Soon some officers and men passed our position and asked us the direction to the plane, and went to his help.

Connolly began to gripe about food now, and it being about thirty hours since we had eaten, I let him go foraging for thirty minutes, while Comfort and I held the position. But after time had elapsed, Sergeant Wagner showed up to repost us in another position, due to the patrols out the night before.

He was angry at Connolly being gone, but consented to wait a few minutes for him.

We ascended the nearby slope a short ways and waited, and in about ten minutes Connolly came dragging two gunnysacks behind him. He had two live hares, a couple of cabbages, and about a dozen raw potatoes in the bags, and a pocketful of salt. We released the rabbits, and soon finished the potatoes and cabbages. And I testify, they made a good meal, dirt, salt, and all.

We turned almost due north onto a rounded, open field, about a kilometer from our old position. We could almost look down on the village of Rembercourt. The territory ahead was devoid of life, except at what appeared to be two concrete pillboxes. And a dirt road led in their direction from our right. I didn't like this position any better, as we again had to lie in the open with no cover.

They gave me the same orders, only now they added; "Division was expecting an attack soon from this direction." Well, I kissed good bye to life and lay wondering what it would be like to die.

We lurked there all day, and the only movement was when Connolly got excited over sighting a couple of Germans shifting from one pill box to the other. Neither Comfort nor I saw them, and in view of his character, we doubted that he had. Connolly wanted to shoot at them; but again I refused, remaining still and quiet was to our advantage; not disclosing our insecure position. Besides, I had about decided that the captain wanted to liquidate us, anyway, due to Connolly's behavior when we left Selaincourt. Not a nice thought, but from the way we had been treated, I couldn't think otherwise.

That night was still, and we heard nothing from the German lines. But, then, anything could happen.

September 16

No word from the company. We were forgotten men. It was getting damned tiresome and lonesome out here.

Shortly after mid-night, we were disturbed by noise and confusion behind us. It was too severe to ignore, and I finally left the men on outpost and went to investigate. I walked erect, and as I approached the woods, I passed an outpost walking his post in the open: I was not challenged nor stopped.

Next, I passed a machine gun crew setting their gun up in the open.

Next, I met two men standing in the open, smoking: "What outfit is this? I barked at them.

"The 78th Division, 310th Infantry," they replied.

"Don't you fellows know anything about war?"

"Well, we were in the trenches in the Alsace Lorraine Sector—what's it to you, anyway?"

"Where are your officers?" I asked.

One of them said, "Over there," pointing into the adjoining woods.

"Take me to them," I snapped. And they complied. From what I had seen and heard, it was no wonder the Germans counterattacked when we made a change of troops at the front. It was easy pickings for them. I was getting extremely nervous about now.

About a dozen officers were sitting on the ground, some of them smoking, and one was telling a joke, at which they all were laughing. I attempted to interrupt, but they were more interested in the story and in their own knowledge of war to listen.

All except one. A 1st lieutenant seemed concerned at my anger, and asked what outfit I was from. I told him I was a buck private of Marines, 2nd Division; that I was on outpost a half mile ahead of them and had come back to investigate all the noise I had heard. I told him how I had walked past their sentry and machine gun crew, without so much as a challenge; how their men were smoking; and how the loud talk and laughter sounded out beyond where we were: and I asked him what he thought the Germans would think and do.

By the time I finished, there was a ring of officers and men around me, all listening. I told them I had been at the front through Belleau Wood, Soissons, and this front, and this was the first time I had seen such utter disregard of the enemy: "I am getting my crew and get out of here fast before the Germans counterattack."

The lieutenant asked me first to stay and help him get his outpost and machine guns posted. And we set to work arranging his part of the line, getting sentries hidden, machine guns placed where they would do the most good, and stopped all smoking, loud talk, and laughter. Then I went after my crew. They said the noise quit all along the line back of them and they wanted to know what had happened.

The lieutenant was waiting for us when we went through their line and again thanked me for helping him. We went down the ravine, passed the burned plane and the commissary building, and came into Jaulny at daybreak.

We were sore at the company officers for not relieving us. And then we ran into Gunner Hulbert from our battalion with about 40 men, who like us had been left on outpost when the division was relieved. They had similar stories to ours about the relieving division, and their opinion of the 78th was low; and we all agreed to "high-tail" it quickly to the back area.

We set out at a fast pace, until we came to Thiaucourt. And then the battle started. The Germans were pounding Thiaucourt with heavy artillery, and we could hear the shell-fire, rifles, and machine guns behind us and above Jaulny. We had got out just in time. We later heard that the 78th was driven back at that point and had to retake the ground. Perhaps they were better troops after that initial "blood-letting"; but they had a long way to go.

We had a tough time in Thiaucourt. The town was ablaze, and the shells tore into buildings, the bursts cascading rubble into the street. We went up the street on the right side, protected somewhat by the walls of the buildings. At certain areas, we lay in the gutter and waited until the shelling let up. The Germans were systematic in shelling; they fired for a brief time, and then waited a like period before resuming the fire. We were lucky in figuring this out, advancing when they were quiet, and laying in the gutters when the bombardment was on. We were glad to get through without losing a man, and took the Thiaucourt-Regniéville road back. We went by Limey to Flirey, south through Bernécourt and Ansauville, to the Fôret de la Reine, where we found our outfit in bivouac.

On the way back, when passing through a forest, Lieutenant Johnson and about twenty men came out onto the road. We halted and looked at them; their uniforms were clean, with no rents, and they looked rested. Some of the men in our column expressed our feeling, "Slackers." And we moved on. Lieutenant Johnson and his men fell in at our rear, but no one talked to them.

We spent the balance of the day in rest at the bivouac area. Toward evening, our galley force served us raised sugar-coated doughnuts as a special treat. Then we had roll call; one killed, Goudy, who had challenged me to the contest with the Sho-Sho, and fifteen, or so, wounded. We got out of that scrap lightly. It was the easiest battle we experienced to date, and it promised to be the worst. Such is the gamble we take at the front.

28

A Farewell to Arms

September 17–25

We lay bivouacked in the woods for two nights before starting one evening our march to the rear. We hiked south on a good road, passing through Mênil la Tour, a sleepy little village with no sign of life, and then on to Toul.

Toul was a fair-sized town, but we were closed up and had to march at ease. Not a light was showing, and the inhabitants were few. The old familiar snarl of army M.P.'s was all we heard, and that at nearly every cross road: "Keep out of this town, if you know when you are well off," they would greet us.

"Shut up, you g---- d---- lousy trench dodgers," was the stock reply, and other remarks less complimentary. It might have gone hard with the M.P.'s if the men weren't so tired.

We plodded on, and at daylight we came to Mont le Vignoble and there were billeted. We drew a billet in the courtyard of a French home. We had bunks, such as they were, the slats mostly broken, and the customary dirt. We were fed, and most of us slept a few hours, and then gathered in the courtyard afterward to "chin."

I bought some dirty goat milk and goat cheese from a French peasant, and I didn't enjoy it a bit: probably the dirt in the milk spoiled my snack. A French woman and her daughter furnished our only amusement that day. They tied an old cow to a post in the courtyard, then disappearing for a short time came back leading a big, black bull, and proceeded to breed the cow. Sergeant Slover helped the women, and the act was accomplished by much laughter and helpful remarks from the gallery.

The balance of the day was spent wandering about town and keeping out of trouble. The next day was Sunday, and we would have the day off. That started a group planning some devilment. Four or five of the men came and asked me to go to Toul with them in the morning. But, sensing trouble, I declined. Then they insisted on my lending them my .45: again, I declined

28. A Farewell to Arms

and asked what was up. The men were still smarting over the remarks made by the M.P.'s and were going over in a bunch to mess them up. Before turning in for the night, I hid my .45 where it wouldn't be found, and decided to get out of camp in the morning to avoid getting in a jam.

In the morning, I went northwest from town until I came to Charmes la Côte and stopped to get something to eat and drink. It was a small village, and I had to follow my "ears" to find a shop that was open. There were several Marines inside, gathered about an ancient player piano, and an old lady and old man in attendance. When I asked for "der kilomètres of fromage," the old couple and the Marines burst out laughing. So I amended that and asked for "der franc of fromage." I imagined that was more eatable. With a bottle of beer and the "fromage" I made out a meal all right.

When I resumed my hike, I climbed a high bluff, and a road led along its edge and overlooked a wide valley. Observing the scene before me, I noticed that the ground was pitted and in each pit a sharpened steel pin. Then for some distance lay ankle-deep, crisscrossed barbed wire. Below the road ran a concrete trench that followed the crest of the hill. Next, came an entanglement over a large area of waist high, crisscrossed barbed wire, followed by a tremendous concrete moat surrounding what appeared a natural rise in the ground.

Before me was the French fortress, Domgermain, and it commanded the surrounding countryside from its lofty height. As I scanned the horizon I also could see other forts and fortresses dominating the valley, and I could see Toul. Studying this defensive system, I could readily understand why Verdun had stood despite the German attack and siege. So, this was the line of forts that blocked the German attack through this area.

Soon I came to a sentry's box and a drawbridge to the fortress, and I decided that I had gone far enough. But I was intercepted by a French soldier. The soldier was middle-aged, as were all the others there, but he seemed friendly, and wished to talk. But I was stymied, as language barred my way. However, by hand motions which seemed to be the correct way in France and with what French words I knew, we managed to make ourselves understood.

I conveyed the information that I was a Marine and that I had been through the battles of Belleau Wood, Soissons, and St. Mihiel. He "O-la-laed" at the mention of Bois de Belleau and shook my hand and gestured and talked a stream of French to the other soldiers standing about. Apparently, I had said the right thing, for they all crowded around me talking, and then led me over the drawbridge into the depths of the fortress.

I was impressed by the thickness of the concrete; it was perhaps 15 to 20 feet over all. They first led me into the crews' quarters, clean and neat; then to various disappearing guns: although all I saw of these were the muzzles from topside. After this, we descended four or five floors, and I saw the munitions lockers, shell rooms, and, finally, the communication tunnels that ran to the surrounding towns. I knew then what the iron grill and gate that led into the hills at Mont le Vignoble was about.

I saw a lot of the fortress, but there was a lot I was not allowed to see, and we made our way back again to the drawbridge and then outside. I made my goodbyes as well as I was able and returned to Mont le Vignoble, arriving there in time for evening chow.

That evening, I saw some of the men who had gone to Toul. They weren't saying much about it, but I gathered there had been some gun play and that some M.P.'s were shot, as well as two Marines. At morning troop, the officers read off an order placing Toul out of bounds; nothing else was said; so I presumed they were willing to let the matter close.

We had an easy day; troop, inspection, and the usual police duties, and by noon we were through for the day. In the afternoon, I felt restless and moody, so I climbed up the nearby hill into the forest. As I followed the fire trail in the woods, I happened along groups of girls and women at various places. They were engaged in the same occupation, that of tying bundles of fagots and piling them like cordwood. The fagots were used by the peasants in their ovens, and they pick up every thing that looks like wood, down to twigs. They all grinned at me and jabbered French, but I was not in the mood to struggle with the French language, and grinned and waved at them as I passed.

After some distance, I came out of the woods and before me lay a great valley. A railroad line ran through the valley, with a train approaching in the distance. I determined then to "shove-off," to go A.W.O.L., so I hopped the freight train and bid goodbye to the 49th. I was on my way to see France from the doorway of a side-door Pullman.

The train puffed and struggled on its way, the funny little whistle tooting at all crossroads, and soon we pulled into a town. The streets were full of troops, standing about in clusters, and they were Marines. I couldn't believe my eyes; I should be going away from them, but here I was running into them. I jumped off, and hailing a group I asked what their outfit was and the name of the town. Blénod lès Toul, 2nd Battalion of the 5th, was the reply. We were billeted in the next town north, so I had gone the wrong direction after crossing the hill: A.W.O.L., what's the use; I might as well hike back and forget it.

Again I got back to town in time for chow, and I bedded down for the night, thinking of the tricks of fate.

In the morning, it was full packs and an all day hike. We hiked for hours into the hills between Blénod lès Toul and Mont le Vignoble, and I was surprised at the distance I must have covered the day before. I had walked completely around the hill in my wandering, but at no place did we cross my trail.

At last we came to a halt near the top of the hill. And, after a long rest, we were started back. I guess the officers didn't feel much like hiking, either. We made the return trip in much shorter time, as it was all down hill, and, like horses, the men knew it was homeward bound. We arrived about the middle of the afternoon and were dismissed for the day.

PART IV: BLANC MONT

29

The One Way Trail

September 25

Today, we were employed in checking our equipment, so I took my gun and crew to one side and spent the time cleaning and oiling the Sho-Sho, cleaning the clips, and wiping off the cartridges.

While working on the gun, the sergeant came by and furnished me with 500 rounds of extra cartridges. He also checked my .45 ammunition, and gave me two extra clips for that gun. He issued two bandoliers of Springfield ammunition, and filled in the iron rations. My load, including the Sho-Sho, was two musette bags with six clips each, approximately 750 rounds of ammunition for my weapon, a .45 with five clips, an ammunition belt with 120 rounds of Springfield bullets, two bandoliers of 60 rounds each of Springfield ammo, a trench knife, a short trench shovel for my pack, besides my personal things and my other gear. It was load enough to kill a mule; but that was what being a Sho-Sho gunner meant. The issue of ammunition and hard tack could mean only one thing: we're going in again. But where?

"49th Company, fall in! With heavy marching order." We were on our way, and we hiked to the town of Domgermain. It was situate in the valley below the fortress I had visited but a few days before.

We had a long wait for the train, so we stacked our arms and shed our packs. While waiting, I purchased a helmet full of filberts, or hazel nuts, I didn't know which, from a French woman for two francs, and made a feast of them. When the train came in, we were loaded fifty men to the car. We must be needed badly, as the cars were all plainly marked 40 Hommes/8 Chevaux. They respected the limit of eight horses: but what are ten or more extra men?

The officers were crabby and their mood spread to the men. With a lot of growling and some sharp remarks, we were finally packed into the cars with barely enough room for each man to sit.

Wedged in, we proceeded to delouse, snapping the cooties between our thumbnails and hoarding the pile of the deceased to brag about. One lad sat watching us with a sneer on his face for our being so "crumby." After several of the men had offered to "wipe the sneer off," and others had made personal remarks as to his ancestry, he consented to "show us"—and he peeled off his blouse, shirt, and undershirt. The sight that met our eyes brought howls of laughter; for cooties he had; he was crawling with them; and long after the rest of us had our shirts on, he was still "popping" cooties with a concentrated effort.

Cooties were no respecter of person or place; they went with the war. The only difference that I noticed was that they didn't like the Germans any more than we did. They "shunned" them and left the field to a smaller flea and louse which were viler.

Another thing about cooties is that they didn't bother us much, until there were enough on our bodies to hold "battalion" maneuvers. And then we got busy. The lad in front of us, however, had enough on him to boast about "divisional" tactics.

Finally night came with the train tooting and jerking on its way. Many of us wondered where we were going. We were traveling west, away from the American Army: was it Rheims? to Soissons with the French? or was it to the north with the British or Belgian Armies? Activities had opened on a big scale, and we could go "in" pretty near anywhere.

We tried lying down. Each man had only his back on the floor, his feet and legs propped across the bodies of others, and his head resting comfortably on someone's torso. When a body couldn't stand it any longer, someone would yell, "Turn," and we all tried a different position.

We passed through Commercy in the night, and at the approach of day, Bar le Duc. And a few men, very few, reminisced over their sojourn here many months before. Then we went through Vitry le François. And after many more towns, and in the late afternoon, we halted at Châlons sur Marne and debarked. So, the Champagne country this time. It will be a tough battle, too.

It was a quiet town, and very few people were on the streets. All the buildings on the street were pock-marked by bullets and H.E. Fragments, the result of the German occupation in 1914. We were not allowed to see much of it, though, as the battalion was marched south out of town to a little wood along the road. And there we were bivouacked for the balance of the day.

We had chow, or what passed as chow, and bedded down in the weeds and mud. A cold rain was falling, and no matter where we lay there was a puddle. Nothing to do but get wet. It was a miserable rest and we found little sleep, due to the rain and the cold. My hands were balled up in fists and cramps in my legs required frequent massaging. Why in hell can't they furnish us with overcoats and warmer clothing? Men in the back areas have been so equipped for some time, and army units at the front were now wearing overcoats. Perhaps, being Marines, we would all be killed off, and they would save their damned coats.

After supper, we settled down to a hike, northward, and surely to trouble. We hiked to St. Hilaire au Temple, where we were billeted. Here our platoon drew a big cow barn. We had bunks (broken slats again) on the second deck. The boards of the floor were not laid too closely, and the odor of cows and manure permeated the sleeping place. Between the odors and the cows below, we didn't get any rest here, either.

September 27

We didn't do much during the day. Several of us stripped to the waist and took an ice cold semi-bath at the old fashioned pump. It felt good, but it didn't help me any, as I was sick and miserable. When I took a deep breath, or stood erect, there were sharp pains in my left chest. I wouldn't answer sick call, as all they did there was issue three C.C. pills, or paint you with iodine and mark you "Duty."

The only thing of interest involved my loader, Connolly. Several men were at their pet past time, playing poker, and a large bunch were watching the game.

Connolly came strutting up and in a cocky manner queried one of the players, "Your name Conley?" Getting an affirmative answer, he then said, "Well, there can be only one Connolly in this company!"

Conley, the player, got up and said, "What you going to do about it?"

They moved off a little ways, and a big ring formed around them. I didn't watch the show, but saw Conley afterward, and he was a sight. His face had been pummeled so badly, that he couldn't see, and he was sick from it. Connolly No. 1 did not have a scratch or mark on him, and he strutted off looking for more trouble.

I was curious about the French people who ran the farm, and I wandered over to the house and looked in. There was but one room, and in one corner stood a brick oven, a huge affair, unlike anything I had ever seen. The madame was working at it, and while I watched, she took a large wooden paddle and reached into the oven and proceeded to remove loaves of bread. The loaves looked strangely familiar; they looked like those we had been issued at Belleau Wood, round and low, with half-inch sawdust bottoms and a hard brown crust. I wondered if the family used a bayonet to open them up.

In the next corner, there was a huge bed, with two or three youngsters on it, playing. Apparently, it was a family bed and all slept there. A table stood in the third corner; on it were many bottles of wine, the usual stamp of a French home, as the water was usually undrinkable. This was the living quarters when raining or when the work was done.

In the fourth corner was a pen, in which an old sow grunted and probably was the source of the barnyard odor that permeated the place. It was a large room, dirty and unkempt, no visible sign of running water, lights, or modern conveniences; just a workshop: and I wondered again, why did the Germans want France?

As I left, I couldn't help thinking of those loaves of bread; how we had to punch a hole through them with our bayonet and string a shoe lace in order to tie the loaf to our pack; how when we ate them, we had to break the loaf with a trench knife or bayonet, and that it about broke our teeth to bite into them. "Oh, the French, they are a funny race, hinkey, dinkey, parlez vous…."

September 28

Today, I went to sick bay. The pains were quite severe and I felt miserable. A large bunch had answered sick call, but, as I knew, I got no help here. Three C.C. pills and marked "Duty."

While there, I noticed that the only thing the doctors were interested in was yesterday's fight. Conley was there with two black, swollen eyes to peer through, and a tale of having fallen out of bed to receive them. The doctors thought it was a huge joke and kidded Conley unmercifully.

As I left, I threw the C.C. pills in the dust and went back to our quarters, and damned the doctors for being indifferent and lazy.

That night, we again fell out with full marching equipment and marched to a cross-road outside town. Here were camions (trucks) lined up as far as we could see. We rode in comfort for several miles, and piled off in a shell-swept town called Suippes.

We were hurried on our way, and hiked north and east to a desolate spot in a clearing in a wood, and there were bivouacked.

September 29

In the dark, we could hear the sound of marching men and the clanking of horse drawn vehicles, but I was tired, and ill, and found some solace in a hazy sleep.

At daylight, I aroused and walked about. I could see countless soldiers asleep on the ground and artillery pieces with their muzzles covering the front. As it became lighter, I saw that the French were on the left of a wagon trail, and American Marines on the right; all girded for battle.

As the men stirred, the difference between the French and Americans was stark. The French gathered for breakfast in groups of from three to five men around a charcoal fire; they brewed a hot drink, cut off chunks of bread and soaked it in vin rouge. The Americans, on the other hand, grabbed their mess kits and fell in a chow line for their food. The French, in their great coats, the front skirt fastened back to give their knees freedom, looked comfortable; the Americans, in summer dress, were huddled up and cold. The French army apparently carried the equipment to prepare a hot meal; the American, on the other hand, was fed from galleys; and once committed to battle, did without, or existed on their iron rations.

Ahead and to the right was a small graveyard, all aviators. Their crosses were made from the broken propellers of their planes; French, British, German, and a few Americans: it was a somber reminder of the cost of war.

That day was a long and difficult one for me, and I was content to lie on the ground and rest. For when I moved about, I would black out and fall to my hands and knees. That night was cold, and I couldn't find a comfortable place to lie. Just before midnight, I got up and wandered about, seeking some dry spot, and the best I could find was a forage wagon. The wheel adjacent to the trail was broken off, but the bed of the wagon was out of the mud, and I curled up on it to sleep.

September 30

My bed for the night was not a wise choice, as countless horse-drawn vehicles rolled passed to the front and others to the rear, and many stumbled as they hit the cart. When they jolted the cart, I cursed the drivers and the drivers would jabber French at me as they continued on. Luckily, they didn't run me over, but I was passed caring about what happened, anyway. I did get some sleep between jolts, but I was awakened once to find a horse astride me on the cart. There was a burst of Gaulic, and I could make out a Frenchman astride his horse bending down and jabbering at me. I cursed the rider and lay still. But I noticed the horse was careful not to move, so I crawled out from between his feet, and the rider rode off, muttering what I supposed were French curses. For the balance of the night, I sat huddled up on my dry oasis. When dawn broke, the drivers all shouted and grinned at me as they passed. How they had missed me during the night, I'll never know.

Soon the galleys were steaming, and I walked over and bummed a boiling hot cup of black java. It made me feel better and it helped to start the day. After chow, sick call blew, and although a large contingent answered, I ignored it; the thought of being doled C.C. pills again didn't appeal to me. But two hospital corpsmen came after me, and I had to go with them. Apparently, someone had reported my black outs.

There were three doctors and a group of navy corpsmen at the outdoor sick bay, and I was ordered to strip to the waist. A strong and damp, cool wind was blowing, and it cut me to the quick. They listened with a stethoscope to my heart and lungs, and then came up with the diagnosis: it seems I had a good case of pleurisy. It was on the left side, and when I breathed deep, the pain was severe. They had me exhale until I couldn't exhale any more, then put a wide strip of adhesive tape on the left side. The tape reached from the center of my body in front to my spine. It did help alleviate the pains, as I couldn't breathe well; and I felt better.

After I put on my shirt and blouse, the doctors then asked whether I wished to go to the hospital or stay with the outfit. The hospital seemed the most logical place to go; I needed the warmth and rest to get over it without complications; but the way they asked me made me angry, and I growled out that I would stay with the outfit. There seemed to be a stigma attached to anyone going to the hospital with anything less than a wound. I had gone once, being gassed, though called "influenza" by the doctors. Well, I could stay with the outfit as long as I could keep on my feet.

The day went by without our doing anything that looked like work. Toward evening, I took a walk to the north edge of the woods and over the crest of the hill. There were a group of French officers there along with Major Hamilton[1] and a group of American officers, who were viewing the French attack a few miles ahead. It was possible to see artillery shells bursting among tiny figures supposed to be French; but I couldn't see much without field glasses. But it certainly looked like hell, and our prospects didn't look too good. According to the men with the glasses, the attack failed. And I wondered whether we would fail when our turn came.

Far off on our left we could see the hazy outline of the Rheims Cathedral, leaving no doubt that we were in the famous Champagne country. Back I went to the bivouac area, and again slept fitfully that night, and was wet and cold. The rain had been intermittent during the day, just enough to keep us wet and uncomfortable, and continued on through the night.

October 1

October First passed as had the days before, wet and inactive. The officers were assembled for a conference in the afternoon. It must be battle orders, and soon we will go. I checked the Sho-Sho and cleaned the six musette bags of ammunition, until I was satisfied. Connolly and Comfort, I ignored.

After dusk, we started and hiked toward the front. Two hundred and forty men in the company were going in: how many would come out? We slogged a ways up the trail, the one way trail for a lot of us, and I couldn't help feeling that a great crime was being committed. Why should we, the rank and file of Allied or German youth, be called upon to kill, or be killed, to satisfy the hunger and greed for power of individuals? To hell with it all; we've got a job to do; and do it we will. God help the Germans: we won't.

As we neared the front, signs of activity increased. We could see other outfits through the dim light also moving up. They looked ominous; men in slickers, helmets jammed down on their heads, a pack on their back, a gas mask on their chest; and all armed.

Coming out from behind a hill, the terrain lay relatively flat, with a road embankment on our left. Beyond the road was a long, low ridge, which merged with our trail at a town. Star shells were constantly being sent up by the Germans, and many bounced over the ridge and extinguished in the dirt. Trenches appeared and stretched as dark strips across the landscape. Shells exploded, all short of our column; but one heavy-caliber shell burst in the midst of a column paralleling ours. There were the agonized yells of the wounded, followed by cries for the first aid men; but dimness shrouded our view, as we continued on. We caught momentary glimpses of French wounded being wheeled back on two-wheeled stretcher carts, and many walking wounded laboring slowly to the rear. We were almost there.

The Germans were nervous and jittery, and were expecting trouble. We entered a town; it was a mass of rubble; all semblances to a living town were gone; a ghostly, eerie, atmosphere permeated the place, and the acrid odor of high explosives and gas sifted in the smoke that blanketed the town.

At a crossroad, the captain signaled a halt. "All men take cover" was the whispered word. But take cover in what? There was none; we lay exposed all along the bank of the road. Sommepy apparently had once been a fair-sized town, but shell-fire hadn't left much, and shells continued to erupt in the mass of rubble around us. Frequently they screamed in—a descending crescendo—to land among the men: yells of pain—cries for first aid—then all was quiet, until the next shell lands. It was a hell of a place to be in. The scream and bursting of shells; the screams of the wounded; the hurrying of first aid men on their job of mercy—and still we waited in that exposed position. What in hell was the captain waiting for?

A couple of officers came up to question the captain. They objected at being halted at a crossroad in the exposed position. But the captain said, "We stay here; we wait for the guides."

It wasn't long before they arrived, two Frenchmen in their long, blue coats, and we arose and followed them. I was directly behind the captain and could hear the muttered talk as we went in: "Pas bon sector," and words expressing their losses here. "Pas bon sector" sounded bad. It was not good: "Pas bon sector," the Frenchmen had said; the worst of this front. It was final and complete—"Pas bon sector."

We moved a scant one thousand yards passed a maze of deep trenches, and entered the Trench des Prussiens. The Germans occupied this trench farther to our left. At each bend or traverse in the trench there was the huddle of blue, three or four dead Frenchmen, caught there by death. A few tall Frenchmen, all that was left of the French forces who had attacked the trench shortly before, hurriedly passed us, going to the rear. As they passed, they shook their heads and mustered—"Par bon sector." They were the tired and worn-out remnants of the attack.

The trench was deep and wide, with a firing bench at the top; and as I came to a stop and looked around, I was amazed at its size and realized that trench warfare was different from war as we knew it.

We relieved units of the French 61st division, XXI Corps, a part of General Gouraud's 4th Army, and henceforth we would fight as part of that force.

October 2

With the coming of day, we could examine our surroundings. Behind us and along the crest of the hill were over one hundred dead Frenchmen. They formed a huge V and lay as they had fallen. At the apex of the V lay three members of a Sho-Sho crew, the gunner in the van supported by his two loaders. All were in action pose; rigor mortis had set in rapidly and froze the men in death. From there back over the ridge their comrades lay, the dead of the outfit we had just relieved. "Pas bon sector"—how right they were. These with the dead in the trench were a reminder that war is a grim reaper. But the only effect I could see in our men was that they became harder, more determined; and not a man was weakened by it.

I stood with a group that was discussing the scene, when one said, "Look," and pointed toward the bottom of the trench. We looked down and saw sticking up out of the floor of the trench a man's left hand. And we wondered how many more were buried there. Then one fellow stepped forward and kicked the hand. Up it flew and out of sight over the parapet. And we went back to our places. We were in the first line of defense, with only the Germans ahead of us; and we settled down to wait for the order to advance.

That evening, men were selected to infiltrate the Tranchée de l'Elba and Tranchée d'Essen, and, stealing off, they successfully drove the Germans out with grenades, pistols, and trench knives.

I was posted as the lone watch on our section of the trench, and I had to get up onto the firing bench and watch the valley for signs of German movement. The men slept in the bottom of the trench, and the only movement was an occasional officer or noncom going to or from the captain's dugout.

October 3

The night was long and no movement of the enemy disturbed me. On taking the post, I was warned to keep my head down because German snipers were active and shot at anything. But I had decided that was the thing to do, anyway.

As dawn was breaking, I noticed a man crawl out of the German trench below and about 250 to 300 yards away and come up the hill. He began to juggle three or four grenades and whistled a tune as though he knew he was being watched and wished to come into our lines. As he neared, I could see that he was dressed in the dark blue of the French Alpins Chasseurs. But that alone did not stamp him as a "friend." The Germans had been known to dress in Allied uniforms and had entered American lines in French clothing; and vice versa. The point he came from was definitely in German hands, and I kept my gun on him with a light touch of the finger on the trigger. As he approached to about 50 feet from me, I challenged, "Halt—drop those grenades; hands up." He complied fast, dropped the grenades, stopped his whistling, and stood still with his hands over his head. I called back into the trench that I had a prisoner; and I was immediately surrounded by men and officers.

An officer told me to advance him but keep him covered: "Advance slowly, but keep your hands up," I commanded.

When he stood about six feet from me, the officer asked me where I had spotted him. And I told him how I had watched him approach, the grenades he juggled, and how he was whistling. The man was grinning all the while as though it was a good joke, and his first remark was general, "Le Boche partir cinq kilomètres." (The Germans have retreated five kilometers.) The officers quickly took him away and later sent out a party into the German trench. It was true, the Boche had fallen back, and the trench was ours.

From the Allied lines a great barrage was now in progress and one shell exploded in a German ammunition dump far back of their lines. First there was a blinding flash through the trees beyond Blanc Mont; then the roar of the explosion, followed by tremors in the earth from the concussion; and then the eruption of a great column of smoke. The surging smoke billowed upward in a huge column and mushroomed out and stood as a giant toadstool in the sky. It remained a long time, and all the men in the trenches were soon up on the firing bench to look. And as it hung in the sky, a mighty roar went up from the men. The barrage was on; all hell was loose, and shells exploded all over and across the German front and rear areas: it was a good omen to start the attack.

30

Into the Storm

The 6th Marines had the attack today, and I watched them go. Troops filtered by our front, then proceeded forward on our left. At moments like these, a man has a strange feeling. One will solemnly swear this attack will be his last; he feels it, and knows it. Another will just as solemnly declare, that he will return from the attack uninjured. He is full of confidence, and eager to get going. I was in the latter group, and I felt that in spite of everything, I was going to be all right in this attack.

The Bois de la Vipère lay straight ahead of us, but the orders said to ignore it. The 9th Infantry was to attack on the right of it, and the 6th Marines were to attack on the left; they would join forces after they had passed the woods: a split attack, something new and to be remembered.

As succeeding waves of the 6th cleared the Essen Trench, they slogged through a hell of a flanking fire from Essen Hook, a strong point in the French zone of attack, telling us that the French were not making a go of it on their front.

Our battalion was the last to leave. We had a grandstand seat, while the three battalions of the 6th moved out and two battalions of the 5th. At last our turn came, and we proceeded down the slope and to our left to bypass the Bois de la Vipère.

We jumped into Essen Trench and filed through it far to our left. While we waited for the signal to advance, the German batteries awoke and began pounding the trench and vicinity. And it was hell. As usual, they had the range down to the last degree, and they poured in their big stuff.

Most of our men had sought shelter in big dug-outs in the trench. I had started down also, but the roof looked too weak, and I had no desire to be buried alive; so I took refuge behind a pile of dirt excavated from the dug-out. The shells rained in, and I crouched there with a couple of fellows who felt as I did.

Soon a 210mm crashed into the opposite side of our dirt pile. The explosion shook us and heaved a mass of earth on top of us. I frantically shook myself free, and cleaned the dirt out of my eyes, my clothing, and from my equipment. I was just completing the operation when a second shell screamed in and exploded in the same spot. Again I was buried, but shook myself clear, and had to clean my equipment again.

While cleaning my gun, a third shell exploded to my left, about a dozen feet away and around a traverse in the trench. Agonized screams of men arose and then the call for first aid. The captain came running through the trench, calling the men out of the dug-outs. Leading the way, he moved us to the left, out of the zone the Germans were covering. As I came around the traverse in the trench, I noticed three men lying on the ground. One was still, and the other two were being tended by first aid men. They were horribly wounded, the shell having badly torn the lower limbs of each.

We soon came to a halt in the trench, well away from the bursting shells. I was sitting down; when I looked up to see a file of German soldiers enter the trench just above me. They had full accouterment, were helmeted, a few had side arms, and they looked mean. They were Prussians. I jumped to my feet, ready to kill or die. But as they reached the bottom of the trench, they shed their helmets and equipment. We motioned them to take places along the trench.

After I sat down again, I studied the Prussians on either side of me. They were big men, and they looked fit, somewhat different than the Saxons, Bavarians, and Austrians we had run into at Soissons and St. Mihiel; more like the troops at Belleau Wood. They didn't smile or weep but looked resigned to their fate. When first aid men called for stretcher-bearers, they stood up and proceeded to make themselves available. They shed their equipment as they arose to go and were business-like in their job. I supposed their willingness to work meant that they would get away from the active front quicker.

We were told to advance, and we jumped out of the trench and dashed across a swale. Machine gun bullets from Essen Hook thrashed all about us. The bullets came in from our left, and to save ourselves, we had to hit the deck. The fire was continuous, and it was bad. I saw an officer rise to his feet and frantically wave a white rag at someone on our left. I rolled over and looked and I saw three small French tanks climbing toward Essen Hook; and while I watched, they wheeled their way onto the top. The machine gun and rifle fire was terrific where they were, and became quiet where we were. One tank advanced toward a nest, the clattering of fire concentrated on it, and the tank spun around on the nest and ground it and the men in it to the dirt. Then the turret opened, and a man climbed part way out and waved an all-clear signal down at us. We again jumped to our feet, and rushed on ahead. But I noticed several forms that we left behind, and still others that stumbled unsteadily to the rear.

We ascended the slope ahead, and I saw that the battalion was stretched out in column. We were moving along the left flank as though expecting an attack from that direction. The 17th Company had left the battalion, and we later heard that it had been directed toward the rear of Essen Hook, to clean out that area for the French. The French had failed in their attack, leaving our left flank open and subject to counterattack. And we were placed in position to repel the enemy.

We slowly advanced and came astride a knoll, when we noticed a German sausage balloon ahead floating serenely over the trees. That meant we would be under observation, as we were in the open. We halted on the knoll and immediately sought cover: and none too soon, for the Germans opened up on us with the big boys, and the deep rumble of ten inch shells came rushing in and exploding with a roar, and a cloud of debris and earth blanketed the company.

I hurried up the slope to get out of the fire, and found a slit trench that would save me from all but a direct hit. As I lay there, I noticed that it was possible to see the shell in flight. There was a noticeable air disturbance preceding the shell; it was concentric, and at the center of the hazy mass, a dark blob, the shell. It was difficult to predict the point of burst, and they all looked as though my name was written on them. It was an eerie experience, and was glad when the captain called on us to move.

Up ahead of us, the 6th had run into trouble, and the reverberation of machine guns and rifles was continuous and made a terrific din. The fire was over a thousand yards ahead and seemed centered on Blanc Mont itself. We moved ahead about four or five hundred yards down a slope, where we found more protection. The Germans shortened their range, but the shells landed a couple of hundred yards ahead of us.

One shell landed in the center of a clearing and burst in the midst of a group of men. It seemed that the entire group was casualties; but soon a few rose to their feet, and began working on the wounded. They were not spread out enough, and as a result they were nearly all killed. There was a file of French troops making their way forward on our left, in the shelter of trees; the shells caught them, and there was hell among their ranks, too.

The captain called on us to spread out and led us across the clearing ahead. We crossed without a casualty, but my trail took me through the center of the group that had taken the burst shortly before. They were a bloody mess, and I scarcely saw a man that wasn't bandaged. And there were those, less fortunate, who were killed.

We turned to the right along an old trench system, and were ordered to take up position in it. We were in the Bois de Sommepy, at the foot of the long slope that led up to Blanc Mont, where there waged a bitter fight to take the dominating height.

The German trench was filthy; human excrement was everywhere, and even the equipment they had shed was filthy and dirty. Our men preferred the natural ground, rather than the safety of a dirty trench, the Boyau d'Augaboury.

Wire entanglements were in front of the trench and along the road in this area, but offered little resistance to our advance. We had moved to the right and across the Marine front, and were now at the apex of the Bois de la Vipère zone; and word was passed, that two companies of Infantry and two companies of the 5th Marines had cleared the zone of German troops.

The 6th Marines were still battling for a foothold on Blanc Mont, and it looked as though the 5th was going to bypass the famous mount. The French on our left were still held up at Essen Hook, and the flank was wide open: not a very good sign to us. If the Germans hit us on the flank, we were liable to be cut off and separated from our supplies. The word was to go ahead, regardless.

Men were sent back to a farmhouse in the Bois de Vipre, to fill our canteens while we waited. It was dark when they returned, and we immediately started forward. We followed the Sommepy-Étienne road for some distance, then up a fairly steep trail to the left, across a trench system, and past a timer shed and camouflaged road: and we were on the front line.

October 4, Midnight

The Germans held the road to our left and the east slope of Blanc Mont and occupied the woods directly ahead of us; and we lay along the ridge, which had sparse cover. About midnight, a German airplane dropped a flare overhead, and it lit up the ridge like day and floated over us for some time. Then with a crash, the Germans opened up on us with heavy artillery. The first burst hit the ground shortly to my right, and a platoon of the 17th Company, which had rejoined the battalion, were the victims. The yells and screams of the men were terrible. And as more shells poured in the area, we were routed out and moved to the left and downhill toward the Germans, where it was safer. I heard that Gunner Hulbert had been killed in that fire. He was the little fellow, well-liked by the men, who had led us back from the St. Mihiel drive. It is tough to lose a man like that.

Since the drive started, we had been following the attacking unit fairly closely, and from the staccato bark of machine guns and the sharp crack of

Springfields, we could tell when they ran into resistance and how stubborn it was. Each line of resistance was a thunder of pieces, until the Marines won. Then it would be rather quiet for a distance: then a repetition of the din. The Germans were fighting hard to hold Blanc Mont, and as yet the 6th Marines had only a foothold on it. The line was bent back for about a kilometer, so that we could hear the crash of small arms to our left, and our left-rear, most of the night.

Toward morning, the 3rd Battalion of the 5th moved forward and took up attack position. The 1st Battalion formed behind them, and the 2nd behind us. As time came to go, German artillery gave us a hammering. In the midst of the bursting shells, I saw one of our "musics" stand up. Several of us yelled at him to get down and take cover. Then one burst struck close and hit him, and he received a hunk of shell-fragment in his back. Even then, he stood and raised both arms and shook his fists toward the Germans, and cursed them. Men nearby ran and pulled him down and applied first aid. It was hard to understand his action, as the shell fragment had apparently smashed his spine.

The 3rd Battalion was on its way. A burst of machine guns and rifle fire marked their debut; but the 3rd swept over them and went on. We were next, the 49th Company leading in column and stretched out in a long line and covering the open flank. With the din ahead and the expected fire from the flank, it was nerve-wracking. But we were lucky, for we experienced no fire from the flank.

There was fierce battle ahead, heavy firing to the right in the path of the 23rd Infantry, and there was heavy firing to our left rear, in the vicinity of Blanc Mont. What in hell was coming off, anyway? It was a mixed mess; the 2nd Division had done it again, we had burst clear through the Germans. If the French units on our left and on our right had been able to keep up, there would have been a rout. A two battalion front had plowed through the Germans; one, marines, and one, infantry; not only whipping the enemy in front of them, but also fighting heavy flanking forces, as well, and repulsing their counter-attacks. And we took position in trenches immediately behind the 3rd.

Mail Call

Then, for some reason unknown to us, mail was passed out to the 49th. It seemed to me that nearly everybody but a guy named Bullis received some. It made me homesick, and I was discouraged and blue. The few letters I had received were months old and didn't tell me much about home. The rattle of Springfields and machine guns continued and became incessant up where the 3rd was, and I moved down the trench until I was alone with my thoughts. I ate part of a box of hardtack to solace my drooping spirit, and then quietly began singing—and my repertoire is very short, as is my singing—but I sang, "Just before the battle, Mother, I was thinking, dear, of you...."

October 4, 11:00 a.m.

"Forty-ninth—fall in!" And we formed a long line abreast the Blanc Mont-St. Étienne road, facing the left flank.

Every sound ceased. It was like the moment before a storm; and we wondered at that. I was on the extreme left flank of the battalion, with Comfort, Connolly, and Corporal Woodard; and Lieutenant Conner directly behind us: and then the shouted command, "For-ward."

As we advanced, we came into a pine grove, and all hell broke loose; machine guns and rifles met us on our left and dead ahead, and indirect fire from our right. It was hell, and no mistake.

There was a burst of fire to my right, and close, and I turned thinking I could stop it; but riflemen rushed in firing from the hip. It was over immediately. And I thought, a few more bastards gone to hell. And I swung back to the left. Connolly and Comfort were now disappeared. Whether they were hit, or not, I didn't know; only I cursed them, for they carried two thirds of my ammunition.

Woodard and I hit the dirt, as Austrian 88's plowed into the ground about us. The 88 is a wicked gun—the burst of the shell comes before the sound. And here it was point blank fire with low trajectory, and limestone surface inches below a thin veneer of soil.

The hell of the next moments will always be remembered—the bursts, the screams of men in agony, and the utter confusion. The shells burst on contact without penetrating the earth and the pieces of shell casing and shrapnel raked the ground. I was prone when I heard a "dud" hit a few feet away. It was a hollow sound—then the most horrible screams arose from the victim. I rolled over to look; the "dud" had torn into Lt. Conner's groin, and he writhed and screamed from agony. I got up to go to him, and almost immediately he relaxed, and was still.

I hit the ground again, trying to "hide under my helmet": Lt. Conner killed; how many more, I didn't know. Off to my right rear, I heard a repeated call, "Joe Carter, Corporal Joe Carter; Lt. Conner is killed." Joe Carter, a short, squat man in our platoon was Lt. Conner's buddy, and they were calling him to care for the lieutenant's body. Why, I didn't know; only I thought it foolish. Lieutenant Conner was dead, why waste men now, when every live man counted?

With that, I took a careful look ahead, and spotted four artillery pieces and the Germans who manned them. They were on a ridge a kilometer, or so, away, and slightly left of center. I could see them swab out the guns and load them; then scatter, as one pulled the lanyard. A burst of reddish-yellow fire and smoke erupted from the guns, and almost immediately the shells arrived and burst: then came the screams of the shells.

Too far away to try for them, I searched the woods across a clearing on my left for closer targets. I didn't see any, but still the machine gun bullets whipped in. From there I looked over the ground ahead in the clumps of trees for action; again, I didn't see anything—and a burst arrived close at hand, a burst of orange smoke two feet in front of Corporal Woodard's head. As I looked at him, he spread eagled on the ground and his entire body quivered, but no sound came from him. I yelled, "Are you hit, Woodard?" As I got no reply, I jumped to my feet to dash ahead. But Woodard also stood up and dashed ahead with me, although he was in shock and didn't know what he was doing. We made about fifty feet and hit the earth again, and looked for those damned machine guns. They sprayed bullets from my left all around us as we dashed forward, but I was unable to detect their positions. They were close was all I could tell.

I arose again and made another short dash, and as I hit the ground I made another useless search. I then turned to see how the rest of the group faired. We were in the open, the trees to our right; I was on the extreme left flank and about a half dozen men in the open with me; and each was making his dash ahead. And I also could see the huddled forms of several men: they were either dead or severely wounded.

After a couple more dashes ahead, all the men shifted to the right into the cover of the trees, and I turned to run that way. I was pressing ahead when something hit me with violence on the left side, spinning me around over 180 degrees. I struggled to regain my balance, but now I could see the guns firing at me. They were about 200 yards away at the edge of the woods. Those were the flanking guns that had been firing into our left flank. There were four machine guns, and each was spurting bluish flame from the muzzle. And all were concentrated on me.

I knew that I was dead. I fired from the hip while walking toward them. I inserted a second clip, and still firing, advanced: a third clip and I stood and fired from the shoulder. My gun whipped me around, but I inserted another clip and concentrated on the two guns still firing. I don't know how many clips I fired, but all the guns were now still. And as I looked, I could see seven or eight Germans stand up and run and disappear into the woods.

I stood dazed. I couldn't believe I was still alive. Ordinarily, thirty to forty men operated that many guns; seven or eight got away: I don't know how many I hit. Then, coming to myself, and realizing I made a perfect target; I turned and ran to the cover of the woods behind me.

31

A Warrior's Boast

When I entered the woods, I saw Comfort lying in the shelter of a fallen tree. There was no one else in the vicinity: "Where's Connolly? I asked. I received a negative answer. I was mad clear through, and I bawled him out for leaving me when the going was rough, and told him to stick close, as I needed ammunition.

I heard somebody yelling for a machine gun, and as ours were knocked out, I decided to go to his aid. Telling Comfort to "Come on," I got up to go, but Comfort said, "You'll get killed, you damned fool."

"That's what we're here for," I said; "I'm going. You can stay here." And I made a dash in the direction of the voice.

It was Captain Frank Whitehead,[1] about 75 feet away; he was alone in an old gun emplacement sheltered behind two trees. He pointed to the target, a German trench about 100 yards away. Groups of the enemy, ten to fifteen men, were leaving the trench and crossing a wagon road to disappear into a second trench.

I got into action, and settling on my knees I fired over the edge of the hole. "You're getting them! You're getting them!" the captain yelled, and pounded me on the back. The vibration of the Sho-Sho is terrific, and I was unable to determine the result of my fire. So to keep on target, I fired in short bursts, re-aimed, and fired again.

When I finished the clip, I ejected it, and a second clip was thrust to me: it was Comfort; he had followed me to the spot and now was feeding the gun. And I felt better.

I fired at several groups as they appeared until there was a pause in the action. Just then a Hotchkiss crew, or rather all that remained of the crew, slid into the hole. One of the men reported to the captain that five men were killed or wounded in coming forward; that they had only three boxes of ammunition, one barrel, a tripod but no seat, and no gloves for handling the hot barrel. The captain told me to keep on target, and told them to use the gun only against a counterattack, and asked two of the men to go back and find ammunition and the missing gun parts.

Just then Sergeant Davis dropped into the hole and two lieutenants, Lt. Johnson and Lt. Lindgren. I fired a few more bursts at the Germans, but they were reluctant to leave the shelter of the trench, and more time elapsed between bursts. Most of the men in the hole with me kept below ground level, leaving me with just my head sticking up and the captain behind the trees. A runner came with a message for the captain ordering all men to close to the right and form on the 2nd Battalion. The captain dashed off, and we remained behind.

Now the Germans tried getting men out of the trench, one at a time. I had Comfort reloading clips and some of the others were helping him. Then the two absent members of the machine gun crew returned with some ammunition they had retrieved; and things became quiet in the hole.

I kept an eye on the target. Individuals still sneaked across, but I intended to stop them. I said to Comfort, "Let me take your rifle." And I set the leaf sight and made ready for the next enemy to make the dash to safety. He left the trench running hard, and I eased off a shot at him. He straightened up, threw his arms over his head, and plunged full length on his face into the dirt: "Did you see me get that son-of-a-bitch!" I chortled.

And before anything was said—*wham*, I was hit and tossed on my shoulders on the other side of the hole. The blow felt as though someone had hit me with a heavy maul. I wasn't conscious of any pain, but I knew it was serious.

I scrambled to my knees and struggled to get my equipment off. Several men rushed to help me: "My God—look at this," said one. My web belt was torn to shreds on my left side, the ammunition pockets were filled with exploded and burned cartridges, my blouse was in tatters, the pocket hung by the seams in front, the back of my shirt was torn off, and nothing was left of my underwear: but there wasn't a scratch on me. They all marveled at the sight, and then I remembered what had happened. I remembered that burst of machine gun fire and being spun about. I had been hit by a burst of several bullets, and only a hair stood between me and death.

One of the men picked up my combat pack, and said, "Look." It appeared as though mice had been at it. It was filled with bullet holes, and the blanket I had was in rags; nothing was salvageable: the mess kit had holes through it, the condiment can was ruined; but there was not a scratch on my back.

Another picked up my canteen; it was holed, too. I marveled that a man could be shot up by so many bullets and still not have a scratch on him.

In the meantime, I stripped to the waist and asked Lt. Johnson where the bullet had come out. He said, "Don't worry, it didn't come out—you're not hit in the lungs, anyway."

I replied, "It's through the lung, all right." I could feel the exhalation of the air on my neck. I didn't bleed very much, at least externally; but I felt that it was extremely bad. And I thought of home, and Mother, and hoped she would understand and not take it too seriously.

The bullet had entered at the base of the neck, and it was some time before they got a bandage on. Then throwing my blouse over my shoulders, they laid me down. I asked that they straighten me out, as I didn't want to die all huddled up.

The men went back to the job of watching and waiting and it became very quiet in the hole. I lay there trying to figure out what had happened. I decided that the Germans had put a sniper on me, and that he had taken two shots. The first had missed, the bullet just grazing my head, leaving a long, thin mark in my scalp between my right ear and my head; and the second shot was in the same spot: but that I raised my head to boast I got it in the base of the neck. I wasn't conscious of much pain, but the wound had sapped my strength and left me weak as a rag.

Silence settled deep in the hole. The men weren't shooting or saying anything. They had just come through a living hell, and were glad enough to be alive, and content to let things simmer down, before going on. They were all under cover but one, and he was on watch. The war was a long way off for me, but even I was brought back when the lieutenant said, "Here they come—we've got to get out of here!"

And instantly, things began to happen. Several came over to me and lifted me to my feet. I looked and saw three waves of Germans approaching at a walk. They were about 400 yards away and in perfect order, spread out, straight lines, and all rifles at high port: "We'll help you back," they said. But I told them to get me out of the hole, and I'd make it": "There are a lot of men helpless—get them out." And they all tore out of there.

I was alone, and I stood and watched the Germans. They came on in steady lines. Their right flank would take in this area: I had to go.

I went about fifty feet and stopped to get my breath; again I eyed the Germans. They were getting closer. I made the trip back in short stretches, and each time the enemy was closer still. I was stripped to the waist, my blouse over one shoulder, without a helmet, a gas mask, or weapon. It looked bad; it looked as though I wouldn't make it.

As I labored on, I passed numerous bodies; some seriously wounded, and others dead. The Germans were sniping at the walking wounded, and I saw several hit again as they trudged to the rear. One body remains fixed as a picture in my mind. He was face down on his knees, his back bared, and he was clutching his fingers at a wound.

I was conscious of the bullets zipping past with a sharp crack, and I still but slowly tramped ahead. One poor devil, wounded, hurried past, only to give a lurch, grab at his back, and plunge to his face. I stopped to breathe and lifted my eyes toward the Germans, now about a hundred yards behind. And I pushed heavily forward.

Soon I saw the remnants of our company along a sunken road, all grimly facing the enemy, holding their fire. I tried to call to them, but I couldn't attract their attention. Womack lay about fifty feet ahead of me but was heedless of my cries. All eyes were narrowed to a slit, all mouths were straight lines. And I thought, God help the Germans.

I suddenly realized that I was in their field of fire, and I hurried to my right to clear them. And as I got out of the way, I stopped again to get my breath and turned to view the scene. The enemy was close now, I could make out the expressions on their faces; they were at high port, the ready position for bayonet attack, and I hurried to get further from their flank.

Woodard hurried past me, the flesh of his left cheek hanging down, baring the teeth. He was in a state of shock, and, ignoring me, he hurried on. As I struggled ahead, the burst of Springfield fire crashed in my ears—the battle was on. The Marines had waited till the last possible moment, and their fire broke the German lines. Then the firing became terrific, as the business of killing went on.

32

He'll Need Those Tags

A first aid station was ahead of me on a knoll, and I made my way to it. Behind me, the battle raged. The vicious crack of the Springfield blended with the reports of the German Mauser: a handful of Marines against three waves of Germans. And the Marines, though out-numbered, were holding their own.

There were three or four doctors and a small group of corpsmen at the dressing station. They were all navy personnel in attendance who accompanied the Marines in their ventures. There were several shell holes to mark the spot, each surrounded by a group of walking wounded, and the ground seemed literally covered with stretcher cases among whom the doctors worked.

I sat in a shell hole, and Harding, a pink-faced kid in our platoon, sat across from me, a round, red hole in his belly, showing where he was hit. A doctor and a corpsman tore off my bandage and replaced it. Then the corpsman grabbed a handful of my belly and shot a big hypodermic needle of tetanus serum in me and marked an "X" with iodine on my forehead. The doctor said to me that if I could walk at all to keep going, as German artillery had been shelling them. Two stretcher-bearers came up then to the station carrying a bad case on the stretcher. As I looked on, I saw him jerkily passing out, and the stretcher-bearers rolled him off and placed another man on the stretcher. I thought, a man can't die in peace here, and I stood up and started down the road.

I wobbled as I went along, first on one side of the trail, then on the other; my knees were buckling, but I staggered on. A lieutenant of artillery and a sergeant, who were observing fire, ran down off the bank of the road and grabbed me and laid me down in the shelter of the bank: "Stay here until the artillery fire is over," they said, and dashed back up the bank again.

As I lay, I listened to the sound of the battle. From the din, it sounded as though our fellows were beating the Germans back. I hoped so, for it had looked ominous to me.

32. He'll Need Those Tags

The lieutenant and sergeant returned and told me it was all right now to go on. But I was helpless, I couldn't get my feet under me; nor could I stand. They said they would get stretcher-bearers, and soon returned with two men and a stretcher. One was tall and lanky, the other was short and stubby, and getting all 185 pounds of me on the stretcher was tough for the four of them. But between them, they hoisted me to a shoulder-carry.

The tall man took the lead and the shorter one the rear, and, swaying and puffing, we went on our way. Soon a light shell came hurtling in and exploded in the dust behind us. The stretcher-bearers fell, and I was tumbled into the dirt. The rear bearer was wounded, and my right ankle was hit. The other bearer went to the aid of his fellow, and when they had bared the wound, there was a lot of laughter—and I also joined in. He was stooped over, his pants about his ankles, and the blood was trickling down from a wound in the center of his ass. It was a minor wound, though painful. It was more an insult than disabling. He was promptly bandaged, and then they looked to my ankle. Three wraps of the leggings plus the top of my tough army boot had stopped the piece. Although I had a sore ankle, there was no wound. I swear that the blow to my ankle hurt worse than the chest wound: at least then. After much heaving and grunting, they raised me to their shoulders, and we resumed our swaying way to the woods and the ambulance we would find there.

At last, we came to the ambulance, and I was shoved into the last vacant place, next to Joe Carter, who said he was paralyzed. Joe had been hit in the thigh while carrying Lt. Conner's body back to safety.

It was after dark when we reached the brigade dressing station. And I was removed from the Ford and laid on the ground. Some time elapsed before they got to me, but finally I was carried down into the underground station. I was laid on a table, and the bandage was removed. One of the doctors started to cut off my dog tags, the string of which was in the wound, but he was stopped by Dr. Boone. Doctor Boone laid his ear on my chest and looked at the hole from which mingled blood and air was bubbling out, and said, "He'll need those tags; take him outside": a blunt ways of saying, He will die.

I was re-bandaged, taken outside, and laid on the ground under the stars. It was cold, and there was a mass of other stretcher cases. I was bare to the waist, and my blouse was thrown over me as a covering. And I waited to die.

But I wasn't ready to die. I was wide awake, and I looked around. I recognized Lt. Lindgren, who was in the hole when I was hit. He lay on the next stretcher but didn't answer when I spoke to him; he was silently contemplating the many stars in the heaven above.

Shortly, the doctor who had removed my bandage came out and knelt down beside me. He inquired about the tape on my left side; and being told "pleurisy," he shook his head and raised me up and placed me on my right shoulder. I cried out; the pain was too great, and I couldn't stand it. But he insisted that I stay in that position. "It's the only chance you have," he said. "You are shot through the right lung, and you can't breathe with that one; and you have pleurisy in the left lung, and it will be hard to breathe with that. You will have to lie this way."

He then called for stretcher-bearers to pick me up and he led the way to another ambulance where they slid me into the bottom right tier so that I would have support for my back. And we started off.

It was a rough, jolting ride; the man in the tier above was hemorrhaging, and the blood dripped down on me—and then—the pain too severe—I passed out, unconscious.

October 5

The ambulance was stopped, and I could hear two men outside talking. Their voices seemed miles away, but I heard them distinctly. One said to the other, "I've been to three hospitals already with this load—what time is it, anyway?" The other replied, "4:30." It was still dark, so it must have been 4:30 a.m. Then they withdrew my stretcher.

Nothing seemed real; it was as though I was floating on air; their voices were far away, yet they were carrying me. They carried me into a long, low tent, past a long line of walking wounded, to the far end, where a couple of doctors were stationed. The doctors looked me over, shook their heads, and motioned them to lay me down at the side of the tent.

As I lay there, it seemed as though everyone forgot me. I heard the walking wounded give their names, rank, company, regiment, and their wound to the doctors; and I heard the assignment to the wards. I heard men of my own company report, and I tried to call to them, but only could make a sickly gurgle.

I lay there for a long time. Then, being uncomfortable, I fussed and fumed, until I attracted the attention of a corpsman. He got down to listen then said he would take care of me. He didn't; he never came back. So, I tried again; and after a while a second corpsman came: he got down to listen, then got up, and called out, "Stretcher-bearers!" And when they came, he ordered me taken to the "non-evacuation ward—immediately."

I was placed on a table in the non-evacuation ward, and two nurses proceeded to cut off my clothing. While they were cutting, a corpsman, who was skulking about, attempted to take my personal belongings, generally being a nuisance. But one of the nurses placed all my belongings in a bag and tucked it under my pillow, and she ordered the corpsman off.

I was completely helpless; I could do nothing; and they soon stripped and bathed me, then rolled me off the table into a bed. And with a good shot in the arm, I relaxed, and went on gasping for breath.

The day was uneventful. All that was done for me was an occasional shot of morphine to ease the pain. I had no interest in the occupants of the beds around me. I couldn't sleep, I couldn't eat, and nor could I move. I appeared to be totally paralyzed; whether from the effect of the wound or from weakness, I didn't know which. The only thing that stirred me was the corpsman, which lurked about and attempted to take my watch, my money belt, and other personal effects: as he said to keep them for me—keep them, hell! He was a grave robber. He slinked away, though, when the nurse came into the ward.

The night was a repetition of the day; no sleep, just a shot in the arm, and the regular visits of the night nurse.

33

Miss Duffy

October 6

More morphine (my arm felt like a pin-cushion), and still another day gasping for breath. I couldn't turn my head, I couldn't lift a finger; and I still couldn't sleep.

Miss Duffy and Miss Schumaker came round to my cot and gave me a bath and an alcohol back-rub. It felt fine. I asked Miss Duffy why they had left me unattended so long in the receiving ward. She paled, and asked me what I meant. And I told her about being laid aside, but when I aroused and needed help, the corpsman wouldn't pay any attention to me. She finally said, "That's the pile for the dead and the dying"; and she wept.

Several German prisoners were working in and around the ward. They seemed subdued and docile, but were willing to work. Miss Duffy told me that there were several badly wounded Germans at the other end of the tent and that she hated to work on them. The saying of the men when passing a dead enemy, "A dead German is a good German," seemed about right.

The night nurse came in, and after taking my temperature and pulse readings, she asked the customary question, "Have you had a bowel movement?" My answer was, "No." She then placed a bowl of thin soup on my chest, ran a rubber tube from it to my mouth, and told me to try and get it down. I managed to suck some in, but I am afraid most of it ran down my neck. After cleaning me up, she gave me a shot in the arm again and left, telling me to try and get some sleep.

I was again sleepless, and watched the activities throughout the night. I had noticed that moveable screens had been set around certain of the cots during the daytime, and now I knew why. For during the night a crew came in, removed the screen, and then a stark body was carried out. After cleaning up the bed, a new patient was carried in. The ward was filled with patients despite the many cots that had been screened. I suppose the night detail was to keep the other patients unaware of the unusually high mortality. The night

33. Miss Duffy

nurse was an awfully busy nurse; between supervising the removal of the dead, and settling in the new patients, she mad periodic checks on the living.

With the coming of morning, Miss Duffy and Miss Schumaker returned to duty. Then came the morning wash and clean up, followed by the feeding of the patients. When Miss Duffy came to me, I asked her if I were going to live or die. She shushed me and placed a bowl of soup on my chest with a tube to my mouth and told me to eat. I didn't get an answer to my question, but after sucking the soup down I felt some better.

Captain Wagner made his rounds and spent considerable time on me, listening on the earphones, tapping my chest, and having me cough. When I asked whether I'd live or die, he ignored me and stood contemplating me as he wrote down his orders for the day. The question bothered me. I'd about got over the matter of dying; and now I wanted to live. Why can't they tell me?

More morphine. As my right arm was sore from the previous shots, I asked the nurse to try the left arm. It was a long day, and I tried to find something to do. I attempted to wiggle my fingers. At first, I had no results. But I kept it up until finally I got a response. And by much effort, I managed to slowly slide my hand up my leg and rest it on my body. I was so excited by the accomplishment that I cried out to the nurse and demonstrated that feat for her. She was as tickled as I was, and in honor of the occasion—gave me another bath.

More cots were screened today, one across the aisle from me and one of the prisoners, as well. I thought of what Dr. Boone had said when he stopped the other doctor from cutting off my dog tags—"He'll need those tags."

As the day wore on, my efforts became more successful; and although I couldn't raise my hands, I got more adept at shifting them. Finally, I could turn my head, to the right and to the left, and felt better about my chances of living.

I noticed cot after cot with the feet of the patient elevated higher than the head, and I wondered about that. Finally, I tried talking to the man on my right whose cot was raised in this manner. When I spoke to him, he turned his head and gave me a wan smile, and said, "That's for shock; I'm coming out of it now." And with the passing of the day, he was almost cheerful, and we had some good "gab" sessions.

After dark, the claxon sounded, and instantly all the nurses and corpsmen were running about in gas masks and tin hats. The nurses quickly checked on the patients and then hurried out to safety trenches. The Germans were on a bombing raid. We heard the drone of engines approaching and pass overhead; and with the passing of the planes we could hear the bombs exploding. They said one bomb hit a tent not far away but that the rest missed the hospital.

When the nurses and corpsmen returned, all excited, we kidded them for running. But they were in no mood to be kidded. And I'll have to admit, if we could have run we would have been the first to seek shelter. So, the Germans do bomb well-marked hospitals; a contemptible stunt: I hope the bombs land in the prisoners' beds, if they bomb again.

After the excitement, the nurse returned with the needle and proceeded to give those who needed it a shot in the arm. After that, I slept.

October 8

This day was long, drawn out, and tiring. One thing that irritated me was the corpsman. He approached me again, persistent in his efforts at getting a hold of my personal items. I finally got rid of him by threatening to call the nurses. And he left with a look that boded me no good. From my cot he crossed the aisle and tried to get things from another patient, and in the struggle to get them struck the fellow across the face. Although we were helpless, those that were able shouted and yelled at him. He beat a hasty retreat as the nurses came in. We didn't see any more of him, as they transferred him to another job and ward.

The captain was pleased with my progress, but he still prescribed more morphine—and morphine I got; however, not in the arm, for I managed to get my leg out in time.

In the late p.m., Miss Duffy came to my cot again and in a somber manner told me I had better write home, as it might be the last chance I would ever have. My heart sank with the thought that the doctor had given me up, and I felt it was unfair to die now. I told her that I couldn't write. And she said, "I know; you dictate, and I'll write for you."

American Red Cross
A.E.F.
Field Hospital
Tuesday, Oct. 8, 1918

Dear Folks:

Am out of the big scrap again. It looks as if it may be for a long time this trip, as the Boche got me with a machine gun bullet. But I am in the hospital and doing as well as being expected. It will be a while before I am o.k. but will try and write you myself next week. We have good care altho' we are in a field hospital, and the song "I never want to get well" seems quite right.

Will be sure and write you regular now as I will have ample time. Address mail as usual but be sure and write often.

Hope all's well at home and above all do not worry about me, as I am well taken care of and feeling better today, so hope and think I will improve daily.

Worlds of love to all
Everard

Passed as censored
O.K.
M.A.W.
Capt. M.C., U.S.A.

Note: This letter was censored by Captain M.A. Wagner, our ward doctor. Miss Blanch Duffy was our day nurse and who went out of her way to make me comfortable. It was very difficult to dictate this letter, as "the last chance" in her remarks sounded very ominous to me. She did not want to write with reference to the song; she thought it rather facetious under the circumstances: "I don't want to get well; I don't want to get well, I'm in love with a beautiful nurse...."

The non-evacuation ward is where you survive or die. The ward remains behind with the more seriously wounded when the hospital moves. This was Field Hospital # 15. After dictating the letter, I was lost in thought about home and mother, and didn't take much interest in the surroundings. In the evening another bowl of soup was placed on my chest, and I sucked it down. Then the night nurse came with the needle again, and I slept the whole night through.

October 9

I felt better this morning, and I could use my hands again. I still hemorrhaged some, and it was more like jelly than blood. It was hard to get rid of, as it was all over my face and hands and hard to clean my mouth. But the nurse was on the job, and soon had me looking "pretty" again.

Doctor Wagner made his rounds and spoke briefly to the ward giving us notice that Major General Ireland, head of the Medical Corps in France, was going to visit the ward and that we were not to speak to him.

The inspection party arrived in due time, the Major General leading the procession. As he was passing by, I gathered my nerve, and said, "Sir, may I speak?" The general whirled and came back to my cot. And I thought here's where I get it: "What is it, boy?" And I told him about the bothersome corpsman and said that he had slapped one of the men yesterday. He immediately asked who had been slapped. I pointed to the man, and the general talked with him. He then gave instructions for the shakedown of the corpsman's quarters and said that there would be no more molestation of the men and stalked out of the ward.

Doctor Wagner looked as though a bomb had exploded, but said nothing as he followed the general out. I later spoke to the nurse and said I was sorry but felt someone should make an issue of it. She said that the nurses were glad I had spoken up, as they had received many complaints about him and now would be rid of him. Several of the men also spoke to me about it later; they, too, were glad. So I guess it was all right.

For supper that night I had soup, and I ate it with a spoon, although it hurt to raise my right arm. The unusual exercise tired me out, and I was glad to get my customary shot, and soon went into a deep sleep for the night.

October 10

A lot of excitement this morning. A hospital train was in and was headed for Paris to a base hospital, and Captain Wagner was selecting the men well enough to make the trip: to Paris, the doughboy's dream; and I wanted to go. The next train undoubtedly would go anywhere in France—but not to Paris.

But Captain Wagner passed me by, and I felt let down. When he passed me again, I spoke up and said, "Can't I go, too?" But he answered, "No, you can't stand the trip."—"Besides," I answered, "it's my birthday."

With that the captain stopped and came back to my cot: "Your birthday?" And he began to check me over while I held my breath. Then shaking his head, he said, "No."

The fellow on the next cot spoke up, "I'll watch out for him." But the captain still shook his head, and said, "No."

I countered with, "I'll be all right; please let me go." Finally, he grinned, and said, "You can go; but you will have to take the responsibility."

Soon they carried my friend out, but I never saw him again. They left me till last, and, finally, I was put on a stretcher and carried outside and placed on the ground by the train.

I lay quite a while, until the pain in my back grew unbearable; and I was cold. We wore the short hospital jackets and were laid on the stretchers with no blankets underneath, and only a thin one as a cover.

I was sure the stretcher had a broken back thus causing the pain, and I put in a call for a doctor. A nurse responded and came and knelt down beside me to help. She had another stretcher put under me; but that one hurt just as badly. So she called for another blanket to soften up the stretcher.

But that was another matter. It was a French train and the "Frogs" wouldn't give up a blanket unless they received one in return: "Non—non." That made the nurse angry, and she went to the pile of blankets and told the Frenchmen off; and then taking two of their sacred blankets, she returned. The Frenchmen just shrugged their shoulders and expressively gesturing turned away from her, as if to say, "Don't argue with a woman." The nurse placed a folded blanket under me and covered me with the other. I felt better, although my back still hurt and I was thoroughly chilled.

The nurse left, and then three or four of the Frenchmen returned, eyeing the blankets. They kept up a continual chatter, and I believe they would have taken them from me if the stretcher-bearers hadn't come to put me on the train.

I was placed in an old third-class coach car which was already filled. That stumped the bearers for a moment, but then they had a brilliant idea and fastened the stretcher to the ceiling of the car: out of the way of everyone, and not accessible for emergences; out of sight of the windows and in a cold draft that swept through the car. But I was satisfied; I was on my way to Paris again, the Mecca of all doughboys, Marines, and sailors in France.

34

A Souvenir

The train started on its way with many jerks and wild tooting. Goodbye, Field Hospital No. 15. What's next?

Soon they started feeding the men. But nothing came my way. I was too well hidden in the upper realms of the car. I called down to get attention and demanded something to eat. That got me noticed, and the fellow who then passed me a bowl of gruel said, "Sorry, I forgot to look on the second deck."

I lay listening to the four flat wheels pounding below and wondered whether I'd be thrown from my wildly rocking perch, or whether the entire stretcher would come down. It would be some tumble, either way.

According to the conversation of those below, we were passing through Rhiems, and I missed the sights that I had hoped to see; the ruins of that famous cathedral and the place where the Germans were stopped.

With the onset of darkness, I was in a bad way; a hacking cough developed, which, along with the difficulty I had in breathing, pretty near finished me. To make matters worse, I hemorrhaged a congealed, jelly-like mass. I tried to catch it in my hands, but it smeared all over my face.

No one noticed my troubles, and I was left alone with my misery. To make matters worse, I needed a urinal badly. I suffered in agony, until, finally, I attracted the attention of one of the walking wounded. He took one look at me and started yelling for a nurse. They were in another car and it was some time before a corpsman put in an appearance and took care of my needs. As he cleaned the gore from my face and hands, he raved about the army and the way they did things. This train was supposed to carry only patients that required a minimum of help, those passed the danger zone; and here I was with a lot of others that required attention they weren't prepared to give.

I was too busy hacking and gasping to argue with him; but the fact was the large number of wounded they received daily was crowding the field hospitals to the limit. The hospital trains and the bases could look for a peak condition now. I knew that if we didn't reach medical help soon, I was done; pneumonia was getting a hold on me and I was scared.

34. A Souvenir

We passed through Château Thierry, and I could hear comments about the fighting there, and I thought of all that had transpired since we were on that front. Not many of the veterans of Belleau Wood were with the outfit now. Also, I realized that we were only about twenty miles from Paris and that I had come from Paris on this road back in June to receive my baptism of fire.

Soon we were there, in spite of my hacking cough, gasping for breath, and the pounding of flat wheels. And the business of unloading began.

After the men in the car detrained, they came for me. And with much cussing and heaving they got me down and carried me into the concourse of the Gare du Nord. It was a large concourse, and wherever I looked there were rows of stretcher cases and hundreds of walking wounded lined the room.

As they put me down, I demanded a doctor, and someone was sent to get him. But a woman came. I was almost in a panic then; I knew I needed medical attention, and I raved at her and demanded a doctor. She grabbed my wrist, and said, "I *am* a doctor." And I quieted down.

The doctor made a quick check and called for stretcher-bearers. As they picked me up, she ordered an ambulance and accompanied me out of the concourse. She had me put in the ambulance and I heard her tell the driver to lose no time in getting me to a hospital. The driver obeyed, and we went tearing out of there and through the streets of Paris at breakneck speed.

Next, we turned into the driveway of a large building, and I was lifted out and my stretcher placed on a rack in the receiving room. And there I stayed.

Finally, between hacks, I called to a corpsman and asked for a doctor, and he leisurely went out to find one. Apparently, he told a nurse who also came at a leisurely walk—but at seeing me she began shouting orders, with the result that I was taken at a rush to the elevator and sent to an upper floor.

On reaching the floor, I was wheeled down a long hall into an X-ray room. The technician, a sergeant, was indifferent, and told me to climb up on the table. I told him I was helpless and would need assistance, whereon he showed a little more interest. And soon he had me on the table and proceeded to take several X-rays from different angles.

"I see it," the technician said, "a little piece of H&E," and he marked my body to locate it.

I wanted to argue, and I said, "It's a bullet; there was no shelling there."

But he was irritated, and said, "I know my business; that's H&E; no bullet looks like that," and I was hoisted on the stretcher again.

I was wheeled out and taken by elevator to the top floor and pushed down a long corridor into a large, well-lit room where I was again lifted off the stretcher onto a table. About a dozen cases were lying on the tables, but there were no nurses or doctors in sight. Finally, the nurses arrived and readied themselves for the work ahead. Three of them came to my table and began to check my papers; and learning that I was a Marine, they all were full of questions. Apparently, lots of Marines from Belleau Wood and Soissons had gone through this hospital and they were remembered by the nurses.

In answer to their queries, I told them I had been all the way from Belleau Wood to Blanc Mont before getting hit. One nurse was Miss Sullivan, one of the head nurses and she stayed with me as the doctors made their preparations. To my right lay a large Negro with a swollen leg wrapped in bandages, who never let out a yelp. Miss Sullivan informed me that they were going to amputate, as his leg was gangrenous.

A group of doctors approached and one of them said, "Let's see this piece of H&E this Marine stopped."

Again I told them, "It's a bullet; I know, I got hit."

They rolled me over and prodded trying to find the bullet. Finally, they took the X-ray, studied it, and proceeded to make measurements on my back marking the spot. They couldn't use a complete anesthetic, so one of them shot a local around the spot; then sitting me up, my hands grabbing my ankles and my head between my knees, they made an incision.

I was watching the doctors operating at the next table and thanking God that I wasn't losing a limb—"Ouch!" they had probed too deeply, and they injected more of the local anesthetic.

One doctor told me to bite hard as it was going to hurt. The first things he removed out of my back were pieces of my blouse, my shirt, and my underwear. They spent some time talking that over, as these had passed clear through me. They offered me the bits of cloth, but one look was enough, and I said, "No—I'll keep the bullet, though." The doctors laughed and answered, "The X-ray shows it to be a fragment: but we'll see."

I claimed again it was a bullet that had been fired by a sniper: "We'll see," and they went back to work with the probe.

"I've got it now; I'll work it out," and in a moment it popped out—"You are right; it's a bullet and well mashed up."

They looked it over and examined the weave marks of the cloth on it and showed it to me. Then, wrapping it in gauze, they handed me the souvenir—a real souvenir they all agreed, and cut some damaged tissue away and cleaned the area.

The bullet was a dumdum and exploded in my body. It passed through the right collar bone, ranged downward, tore through the apex of the right lung, crashed into my ribs, ricocheted to the right, and stopped in the muscles

34. *A Souvenir*   181

near my shoulder blade. In passing through the clavicle, it apparently just missed the great artery that lies behind it; and if it had hit that, I would have bled to death. After passing through the lung, it crashed into the third and fourth ribs, pulverizing them about a quarter of an inch from the spine, and cracked and smashed the second, fifth, and sixth ribs, before coming to a stop in the nerve center of my back. The cupro-nickel jacket disintegrated, leaving a large section in my lung and another in the muscles of my back, with countless small pieces embedded in my spine and in my ribs. No wonder I was paralyzed from the blow, and I was extremely fortunate in being able to walk out in front of the attacking Germans.

The nurses bandaged me leaving a tube in the wound so that Dakin fluid could run through and help heal the wound. I was wheeled out and taken down to the first floor into a large ward, where I was placed in a bed and made comfortable.

All in all, I thought that my twenty-second birthday had come to a fitting close, and I prayed that no more presents of that nature be given me.

35

A Salute

October 11

The hacking cough improved by morning, and any immediate chance of contracting pneumonia was gone. Miss Sullivan stopped to see me and explained the reason the nurses and doctors weren't there when I was brought in. They were gone to their quarters for rest after three days and nights in the operating room, taking care of new patients—only to be summoned again when I and the others arrived. And we felt that we were exploited: I stand at salute the many doctors and nurses over there who took care of the wounded.

The Ward

There were about sixty to eighty patients in the ward, arranged in four rows of beds, the length of the room. The occupants of the beds were well mixed, both French and American, all wounded in battle. A French Infantryman was on my right, who was badly mangled by a shell; and an Alpine Chasseur was on my left, a dispatch rider who crashed on his motor-bike.

The ward was one of many in the three to four story building which housed the American Red Cross Hospital No. 1 and which formerly held the famous Louis Pasteur Institute of Paris. The hospital was situated in the beautiful suburb of Paris, Neuilly, outside one of the seven gates of the city.

It was not an American military hospital, but one sponsored by wealthy Americans. The various wards were sponsored by great organizations, such as the National Geographic, and the beds were financed by rich Americans, whose names were on bronze plates over each bed. The head sponsor was Mrs. W.K. Vanderbilt, who was the leading lady of the 400 social elite of New York. It was probably the foremost hospital in France, and the patients were fortunate in being there.

The events in a hospital are such as cannot be recorded day by day, so

35. A Salute

only the more interesting occurrences shall be observed. The first few days in the hospital were uninteresting, as I was preoccupied recovering from my wound and the trying trip across France.

There were many nurses and auxiliary nurses in the ward, French, American, Belgian, and British women; and between them all, the patients had good care. As for the Red Cross nurses, they were always busy and the patients saw little of them except when they accompanied the doctor on his morning rounds to the patients. The auxiliary nurses had the various jobs of bathing the patient and making him comfortable, while the other women cleaned the wards and did the dirty jobs about the hospital.

In a large ward as this, the attention we received was quite impersonal, but adequate, and our interests were in watching the other patients and noting the variety and types of wounds they had. It seemed most were hit by shell fragments, small pieces and large, and they made horrible, painful, and disfiguring wounds. Most of the patients were quite cheerful despite their injuries; a few felt sorry for themselves and were quite fretful; and a very few were downright "babies."

One American soldier, who had a bed in the corner, had both buttocks torn away. It was a painful and extremely embarrassing wound, and it turned him into a complainer and whiner, which was at its worst when the doctor and nurse were dressing his wounds. Despite everything they did for him, whines were his only answer; until, finally, they approached him with sneers for his mental condition.

The Frenchman on my left was very solicitous over my condition and always tried to anticipate my needs. Although he could speak no English, he kept up a steady patter, smiling and gesturing all the while. One day, he took out a small case and opened it and showed me his medals. He was from the famous Alpine Chasseurs and had been in action four years. Among his medals were several Croix de Guerres, the ribbon well covered with palms and stars, and other medals, as well. There were three fourrageres, one green and red, the Croix de Guerre colors; one blood-red; and the other yellow and black. All these showed a remarkable and courageous regiment and typified the commendable fighting they had performed. After showing me the medals and cords, he insisted on my having one of the Croix de Guerres, and tried to pin it to my bed shirt. But I convinced him that they were his and that I had no right to wear one: at which he threw out his arms in Gaulic gestures and spoke out his mind.

When he had visitors—and they all appeared to be relatives—he had them sit on chairs and on both my cot was well as his. He made much in introducing them to me, but it was near impossible to gather the relationship;

although I was able to determine that one was his wife and another his daughter. Often they brought a spread and cakes and cookies, and again I was enjoined to share in them with the group. And all the while they chattered and talked as one, and included me in their conversation. It was tough at such times to be a "foreigner," and not understand or appreciate the friendliness that they showed me.

The Frenchman on my right was a comic, always laughing, who insisted on exhibiting what he could do with his badly mangled leg, to anyone who would watch. The left hip, knee, and foot had been shattered, leaving him with the foot turned inward to about ninety degrees and stiff. The knee also was stiff as a board, while the hip seemed to be free with no restrictions. It was nothing unusual to see him raise the leg high overhead and pillow his head on his foot; and then he would guffaw his delight.

In the opposite corner of the room and across from me was another Frenchman. He was young, good looking, and cheerful. He, so I was told, was a gunner in a tank, and had been shot through the chest by an anti-tank bullet. He was able to sit up and was intensely interested in me; for whenever I looked in his direction, he smiled and waved. One day, he pantomimed for me that a shot had taken him through the lung; for he knew that I had been wounded that way, too. A kindred spirit and I responded to it and often waved to him.

I was very weak and gaunt the first week there, and to make it worse, I had continual diarrhea so that I lay on a bed pan, morning and night. They gave me medicine to abate it, but it did no good. Finally, a crippled nurse limped in one day and put up screens about me and proceeded to give me medicated enemas. While she was about it, she asked me my name and where I was from. On getting the reply, she said, "I'm the office nurse of a Dr. Bullis in Rochester, New York." I replied, "Dr. Bill Bullis?" And at her startled look, I added, "I've often heard my Dad speak about Dr. Bill Bullis: he's a cousin of mine, although I've never met him." After giving me repeated enemas, she removed the gear and screens and bid me "Good-bye," and I never saw her again.

During this period, it was the habit of two frail, elderly women, Americans, to visit the ward each day. They came in carrying an armful of roses, American Beauties, and it was their habit to sit by each patient a few moments, present him with a rose, bid him "Good-bye," and go on to the next. This day, when they arrived at my cot, I was lying on a bed pan and couldn't tell them that I wished to be alone. As they sat down, they sniffed—and it wasn't roses they smelled—and after a few agonizing minutes, they arose, offered me their token, and hurriedly made their way out of the ward. I took a lot of good-natured ribbing from the men about this, and for several days they kidded me about "roses." But it was the last we saw of the two ladies in that ward.

One morning, I saw Lt. Corbett[1] passing by my bed, and I called out to him. He came back, looked down at me with horror on his face, stood a few moments, and said, "For God's sake, who are you?" and didn't want to believe that it was I. He had been wounded the same time as I and had recovered from a broken leg. After talking a few moments, he left, shaking his head in disbelief. I was shocked, because I didn't think I had changed that much. So I borrowed a mirror from the Frenchman next to me. Who was I? My eyes were sunk in my head, I was gaunt and drawn, and the face reflected back at me was unreal: if that was me, what had I gone through to bring that result? I looked in the mirror time and again, and marveled at what I saw. Finally, I returned the mirror as unwanted and lay and thought for a long time.

One day the doctors came to my cot, wheeling bottles and rubber tubes and told me they were going to aspirate, all of which confused me more than ever. As the nurses were getting me ready, one doctor explained that they were going to pump the blood from my pleural cavity, so that I could breathe properly again. Anything they did that would improve my breathing and stop the horrible gasping for breath I was experiencing, I was quite willing. The nurses held me in a sitting position with my hands grasping the rail at the foot of the bed and gave me a rubber pad to bite on. I was so weak that it was difficult to sit up. They said it wouldn't hurt much and wouldn't take long. Then the doctor took a long, hollow needle, about eight inches in length, and proceeded to insert it in my back. It hurt; and I could feel the needle tearing at my insides. After a while it was withdrawn, as the point became clogged. After clearing the needle, the doctor pushed it in a second time. Then moving it around to clear it, they put on a pump and proceeded to withdraw blood. They showed me the result after the needle was withdrawn; a pint bottle nearly filled with a blackish, thick mass, blood that had filled the lung cavity—no wonder it was so hard to breathe. After they laid me down again, I bawled like a baby, and Miss Sutherland attempted to soothe me; but it was the relief I had looked for, and I felt better for the good cry. So she tucked me in and left.

36

The Salvation Army Girl

The doctor brought me a present, today—two five-gallon water jars. They were connected by tubing, and one was filled with liquid. He said I was to blow the water from one jar to the other, then back again. This, he told me, would bring my lung back into use again.

The contraption looked interesting, not only to me but to my bed companions, as well, and I proceeded to entertain them. But after a while, I grew tired of blowing the water back and forth, and let it run by gravity. The nurse saw what was going on and came over and scolded me, and said it was given to me for improvement, not for entertaining the men. So, I blew again and again, and for the next few days the contraption was rolled up to my cot, both morning and afternoon, and I religiously blew the water from one jar to the other, until the doctor said I was using both lungs and wouldn't need the jars any longer.

One day, I noticed a young lady in the ward. She was visiting each man and appeared to be taking notes in a book she carried. I naturally was interested, and when she stopped at my cot and introduced herself as a Salvation Army worker, and asked me what I needed, I complied. I gave her quite a list of things; a comb, a toothbrush, toothpaste, shaving soap, and many other articles. She thanked me, and went on to the next man. And I promptly forgot all about her as just another war worker.

But in a couple of days she came back with a big bundle, which she opened and gave each and every article I had asked for. She seemed quite friendly, and while she talked to me I reached into my money belt and asked how much I owed her. She seemed startled, and then broke into tears, and, sobbing, said that it was all a gift from the Salvation Army and she wouldn't take any money. I told her that I was sorry that I had asked for so much but thanked her for all she had done. She then smiled at me and was on her way.

October 22

Time hangs heavy. I sleep all night, and sleep most of the day. Little happens to cheer us—only the "agony" cart pushed to each patient by the nurse. They wake us early in the morning, put water to wash with on the stand, remake the beds, take our temperature and pulse, and ask the inevitable question, "Have you had a bowel movement?" and then serve breakfast.

After breakfast, all are expectant, awaiting the doctor's visit. No man envies the other, and it is an ordeal for all. But most of the men are stoical while having their dressings changed. It takes quite a while for the doctor to make his rounds and it is hard not to suffer with each patient as old adhesive dressings are torn from the wound and new ones replaced.

This morning, he removed the tape from my left side that was placed there to ease the pains of pleurisy on September 30. He was quick and merciful and I did not feel it too much, and I was glad to lose it. As he was leaving, he told the nurse that I should be kept quiet as I had "influenza" and mentioned the oxygen tent as a means of helping me breathe.

After he left, I fell to brooding: pleurisy in the left side, a wound in the right lung, and just as I am recovering, influenza again: and I remembered the tough time I had after the Soissons battle. Well, I guess I'll write another letter and send my coupon home for a X-mas package. Perhaps that will make me feel better.

October 28

The Marine paymaster came round today. I don't know where my field records are, or whether I have any, they were supposed to have been blown up by an enemy shell; but the paymaster, a Lt. Woods of St. Paul, didn't seem to care about that; for he automatically paid me a hundred francs. He said the Marine Corps was appreciative of our efforts in the war, and he would be back in a couple of weeks to give us additional pay. I celebrated by buying a jar of stick candy, the first in several months. So, here goes (sucking on candy-sticks like a little boy)—they taste fine.

October 29

Lieutenant Border is censoring letters at a table in front of my cot and seems to be doing a lot of cutting. He now has my letter to Mother and turns to kid me about my prediction that Germany will be whipped in a few weeks. He says "No peace this year, but by next summer the war will be over." To emphasize his statement he takes a snip out of the letter. Well, all he cut out was "Neuilly, France"—and who cares?

Moving time is here again; all cots are out in the aisles. Those with limbs in a tractor go to one ward; those with the loss of sight in one eye or both are headed for another; chest cases are headed for a third; and other cases are being collected into separate wards.

Finally, four orderlies grabbed separate corners of my cot and picked me up. They carried me, swaying, through another big ward down a long hall into a small room where they set me down and left.

An auxiliary nurse, Miss Smith, hovered over me. She was crying her eyes out and sniveling, so I asked her what the matter was. She blurted out with another sob, "They have taken my Marine away from me."

"Well, cheer up," said I, "you have another Marine now to take care of." She changed immediately and was all smiles, as she asked, "Are you a Marine?" And I assured her that I was; whereupon my cot was placed in a choice position by the window.

After I was made comfortable again, she said that her name was Smith, and she took off her jewelry and watch and gave them to me to hold while she busied herself with other new arrivals. When she left the ward, the other patients began to kid me and told me that I was her elected "pet," and would get all of her attention, and that, as usual, the Marines came first and took all the honors, in war and in love. I just grinned, but saw that I would have to be careful in that ward, or I would be resented by the others.

In the cot to my left lay another Marine, Leonard Ophien. He had been invalided in bed since the 19th of July with seven wounds in his body. To his left was "Red," a big, husky fellow who had been struck by a large piece of shell-fragment inside his thigh and which had torn quite a chunk of meat away. To my right was an American Indian with his right arm in a tractor, who, gazing up at the ceiling, seemed unaware of the others in the ward. On his right was Felnore, from the 6th Engineers of the 3rd Division, and who was always talking. On the next cot, there was a large American, a corporal of the 89th Division. And next to him a man who spoke broken English and who had a broken leg by a bursting shell. There were others, but they did not partake much in the life of the ward.

Miss Smith, the auxiliary nurse, who had cried about "losing a Marine," was in charge of the ward. She had a helper, a Miss Crackle, and between them they covered several adjoining wards. The nurse in charge was Miss Bowser, who came from "Toity-toid and Toid Streets, New Yoick," and who could speak good English: or lapse at will into the lingo of New York's East Side. It was a "chummy" ward, and we soon got to know about one another, which made our stay enjoyable.

November 1

Turkey has surrendered—the war looks about over—and the hospital is filled with American wounded. The Argonne has been terrible; untried troops have been "fed to the wolves," and the effect is shown in the casualties that are coming in now—rather glad I am out of it.

The Salvation Army girl came into our ward, today. She remembered me, and she waved and smiled as she took down requests for supplies from the men. At my turn, she asked, "And what do you want, today?" I grinned and answered—"A lemon pie." That didn't stop her, and she counted the men: twelve of us in the ward. Then she said that we would have to keep it quiet from the other wards. A lemon pie—*wow*.

Mrs. W.K. Vanderbilt came in and exclaimed, "The war is over!" But we wouldn't go for it and told her we knew it wasn't; it sounded phony to us. She tried to argue the matter, but all she got was good-natured ribbing. So she left. There was a good deal of excitement outside, too, but soon she returned, and announced, "It's a mistake—Turkey surrendered; that is all." So we settled down quietly again and forgot it. But she is a grand lady, anyway, and the men all fell for her.

A young lady came into the ward. She had on swell clothes, neat and trim, and she looked quite out of place. After looking over the patients, she came to my cot and sat down on the edge. She said she was supposed to bathe some patient and that I was elected. We both blushed, but I told her I was willing.

She arose again, put screens about the bed, carried in a basin of water, soap, and towels; then removing her jacket, she handed me her rings, and said, "Well, I've got to do it." She was embarrassed, so I uncovered my left leg, and she washed that. After drying and covering the leg, she then helped me remove my bed shirt, and uncovering me to the waist proceeded to wash my arms, chest, and stomach. As I needed help in sitting up, I put my arms about her neck and clung to her—it was much better that way—then she washed my back. After drying my back, I fell back on the pillow, and she moved to my right side and completed washing me. She was over her embarrassment by now and became friendly, and she asked me my name, age, and outfit that I was with; and then she told me her name and age. She said that she and her mother came to Paris to be near her father who was in the army. She was the daughter of General Bullard, one of the three highest ranking generals in the American Army.

As she gave me an alcohol rub I lay passive and wished it would go on for ever. I fairly "purred" with pleasure. She said she was scared stiff when she first came into the ward and picked me out as the youngest and best looking and decided I was to be the one. When she put my shirt back on and tucked me in, she said, "I am coming in again to see you," then putting away the screens and basin, she waved good-bye.

November 2

The Salvation Army girl returned today bearing a well-covered package. She placed it on the table, and the nurse came in with plates and forks, and, after closing the door, they began to cut and serve the *lemon pies*. It was delicious, with plenty of meringue on it, too. She said she had an awful time finding lemons in Paris, and had been up most of the night in making them.

I called her over to my cot and offered to pay for them, and she said she had paid for the materials herself but that she derived so much pleasure in making them for us that she refused to allow me to contribute. I thanked her, and told her that she was a "dear" for being so nice.

As she was leaving she asked what else we would like; but as no one answered her, I grinned and said, "Well, I know what everyone would like, fresh fruit; something we haven't had since we left home." She said, "All right—but again, don't tell the other wards about it," and she left.

November 3

I asked the doctor as he wheeled the "agony" cart by if I could get out of bed. And I received a sharp "No; I don't want you up, yet." That's that, although it will be a month tomorrow that I've been in bed, and I'm getting restless.

The general's daughter came in this afternoon, and I alone received another bath and back-rub. I was glad to see her, and we both got along swell. She is a mighty nice girl, and even if the introduction was through the "baths," I will always remember her.

Felnore, the 6th Engineer, apparently was jealous, and kept making sarcastic remarks; about me, the Marines in general, and the publicity we received as a result of Belleau Wood. I took it quietly for some time but then snapped at him to "shut up" and mind his own business. He countered with a remark about the general's daughter, and I started to get out of bed to take him apart. But Brigman was up and got to him first; and Felnore, sensing he had gone too far, offered an apology. So things were some better for a time, but I determined to watch him, for several things he said had smarted.

November 4

Not too much to write about. The nurses tended the wounded, and the auxiliary nurses made the beds and cleaned up the ward: just another day.

In the afternoon, I had two visitors, the general's daughter and a friend she brought, and with them, a beautiful, large dog on a leash. They sat on my cot, and we talked quiet a while. Then they asked me if would hold the dog's leash, while they visited other wards—and I was left with the dog. Not so good; I would rather have held the girls: although the dog was well behaved.

Felnore got in a few barbs at me to relieve his tension. And when I didn't react to them, he changed his attitude and told the ward he wished he had been a Marine. He went on and explained that the Marines were a great outfit, and "good guys"; that they had done a great job in France. I could only add that we had been a part of the Second Division, and the regulars of the division included doughboys, and that they were just as good as the Marines. So, I hope the age-old controversy ends at that.

37

They Never Failed in Assignments

The days all seem alike, the routine in the hospital the same. We see the doctor for a few minutes in the morning, then the nurse comes in and says hello, and disappears to work other wards with newer, needier patients: while we just lie in bed doing nothing. The only variation is Mrs. Smith, the general's daughter, a kindly, elderly lady who comes in to mop the floor, a Madame Rose, and a Belgian girl who delivered us chow three times a day.

Mrs. Smith is an American who had come over before we entered the war. Her husband was an ambulance driver and belonged to the famous Norton-Harjes[1] unit. When that unit was broken up and the drivers assigned to American units, Mrs. Smith continued her hospital work: and thus I came to know her. She was a hard worker and was kind, but she sure did have a preference for Marines. And I came in for a good deal of special treatment and attention while in the ward.

Miss Bullard, as I have mentioned, came over with her mother. I am told she also had a "sweetie" in the service, a regular army officer, and she came in every second or third day to do her stint—rather as a must, and not because she liked it.

The elderly lady who mopped the floors, I did not get particularly acquainted with, but was told that she was the wife of a New York millionaire. One day, I asked her why she did the menial chores about the place and why she didn't do something more appropriate. She was on her knees scrubbing at the time, and she looked up at me and smiled, and said, "Why, because I would do anything for you boys," and resumed her scrubbing.

Madame Rose, a good-natured woman in her late forties, was a Belgian refugee, whose home was in German hands. She, according to her own count, had already lost six husbands in the war—and was about to acquire her seventh. Although she spoke only Belgian and was always chattering, it was not hard to get the drift of her talk and her meaning, as she always went straight

37. They Never Failed in Assignments

to Felnore's bed, ruffled and mauled him, and took liberties with him. The seventh husband could look forward to a good bed-mate when they were married, although it was doubtful if he could satisfy her.

As for her companion, no one got to know her, as any remark, friendly or not, always unleashed a barrage of tears. As far as Madame Rose could tell, she had been captured by the Germans in her native Belgium and was abused by them. She had escaped into France, but she knew nothing as to the whereabouts of her family, and it was supposed that they had all been killed.

Occasionally, there were visitors. They came in groups, and were there, it seemed, out of curiosity and pity—of which we wanted none. They usually were conducted by Major Powell, who was said to be a famous surgeon from Denver. And when they came to the door of the ward, it was his wont to stand with his chest sticking out and gesturing, pointing with his arms—"That," he would say, "is my only American lying there." And the visitors would gawk in wonder. "That" was Charley Thomas, a Choctaw Indian from Oklahoma. And after the group was escorted along, Charley would come out of his stoical trance and turn toward me, and say, "Ugh, him talk too much."

One day, Mrs. Smith came rushing into the ward, and bubbling in excitement exclaimed, "General Pershing[2] is going to visit the hospital tomorrow." As she had many times told us about the general being a personal friend, which we doubted, we all told her to "bring him in and show him off," thinking that would stop her from boasting about her friendship with him. And she said she would do "just that."

The next day, there was some undue excitement and the ward was made some cleaner and the patients were "slicked up" and "polished." Mrs. Smith was conspicuous by her absence—but now, there she was in the doorway, hanging on the arms of General Pershing, "bubbling" up to him, and he smiling down at her. No doubt now, the proof was there for all to see.

They entered the ward, and, I must admit, he was all soldier. He stood erect, slim and neat, with a big grin on his face; not the stern taskmaster I had pictured. He advanced to each cot in turn and asked the name of the soldier, his organization, and the front he was wounded on. He approached me after passing two other Marines, and on my reply, "Private E.J. Bullis, 49th Co., 5th Regiment Marines, 2nd Division, a serious stern look appeared on his face; he stepped back a pace or two and paid a glowing tribute to the Marines and the 2nd Division; for Belleau Wood, Soissons, St. Mihiel, and Champagne, and said, "They have never failed in assignments."

After he left the ward, I thought of the remarks I had heard during the Belleau Wood battle, when it was reputed that he had said in an argument with Senator Stone of Missouri, "I'll put the Marines in action, but I'll guarantee there won't be enough to go home in a row boat." In Belleau Wood it looked as though that remark was coming true. But his tribute in the ward belied the reputed statement and convinced me that he made no difference between the Marines and the doughboys. He was appreciative of all and had no preference one over the other: we were all American troops to him. When Mrs. Smith returned to the ward, she was kept busy talking to us about the general.

November 10

I asked the doctor again if I might get up today, but was turned down in a short but definite way. I was determined, though, and after he had moved on to another ward, I made my attempt. I edged out on my feet and stepped gingerly about my cot, hanging on, and was quite glad to slide back into bed on the other side. I stumbled on rubbery legs, and felt as though they would buckle at any moment. But I made it, and it was a momentous occasion for me.

The Salvation Army girl was here today and she presented the men in the ward with a basket of fresh fruit. She passed it around, and finally sat down herself and enjoyed some, too. It sure was good, and everybody enjoyed it and we thanked her very much: but we had previously agreed that she had done enough for us, and we told her so. She was a mighty nice girl, who did everything for the boys that she could.

38

The War Is Over!

November 11

    Yesterday was too much for me, so I'll stay in bed and get my strength back.
    Mrs. Vanderbilt came dancing into the ward this morning, and cried out, "The war is over! the Armistice has been signed! It goes into effect at 11:00 a.m.!" We remembered the excitement on the First, but this time we weren't so sure. We'll wait and see what happens next. Mrs. Vanderbilt was disgusted with us, as we showed no inclination to shout and celebrate, and said as she left the ward—"Wait, you'll see."
    The men spent the next two or three hours quietly, neither hoping nor accepting the announcement. But at 11:00 a.m., there was the boom of one gun followed by a fanfare of artillery and the clanging of church bells. It was true.
    The din continued, and thousands of the population of Paris surrounded the hospital, with "Viva!" everything. The boys that were up and around helped me to the window so I could look. The streets were jammed with French people as far as our eyes could see. They yelled, they waved, they cheered, and they finally settled down to serenade us with renditions of "The Star-Spangled Banner" and the "Marseillaise." Everyone in the hospital that was able headed for the city, and the rest of us envied them and wished we could go, too. I felt that I could celebrate by writing home, and so busied myself in composing a letter.

    A.R.C. M.H. No. 1
    Neuilly sur Seine, France
    November 11, 1918
    Dear Dad:
        This sure is a great day for the Allies. With the signing of the Armistice this morning, everyone in and around Paris went wild with excitement and joy. At eleven, all the bells throughout the city rang and cannons sounded their final shots of victory. The French people are running in the streets and singing the "Marseillaise" and yelling

American Red Cross Hospital #1, located at Neuilly sur Seine on the outskirts of Paris. Before war it was College Pasteur, a prestigious school. Everard was hospitalized here from October 10, 1918, until approximately December 20, 1918, when he was transferred to the American base Hospital # 65, located near Brest (Brittany) in the small town of Kerhuon, before returning to the USA (courtesy Gilles Lagin).

A view of the hospital, probably fall of 1918 (courtesy Gilles Lagin).

"Viva l'American! and Viva" everything else. Allied flags are up on all the buildings and everything is being decorated. They say the streets of Paris are jammed with the celebrating population. It certainly appears I will soon get a chance to look the Statue of Liberty in the face; at least, I hope so.

Sunday, I got up for the first time in thirty-seven days, and believe me, it certainly feels fine to be on one's feet again. I staggered around like a drunken man at first but soon got my sea legs working and navigated in fine shape. I am feeling great now, although I am still pretty weak. I am to be sent to a southern convalescent area soon, where they will build me up again.

Will close now, with lots of love to all, Everard

Part V: Looking Westward

39

Let the Big Boys Take Over

Dec. 9, 1918
A.R.C. M.H. No. 1
Neuilly sur Seine, France

Dear Mother:

It is now 9:30 p.m., and I am sending a few lines to let you know everything is all right with me, and that I am having a great time. I wish that I could be home for Xmas and New Year's, but I am afraid it isn't possible this time. There are so many ready to go home now that we can't all go at once and have to wait our turn.

Last Thursday I went into Paris and saw the "King pass by." A cool and drizzling rain fell, but that didn't stop the people from turning out to see King Albert of Belgium, Queen Elizabeth, and Prince Leopold. The city certainly did give a rousing reception to this soldier-king and queen, and believe me, they rated it.

Well, that is about the only excitement I have had this week and last. If I don't start the homeward trip soon I shall see our own president & wife, as well. I don't know which I would rather do; go home, or see the president. (Of course, I would rather start home, but I would like to see the president, also.)

I will enclose a picture postcard showing a view of the hospital I am in, and I hope you get it. Where I have marked an X is the ward I am now in. It is a small ward containing twelve beds, all full, though none of the patients are very bad now. In the bed on my left is another Marine, who was wounded at Soissons on the 19th of the July. On my right, is a real American, a Choctaw Indian from Oklahoma. He's a fine chap, too, with a wife and three children at home. There is an Italian, a Romanian, a Pole, a Greek, a Frenchman, and a Swede, and the rest are pure Americans; but we all get on harmoniously at that.

The chap I go around with is a Virginian, about the same height as I but a good deal heavier. He and I must be a comical pair, at least to the French; for whenever we are out they all look up at us and smile. You see, we are both about 6ft. 2in. tall. He is broad while I am more like a match, or rather, of the dandelion variety, and we tower way above the people over here.

I haven't decided yet as to whether I should bring home an orphan or a French mademoiselle. The latter are sure tempting, though, with their great big beautiful eyes, etc., etc. But even at that, I think I will take my chance with an American lassie. (Don't let this worry you, for I am still as afraid of the "gals" as I was when I left home.)

39. Let the Big Boys Take Over

I received a letter from you and one from Dad both written the last of September, and I am now waiting anxiously for some more recent ones. Dad spoke of Nellie as having been to see you. It sure made me glad to know he was well and back home, for I had given him up as "pushing up daisies" (as we say) "somewhere in France." He certainly was one of the best "buddies" I have ever had, and I sure felt lost when he disappeared so completely last June. I hope he wasn't wounded very badly and that he is entirely recovered now.

It is about 10:30 now and high time I was in bed, so I will take the record off, put on a new needle, and start making a new record for the next week (if I don't start home in the meantime).

Kiss the girls for me and give my love to all, worlds to you & Dad, Everard

It was all excitement in the ward today. The doctors were classifying the patients for their discharge: "A" for healed wounds, and the man able to go back to his outfit; "B" for the man with a healed wound, but who would need time and rest, to be sent to a replacement camp before returning to his company; "C" will go to a large rest camp in the southern part of France; and "D" cases are unfit for further duty, and are to be sent home.

How will I be classified? The doc says I will probably be sent to a rest camp. But I would like to rejoin my company in Germany. Then, too, I'd like to go home—well, the doctors will soon settle the question for me.

A bunch of the fellows have already been before the re-classification board. Some returned with a long face, and said they were "A's" and going back to their company. Others reported that they were headed for a replacement camp. While only a couple were to be sent south for a long rest. The only "D's" are amputees, crippling wounds, and those with the loss of sight, in one eye or in both: it looks as though it shall be a "C" rating for me.

At last, my turn arrives, and I report for the verdict with mixed emotions. As I enter the doctors are poring over my file; they arise smiling, and the head doctor announces, "D"—you are going home, Son. Good luck."

I don't know how I got out or what I said, but I found myself headed for the ward, muttering, "Going home—a 'D' case; and I'm going home." It didn't seem possible: Belleau Wood, Soissons, St. Mihiel, and Blanc Mont in the Champagne Battle: alive, and after all that I am going home. Two legs, two arms, and two eyes; nothing wrong with me that time won't heal; no amputations, no disfigurements: and I am going home.

As I entered the ward I was greeted by a chorus of voices asking me what classification I received. "D" was my answer, and the ward to a man shouted for me.

Tomorrow was the day, and we were to travel by regular transports. No amputees were going; only men who could handle themselves were on the list.

The day in the hospital was endless; and although I was the only one in the ward to be sent home, others also were getting ready to leave, while the bed-ridden were bemoaning their fate. Charley Thomas, the Choctaw Indian of the 36th Division, laid in bed his right arm in a tractor: he lay unperturbed. Ophien, a 6th Marine, who had been in bed since the 19th of July as a result of seven wounds, was feeling blue. Felnore, of the 6th Engineers of the 3rd Division, who walked doubled over from a kidney wound, was cheerful though remaining behind. And Corporal Brigman, of the 89th Division, an "A" case, was going back to his outfit: and the others in the ward were silent as the time to leave approached.

Finally, the "D" cases were called. We left the hospital by ambulances and were taken to the Gare du Nord depot where an American hospital train was waiting. It was evening and we filed aboard and found that for the length of the trip we were to be tripled together, three men to sleep in a bunk made for one. But we didn't object; we were homeward bound.

While the attendants fed us, the nurses busily took our temperatures and did what nurses must do in getting us bedded down for the night. I lay on the aisle-side of the bunk on my side; behind me lay the second bed-mate, a rather large man; while between us were the feet of the third. At that we two had the best of the deal; we had only two feet to comfort us; but the third man was nestled between four.

We had traveled for quite some time when the nurse aroused us and said we were about to pass the president's Special. We all crowded to the windows of the car for a look, and soon a flag-bedecked locomotive leading a few cars puffed by. President Woodrow Wilson had just landed in France and was headed for Paris and the Peace Conference: but all we saw was the flag-draped locomotive. We got settled back into bed again, thinking: we had fought the war, now let the big boys take over; we are going home.

We detrained in Brest the next day and were met by ambulances that took us to the hospital center at Kerhuon. This was a little village on the bay about seven miles from Brest and where we stayed for the next three or four days.

It was rainy weather at Kerhuon, and a worse mud-hole I have never seen. It was ankle deep and only a few "duck" boardwalks were in evidence. It was cold and miserable, in the wards and without, and we were left to our own resources while there.

Here, the nurses were indifferent to the care of the men and hospital corpsmen were hard to find. The nurses seemed interested only in the nightly dances held with the officers, and in the daytime were too sleepy to be of much use. They were short-tempered, and when any of their patients complained, they would threaten him with a court martial, or, as a punishment, would deny him an early chance to go home. It was a far cry from the way we were treated in the hospitals serving the front. Too bad the nurses here had to lower the opinion of the men. But I'll keep out of their way; they can "drink and be merry" for all of me.

The nurse in our ward came in one afternoon, smirking and gushing, and told us to gather near her office. She then introduced to us a Broadway celebrity and said he would sing for us. We listened for a few seconds to "Oh! how I hate to get up..." and while he "murdered the bugler," one after another drifted away and left a "corporal's guard" to do him honor.

Random Harvest

I spent some time on the cliff overlooking the bay, watching the tide ebb and flow, looking westward and home. Behind me was a building with barred windows, behind which stared through countless empty faces. It was the ward of crazy, shell-shocked soldiers. Some of them were violently insane, hopeless, doomed to a life apart from man. When orderlies entered the building, hideous yells disrupted the peace, and I was glad to leave the scene and go back to my ward.

40

Shipwrecked!

December 24

    I was among the lucky ones, and I packed my tooth brush, all set to go. We were tagged, "Hospital Center, Kerhuon, List No. 1149, Ward A-5," loaded in trucks, and conveyed to the pier at Brest. The bay was fogged in, and no ships were to be seen, only thousands of wounded waiting to go. The only activity was an occasional lighter loaded with men, pushed out to sea by a tug, then absorbed in the fog.

    There were rumors afloat that no more men would go: the ships were loaded; and our hearts sank at the thought. Night approached, darkness was settling in; we were tired, hungry, and discouraged, when our detail was finally called.

    We happily wended our way through the horde of men, and entered a fenced-in area. On giving our name and list number and having it checked O.K., we stepped into a lighter. When we were loaded, a tug nosed up against the lighter, and we were pushed slowly out into the fog. It was an eerie feeling. The fog blotted out the men a few feet away; only the swish of the lighter through the water told us we were moving.

    A dark shape loomed high above us, and a mega-phoned voice told us it was the USS *Mauritania*. The voice also told us that she was fully loaded and no more passengers would be taken aboard; she was weighing anchor, and departing.

    We were a disheartened bunch of men as we veered away in the dreary fog. But as we plied shoreward, another mega-phoned voice hailed—"Lighter, ahoy! Bring lighter alongside; USS *Northern Pacific* ready to load." A cheer went up from the men, and all was well with us, as we turned toward a great ship in the fog.

    We edged up to a gangway on the port side aft, and climbed up the ladder onto the deck, where we were met by a group of Red Cross women. They greeted us, and passed out an instruction sheet on which was stamped our bunk number and the troop space we would occupy. My bunk was No. 612, and I was allotted to troop space 7C. Then one of the workers handed out a bulging Red Cross bag to each man, and another directed us to our space.

As directed, I filed down a large gangway to the deck below, turned left into a large compartment, and located my bunk. I was lucky, portside one deck below topside, one bunk away from the port holes: couldn't be any luckier than that.

Shedding my coat, I investigated the contents of the bag: roast turkey, fruits, several pieces of fruitcake, candies and cookies, besides several useful toilet articles. What a feast! I gorged myself then and there. It had been a long time since I had such food. Christmas Eve and going home; and I crept into my bunk and slept.

Christmas Day, 1918

I awoke to the "jimmy legs" pipe and shortly made my way down the gangway into a great salon, where we had chow. As we filed past the K.P.'s, our tins were filled with good wholesome American food, and our cups filled with good old navy "java." Only one thing prevented our gorging; that was a promised turkey dinner later.

After chow, I went to prowl the ship. We were still at anchor in the bay, taking on men. But to me the feel of the deck beneath my feet was heaven, and I remained there until the noon chow was announced.

Turkey dinner, mashed potatoes, green peas, fruit salad, buns, dressing, coffee (with sugar and cream), topped off with mince pie: and speaking for myself, I made the rounds twice and gorged until I could eat no more. And I went up on deck and walked until we heaved anchor and were underway.

The ship steamed out about 4:00 p.m., and the sky westward was dark and threatening. At first the ship plowed on in an even keel, but soon the seas grew heavier, and the waves caused the ship to roll. Aft, I watched the shoreline fade away, and the thousands of lights flicker out, and France became but a memory to me.

Turning from the scene, I noticed that the ocean had grown worse. Great tumbling waves were heaving the ship. One moment the prow raised heavenward, the next it plowed down and buried its nose in the sea. And I wondered if I were going to be sick. I wandered midship on the starboard side, selected a sheltered spot, and sat on the deck with my back against the cabins. No, I wasn't sick; I just felt that way.

For a long time, I sat trying desperately not to watch the angry sea. A lot of other soldiers were wandering about on deck, too, and some had elected to sit as I was. But there were a number at the rail. I pitied those at the rail. And every time they heaved, I gulped in sympathy.

One by one those on deck disappeared to their quarters, but I sat huddled and cold. Only a few remained at the rail, silently contemplating the rise and fall of the sea; and now and then they heaved in anguish.

It was near midnight when I ventured to move. As I arose, and made my way to the gangway, the impulse got the best of me, and I dove for the rail—just in time. I heaved until I thought I would turn inside out; and then I heaved some more. All that turkey, fruitcake, and pie, gone—but not forgotten.

At last, I thought it safe to make my way to my quarters again, and I staggered down. The ever thoughtful gob had prepared for the deluge. At the foot of the stairway was a big G.I. can and huddled around it a mournful group. The suggestion was well meant. I made the can, sat huddled on the bottom stair, until I was forced to visit the can, again and again.

We sat till the small hours of the morning, when I tried to get to my bunk, but another G.I. can and its waiting group was in my way. I stopped and joined the fellows there. After a while, I stumbled to my bunk and rolled in, exhausted.

December 26

The ship heaved and pitched, and as it dove into the sea the ship shuddered when the waves hit the front of the cabins and the prop rose to the surface and raced. It didn't seem possible that the ship would weather the storm—and I didn't care much whether it did. I lay in my bunk that day.

December 27–31

The storm continued unabated. I forced myself to get up and go to chow and then out on deck for fresh air. I felt ragged, but was not affected by *mal de mer* anymore, and found the fresh air a good medicine.

Men wandered on the pitching deck, or stood in groups, talking over their experience or chatting about the storm. There were only a few Marines on board, and they were well scattered among the passengers. At last, I found someone I knew from the hospital in Paris. I knew him only by his nickname, "Whitey," and had a short visit with him.

40. Shipwrecked!

Whitey, in token of a crown of whitish hair, was the man who threw a heavy cup of java in the face of an orderly. After a terrible fight with him, he was transferred out to a replacement camp. He didn't recognize me, as I was still a bed patient when he was there; but after recalling the fight to him, he grinned and was friendly and asked about several of the patients. I gathered that his one aim in life was to run into that orderly and finish the job. However, I supposed that when the two met in civil life, they would throw their arms around each other's neck and be bosom pals.

Next, I ran across Neff, who was in the same group as I going into the Belleau Wood fight. He was in the same company and shortly after reaching Belleau Wood was wounded. He recovered and returned for the Soissons scrap: and was wounded again. Then he returned in time to be wounded at St. Mihiel. He healed and was re-wounded for the fourth time at Champagne. He had had enough and wouldn't talk about his experiences other than state, "I didn't see any of the war; I'd just get up—and then go to the hospital with a wound." Well, war is like that. Some get all the fighting, and others are just "cannon fodder." Personally, I think he was lucky; four minor wounds and practically none of the hardships that goes to the front-line soldier.

Then there was Cooper. I ran into him when the trip was nearly over. He was a little fellow, good-looking, good-natured, and quiet; one of those fellows who doesn't have much to say, but smile at the quips and banter that goes on in a group of men. Here he was with a lopsided grin on his face. He remembered me instantly, although we had met only briefly before going to the front. There were nine of us in the third-class coach on the rush trip to the front, and we had agreed to keep in touch with one another and notify the parents if the worst happened. We hadn't, as conditions did not permit; although Cooper had news about most of the men. Miller had been killed that night going into Belleau Wood, in the heavy shelling we took in Champillon. He was the only one of the group killed. Kopfa, who was the company clerk of the 49th, was neither wounded nor gassed; probably his duties as clerk kept him out of most of the fighting. The other seven of us had been wounded. Rather rough, though I think we were fortunate in view of the high casualties in the Marine Brigade. Cooper himself had been shot through the jaw, tearing out several teeth and part of the jaw bone, the bullet finally lodging in the vertebrae of the neck: hence the lop-sided grin and stiff neck. They were all that I met on the boat.

In the meantime, the storm continued in all its fury, and at times we were sure the ship would founder. I couldn't believe the waves could be so huge or that a ship could withstand them. As the ship climbed heavenwards, it seemed as though it were trying to climb out of the sea, only to hang poised for a moment then plunge downward with a sickening roll. The ship slid down until its prow was buried in the sea; and as the tons of water rushed against the forward part of the superstructure, the resultant crash made the ship shudder throughout. The props breached the surface in these plunges and seemed to race, accompanied by weird noises. To the men at these times, we were sure that the shafts would break, leaving us without propulsion and thus leave the ship to broach in the sea.

The men on deck took all this without apparent fear, and there were no orders from the bridge indicating anything like disaster. There wasn't a spot on the deck that was not covered by spray or any place where you could find a level spot to stand. Throughout it all we enjoyed the storm and the sight of the great waves—but being a landlubber, I would rather have been on shore.

There was little to do, no entertainment for the men. The only thing attempted was offered by a "Y" secretary, who tried desperately to lead the men in singing. He offered a chocolate bar to those who did, and managed to gather a few about him. The rest of the men avoided him like a plague: the "Y" was reaping the fruits of its labor.

There was an announcement on New Year's Eve that the big salon was out of bounds. The officers were having a dance there with the seventeen nurses who were on board. The men were resentful about the discrimination and were plenty mad about it, but there being nothing we could do; we turned in early for the night.

Around mid-night, I awoke to feel the ship drag, slide ahead, then drag again. And then I heard the anchor chain as it slid out. I immediately jumped to the port hole, when I heard the blast of the whistle; but all I saw was the beam of the searchlight being reflected back by the fog. I yelled, "We're in Hoboken!"—only to be told to "pipe down," and, "go to sleep." And after other remarks, I went to bed again and back to sleep.

New Year's Day, 1919

I felt great when I awoke on New Year's morning: in Hoboken, and soon we will land. The engines of the boat were silent and everything was peaceful at last. I heaved a sigh—but just then a doughboy came rushing into the quarters, and shouted, "We're shipwrecked! the ship is aground!" He was told plenty by the rest of the men, but in defense, shouted, "Get up and see for yourselves." I got up and immediately noticed the slant to the deck. Dressing hurriedly, I sped up the gangway. He was right, the ship was aground. Outside the breakers keeled over to port with enormous waves smashing against the ship.

40. Shipwrecked!

The fog had lifted, and we looked shoreward to a strip of sand and a lighthouse up the shore. In the distance, we could faintly see the shadows of Long Island—a nice New Year's morning. To seaward, a couple of ships appeared heading our way and an aeroplane circled overhead; nothing else was seen except the great waves.

All portholes were battened down on orders, and only at certain times were we able to get a drink. The "heads" were not operating and we cold not wash; and a terrible odor quickly developed throughout the ship. We later learned that they had flooded water into some compartments to settle the ship in the sand, and that the prow and forward third of the ship rested on the bottom. The balance of the ship hung suspended over deep water and there was danger of the ship breaking up in the heavy seas.

The lifeboats hung in readiness on their davits, but that lent no courage to the men. We looked at the stretch of water between the ship and shore and wondered how a lifeboat could navigate through the breakers. An ever increasing horde of people began gathering on Fire Island, and more ships appeared in the sea around us, but the *Northern Pacific* was isolated from all.

Chow: turkey dinner again with all the fixings. We couldn't do anything about the ship's predicament, and if she broke up we might as well go down with a full belly, anyway. We went down to the salon, emptied of its tables and benches, and filed ahead to have our plates filled. The deck lay at a sharp angle shoreward and there was a great pitch crosswise and toward the shore. As we went by the cooks for our helpings, we had to climb hanging on the railing while they piled our plates high with food. After completing the climb, we turned to go into the salon again, and we found ourselves on the high side. Some fell and slid across the room, their food greasing their slide. Others sat down, and holding their plates in a safe position slid on their fannies to the far side. The line of men going for food was now mixed with the fallen and the sitting. Others of us minced along and kept upright, then sat down in the center of the slanting deck, and there ate our food with relish.

There was a great deal of hilarity accompanied by the cursing of the fallen, but even they had to laugh at the spectacle they made. Those soldiers who still were seasick and the worried ones did not go to chow; hence, those of us that did could have all we wanted: and I took two heaping helpings of turkey, dressing, mashed potatoes, and other good things to eat. It was one of the grandest meals I have ever had, despite the conditions under which we had it. For the evening meal, I tried it again and had nearly the same meal as before, but with the deck on a leveler keel again.

I went up on deck in the afternoon to watch the spectacle. More ships, big and small, were anchored to seaward. There was the cruiser *Columbia*, the hospital ship *Solace*, a dozen destroyers, submarine patrol boats, submarine chasers, tugboats, and several others. They all were in anxious readiness to help, but because of the storm were forced to idleness.

Shoreward, hundreds of people were crowded along the beach. Several large fires had been kindled to warm the toes of those in need, and we could see Red Cross workers trying to keep busy. The life guards of Sandy Hook were there with their little cannon, and were trying to shoot a line across our ship. They kept up a steady bombardment of ropes, many falling short in the ocean, while others parted their line and sailed over the ship and were lost. And then one wildly struck our aerial and tore it down. With darkness coming on, I turned to for the night.

41

Officers First

January 2

    The storm continued in all its fury and the men were just as stoical as ever—and we were still above water. Some of us went to breakfast, and then prowled the ship to see our status. The Coast Guard was again attempting to get a rope to us from shore and destroyers had closed in and likewise attempted to get lines to the ship. On shore, a great crowd was on hand to view the spectacle and they had enormous bonfires to warm by.

    The wind whipped the lines away from the ship, until finally one was shot to us from shore. It was made secure and then additional, heavier lines were rigged: and then the fun began.

    After a breech buoy was rigged up, many crowded forward to be the first to ride it, but we were out-maneuvered; officers only was the word. Our place at the prow was taken by all the army officers who had visions of going ashore via the breech buoy.

    At last one was seated and they heaved on the lines. At first, his ride was high and dry, but about a third of the way to shore the sag was too great and he sank and was dragged submerged for quite a distance. Then he re-surfaced to ride soaked above the water to shore: a drowned rat.

    In the beginning the men were quite resentful that officers should have preferential treatment. But when the first "hero" was dragged into the sea, a great shout of glee went up from the men. The officers began to back into the crowd on deck but found their way blocked: if they wanted to go ashore, they would go. So a second victim was chosen and he reluctantly advanced to the chair: only to be well ducked on his ride in. A third officer was selected but he didn't wish to go; but the catcalls drove him on. As he neared the water he tried to scramble up the line, but to no avail, and he, too, was dragged through the water to reappear as a drowned rat.

    The Coast Guard called a halt to the operation and moved their end of the line to a high bank on shore, re-rigged the chair and that was the end of the impromptu baths. Each officer afterward rode to shore in comfort and in style.

In the midst of this operation a semaphore message was signaled to the ship. A private was being paged. So word was passed and finally the soldier reported to the front. His parents were on shore and wished him sent to them by the chair. With special permission of the ship's captain, he was transferred ashore and was immediately swallowed by a welcoming group: and there was not one of us that didn't wish the scene duplicated with his own parents.

Several lines were now strung from land to the ship so we wandered about to see what the next move was. Soon a boat, a famous double-ender, was attached to the line. It was filled with coast guard men, all oars set in perpendicular fashion, and was drawn toward the ship.

All went well until they reached the breakers, then over it went, dumping the men into the sea. The men made it back to shore safely, and they re-rigged and manned the boat again; but again they were thrown in and washed upon the beach. But they persisted and were finally drawn into quiet waters alongside the ship.

Almost immediately, a line of casual troops were climbing down the rope ladders and boarding the boat to go ashore for guard duty. At the breakers, they all were spilled into the raging waters, lifesavers and soldiers alike. It was a horrible sight, especially to the men on the ship. We could see their heads bobbing on the sea, and one soldier attempting to crawl on the overturned boat, but knocked back into the water by a lifeguard. But shortly, most of the lifeguards were sprawled on the overturned boat and dragged to shore.

Then a long line of men from shore formed hand in hand and waded into the sea, and by this life-line nearly all the soldiers hand over hand made it to the safety of the beach. One lone soldier floated back toward the ship, clinging to an oar. We could see him at first, but the next moment only the oar protruding from the water. A sailor on shore saw his predicament and dove in and swam out to help him. He labored through the breakers, reached the drowning soldier, and towed him back to shore. When they reached land, a great cheer went up from the men on the ship.

In the meantime, the lifeguards were busy with the boat, up-righting it, and dragged it out from beneath two nearly drowned soldiers. We could see them carry their inert forms ashore and roll them over barrels until they came to. The men on the ship were yelling and cursing the lifeguards, and I am afraid it would have gone hard with them if they could have got their hands on them. However, in all fairness to the lifeguards, they had a job to do; it was important that they live in order to save others. The lives of the soldiers in the boat didn't matter as much then, as it was still possible that

41. Officers First

the ship might break up. After a final check on the men, it was found that they all were safe; and aside from a couple being rolled over barrels, they were in good shape, despite their experience.

Activity of the rescue detail subsided for the time being, so we rushed to the stern in time to witness another thrilling episode. A motor launch from the cruiser *Columbia* attempted to get around our stern, but its motor was drowned out in the heavy seas. The boat missed our stern by quite a distance and the men worked their oars to control it. The breakers became threatening and they managed to steer the boat away and drop anchor. But the wind and waves swept them back into the breakers. The boat swamped and all the occupants jumped into the sea. And for a second time that day, a long line of men joined hand to hand and successfully saved all from the boat. The swamped launch was washed onto the beach and was pounded by the seas while we were there.

It was still the same on board the ship, and there was no fresh air to the quarters. Scuttle—or rather—drinking butts were only on for a short period, and there was no water to wash with. Nor were the heads working and about a foot of water sloshed back and forth in them, so that it was nauseating to the men, and the stench was terrible in the battened down ship. The kitchen still regularly put out grand meals for the men, and during the day we remained on deck in the fresh air.

The seas still slammed into the ship and the spray dashed over its deck, but there was a noticeable abatement of the wind. In the meantime, rescue operations continued, and the officers and casual troops went ashore in the boat, as did the nurses; but all the wounded remained aboard.

On the seaward side, seven destroyers and tugboats were cabled to the stern attempting to yank the ship out into deep water. They were cabled with big rope hawsers, and when the pull was made each boat first backed until the hawser dipped into the sea—then each boat put on full power ahead; and as they reached the end of the hawser, it was nearly a straight line—and then it snapped, the loose end of the hawser whipping back, hitting the ship with a mighty bang.

The ship never budged during these operations; it was bedded down deep in the sandy reef. They tried four inch hawsers, then six inch, and, finally, strung a new eight inch manila hawser: they all broke under the strain. The authorities finally chased us away due to the dangers from the snapped end of the cable, as it could have killed scores if it flew back on deck.

That night we went to chow in our shirt sleeves. After a grand meal, I sauntered to the gangway, but found it blocked with angry troops. At the head of the gangway was a soldier on guard; he was a raw recruit that didn't know his business, and was confused; and nor did he know what to do, nor how to do it. He stood in the gangway and wouldn't let anyone pass, and said we had to go topside and come down to our compartment the back way. That meant we had to go out in the wet, traverse the ship, and climb down two narrow gangways to reach our compartment: not the best way to keep warm and dry.

The angry yells of the men soon brought the lieutenant of the guard, who inquired about the disturbance. And I, sticking my neck out, attempted to explain and suggested that he move the guard and allow the men into their quarters. Like most lieutenants, he huffed up and ordered us to go up and around, and, eying me, yelled something about a court martial for disobedience of orders while in disaster status, and about death being the sentence.

I bridled up and reminded him that he had put a question to us, and I merely had given him the answer; that there was no question of disobedience of orders.

He blustered again, and said, "We'll see the captain." And I asked, "The captain of the ship?" And he replied, "Yes." And we started off.

I knew that the captain of the ship would have more important work to do than listen to the lieutenant, so I didn't worry. He stalked ahead, and I followed, but by his actions I knew he wasn't trying to find the ship's captain. So I reminded him that we would find the captain on the bridge. But that didn't help him, either. Finally we found an army captain, and he "sang" his song to him. I remained quiet until the captain said he would go back with us, and he turned and asked me a question or two.

When we reached the entrance to the compartment, there was a much larger and louder group of angry men, and the captain asked the guard who had placed him there and what his orders were. The guard replied, "The lieutenant," and his orders were to keep the men from going into the compartment through the gangway. The captain then said he knew nothing of the order, nor why the sentry was there; but that we had better do as the sentry said.

I was mad clear through by then, and said, "To hell with it; I'm going through," and shoving the sentry aside, I went into the compartment, with a cheering and clamoring crowd behind me. When inside, I put my coat on and went out the other way, making myself scarce in case the guard should turn out and search for me. Later, when I returned, the men laughed and told me the sentry was removed and nothing more came of it.

January 3

All was quiet within the ship; there was still no water and the heads were a floating mass of sickening matter from which a terrible stench arose. The crowd of people on shore had thinned out and the lifeguards plied ship to shore and back again with clock-work precision. Seaward, the cruisers, destroyers, and hospital ships rode at anchor; only the submarine patrol boats were moving in on us, and the seas were some calmer and there was less wind.

At last, they were to commence rescue operation on a big scale, and we were to be taken out to one of the waiting ships. And we were ordered to our compartments to await further orders.

Shortly after noon chow our compartment was called and we assembled on the top deck, which listed quite heavily shoreward, and were given instructions what we were to do. We were in turn to lie down on the deck with our heads inboard and crawl backward to the shoreward side of the ship to the rope ladder. Two sailors, one on each side, would steady us and keep a sure grip on our shoulders as our feet dropped over the side. We felt with our feet until we could stand on the rope ladder; then grabbing the sides of the ladder, we descended. It was tricky, for as soon as we put weight on the ladder our feet swung in and we were jack-knifed over the water.

After a couple of steps down I grasped the situation and supported my weight by my arms, allowing the ladder to hang straight. I halted briefly to look below; it was a long way down and directly below was a whale boat, manned by life guards. I glanced along the side of the ship to see stretcher cases being lowered to the deck of submarine patrol boats.

Starting down again my right hand grasped a knotted rope at the side of the ladder; and as I had only one foot on the ladder, I swung outward, grimly holding the ladder with one hand. Officers on deck noticing my predicament yelled out, "Clear away below." And the men in the lifeboat frantically pushed the boat away from the ship to allow me a soft landing place. I made a desperate grab for the ladder with my free hand and somehow grasped the side of the ladder and safely made my way down into the lifeboat.

I was the last man in the boat and was seated in a single seat in the stern, and we headed out to sea. It was nice rowing in the semi-quiet waters in the lea of the ship, but as we neared the end of the *Northern Pacific* there was a standing wall of water cascading off the seaward side. It was fully twenty feet high; and as we topped the crest I was sure we were going to roll over, but the lifeboat straightened and slid down the other side of the tumbling wave; and we were away.

The ride out to sea was interesting; one moment we were on the crest of a wave and could see all the activities around, and the next, we were in the trough and could see nothing but an enormous wall of water about us. The waves seemed gigantic in size and must have stood twenty-five to thirty feet in height. It was up and down with a steady progress, until presently we drew alongside a destroyer, the USS *Upshur*. It was riding anchored fore and aft, and rolling in the heaving waters.

The lifeboat drew to port side aft and attempted to maneuver to the ladder at that point. But the suction was more than the rowers could handle. As the ship rolled to starboard, our lifeboat settled in the trough of the wave until we could reach out and touch the bilge keel, the long, semi-circular bulge on the side of the vessel. Then the ship would roll to port, and we would ride on the wave until we were nearly level with the deck. There was hardly room enough to slip a sheet of paper between our boat and the destroyer, and it became apparent that we were in danger of hooking the bilge keel and being rolled over and crushed by the ship on its next roll.

The lifeguards were attempting to push our boat away from the ship with pike poles, and it seemed certain we would be crushed at each roll. Up and down we went, and each time missing the bilge keel; and the officers on the deck of the destroyer yelling at us: "Keep your hands and arms in; keep still in the boat," and a lot of other useless advice.

Meanwhile, I, sitting alone in the stern, eyeing the deck rung of the ladder, calculated the risk. I counted cadence with the rise and fall, and knew if I grabbed the deck rung at the proper instant, the lifeboat would drop away, leaving the side of the ship high above any danger; and I would be on deck before the next roll. I waited for the right instant then reached and grabbed the deck rung and scrambled on deck. I was promptly bawled out by the officers on deck, and ordered below. I went, glad enough to be safe on board and out of the lifeboat.

The first thing that struck my eyes when I entered the quarters below was a large G.I. can, sitting in the center of the room. Even on destroyers, the ever considerate gobs were thinking of our comfort. But I had no intention of getting seasick again. And I entered into conversation with a C.P.O. and several gobs.

Soon, one by one, the others from the lifeboat came down; and as the room became over-crowded, I departed through another gangway to the deck. Several more boats arrived and transferred their passengers, and, power on, the destroyer took on life, and we were away.

It was my first ride on a destroyer, a thrilling ride, and one I wouldn't have missed. I remained in the stern at the taffrail for a long while, the depth bomb guns ahead of me, and a couple of bumpers cutting the waves on either side; and the sea high overhead. The stern seemed walled deep in the sea, and the deck slanted up toward the bow; we were making "knots" toward New York.

There were safety lines running about the deck and in the direction of the bridge, and, after a time, I grabbed on to a line and pulled my way forward to mid-ship, where I sat on the super-structure over the boilers. From here, I could look down on the engines and see the sailors at work; I could look out to sea and watch the traces of land roll by; and I could watch the deck crew doing their work about me.

One sailor came over and sat beside me, and told me that the *Upshur* was just finishing her trial run. She was brand new, and that on her trial run she had made 39 knots, (approximately 45 miles per hour,) a top speed as far as destroyers are concerned. She was a four stacker, trim and neat, and was an improvement over the ones I had seen in the yards in Philadelphia.

We approached and passed Coney Island and the cluster of villages that lay near New York. Then the famous Lady appeared, the Statue of Liberty, and the busy harbor traffic about the city. We passed the USS *Siboney* with a quarantine flag flying, as she approached a berth to land troops from France. The *Siboney* was in our convoy going over, so, of course, she was of interest to me.

The deck was now covered with troops. They had gained their nerve now that we were traveling at a much slower speed. As we gazed at the New York skyline we spotted the mayor's welcoming-boat approaching, with a band playing and many people waving and shouting. We naturally thought we were to be honored, being the first boat load in from the stranded *Northern Pacific*[1]; but she passed us by without a wave of the hand or fanfare from the band.

We were disappointed, but soon found other things to hold our interest; the *Leviathan*, a huge transport, formerly the *Vaterland*, queen of the German merchant fleet, docked at a Hoboken pier; and the many ferries plying between New York and New Jersey, and the tugboats and boats about the harbor.

The ship slowed, tugboats nosed against us, and we were edged to a Hoboken pier. When we looked down from the deck we saw a Y.M.C.A. worker, and the men remembering their activities in France shouted to a man, "Who won the war?" and answering their own query, yelled the answer, "The Y.M.C.A.!"

Next a band appeared and began to serenade us, but the men had had enough and moved back from the edge of the deck. A horde of newspaper correspondents then came on board, and they asked endless questions and wanted stories of our experiences; but again, the men went into their shell. Finally, one reporter approached a group of us and asked our names and where home was. He said he would telegraph our folks of our safe arrival. We gladly gave our names and the addresses of our parents, as that seemed to be the solution to our problems.

42

Look, Marie

Shortly afterward, we Marines were separated from the doughboys and marched to the pier, where we would wait for a navy yard boat that was being sent for. Well, we were good at waiting, too.

It was dark, and the brightly lit offices showed through the windows at the shore end of the pier, and we could see many girls inside at work. But that was out of bounds to us; we were in quarantine and must stay cooped up in the dark, dreary shed that constituted the pier, and we were disgusted.

Many of the Marines lay down on the dirty planks, and went to sleep. Others of us looked through the windows and envied the freedom they represented. While others still sat on the floor, their heads on their knees, and silent in their thoughts.

But we were not left to ourselves for long, for a great many girls from the offices came out to look us over. At first, we welcomed them, but noticed that they were only out to satisfy their ---- curiosity. They would stop in small groups, and exclaim—"Oh! look at him, isn't that terrible? Marie, come here, and look at this one."

At first, those of us on our feet were disgusted. But finally, we were agitated, and drove the girls back to their offices. The mutilated men felt terrible for the girls' thoughtless remarks and became morose. And who would blame them? For in France no one made remarks about disfigurations; each was accepted as a wounded veteran.

I looked curiously at the men. One had received a shell fragment in the face, his upper lip and nose being badly scarred and disfigured; another had been hit in the left cheek by a bullet, the left eye was gone and his cheek was covered with livid scars; and one had part of his lower jaw removed, giving him a gruesome appearance: no wonder the girls made their remarks; they weren't used to such sights. And I didn't blame them.

I walked to the windows again and looked in. The girls all smiled and waved at me, and I smiled and waved back. But it wasn't the girls that interested me; it was the phone. There it was within reach, though out of bounds.

42. Look, Marie

How nice it would be to call home and talk with Mother, to let her know that I am in the country again, and that I was all right. But then a C.P.O. yelled out, "All aboard," and the men were crowding to go aboard.

The boat soon backed away from the pier, and we rode down the Hudson, cutting through the river traffic, around the Battery, and up the East River to the Brooklyn Navy Yards, where we were met by private cars and promptly whisked to the naval hospital. Our trip, with all its interesting and dangerous events, was now a thing of the past, and we were ready to take on the events of the future.

Western Union Telegram
19 Jan. 4:25 A.M.
New York N.Y.

J.J. Bullis
1301 Raymond Ave. St. Paul, Minn.

Landed New York. Am well. On Board USS Northern Pacific. Letter following.

Pvt. E.J. Bullis
Brooklyn Naval Hospital

We made an inconspicuous entrance through the basement. We were assumed to be a "crummy" gang and we had to first have a bath. We stripped in a large room, with our outer clothes going in one pile and underclothes in another. The nurses and orderlies passed out disinfectant and soap and told us to "go to it." They were afraid of "cooties and lice." Apparently they had heard about our "pets" at home. And although it was long since we had been infested with them, we had to make sure. After a good hot shower, they gave us pajamas and our personal belongings and directed us to the second floor, where we were given assigned bunks.

After a good night's sleep, I got up and wandered about the ward in my pajamas. I found a glassed-in porch where others were congregated, and so I joined them. Two of the men I had known in France who had been wounded in Belleau Wood and the rest were all strangers, about evenly divided between the Corps and the Navy.

One of them introduced me to a gunnery sergeant who was from the 49th and who had won the Medal of Honor in Belleau Wood. He was Charles F. Hoffman, an alias to cover a previous enlistment in the Corps. He was a little, dried-up old-timer, who might have been tending chickens somewhere rather than fighting with the Marines. He received the medal due to his actions on June 6 while fighting on hill 142. He single-handedly charged twelve Germans armed with five light machine guns, bayoneted several, and caused the rest to flee: quite a job for the "dried-up old-timer."

The patients here in the Brooklyn Naval Hospital seemed complacent and content with life in general, and were not full of "pep" like the men I was used to.

The next three or four days were a nightmare. We were in quarantine shut up in the hospital and confined to the ward with no clothes, and time passed very slowly for us. The things that did happen are not worth recalling, except for the following incident.

There was a patient there, a good-looking gob; he was good natured and moved among the men alt will—until he was in need of his medicine, or, "appeaser." He was a "dope" addict. He had acquired the habit in China, and of his own free will. As he put it, "A bunch of us went into the dive and got a 'shot,' to see what it was like." He found out all right, and now he was in the naval hospital occupying a bed that might better have been filled with a wounded man.

When the time approached that he should need his "medicine," he grew jumpy, nervous, and broke out in a cold sweat. Then he would call the orderlies to get him into a straight jacket. When in the jacket, he was placed on his cot where he would go through some terrible moments writhing and struggling. Then the nurse would appear with the hypodermic needle and apply the "dope." He would lie quiet for some time, and afterward they would remove the jacket. And after a long rest, he would be up and around again. The men didn't have much use for him, and when he was in a crowd he made reference to the "butterflies" and other hallucinations of people thus afflicted.

Nothing to do except write letters and wait for news from home—which never came. It was enough to make a man "jump ship" to get away from it all.

43

Hilarious Celebration

January 7

Well, we are moving again; always a move, a change of address—and still no mail from home. If I didn't know better, I would quit writing, and stop worrying.

Private cars picked us up and dropped us at a pier, where we went aboard a navy yard boat. We started out by descending the East River, cruising under the majestic Brooklyn Bridge, navigating around the lower end of New York, then cruising up into the Hudson River. I didn't know what to look at, the skyline of New York, the river traffic, or the many ships in the harbor—so, I took it all in and enjoyed the ever-changing scenes.

Ascending the river, the water traffic thinned out, and I saw our destination. A part of the fleet was anchored ahead, mostly destroyers, but stationed among them was the hospital ship *Solace*. It was anchored off 74th Street, and we came alongside and boarded, and were assigned bunks in a ward. This was to be our home for a while, and I didn't like it; for it meant going to sea again, to get to Washington, D.C.

I didn't know a soul on board. I didn't mind that in the hospitals in France, but now that I was up and around it gave me a strange feeling to be among strangers. I roamed the ship, and everyone seemed lost, and like I, alone. Although we got along with one another, it was lonesome.

After chow, most of us stood at the railing and looked at New York. Grant's Tomb was upstream a short ways, the city proper, down. And as the lights of the city came on, they lit into a blaze of glory. The many destroyers swinging gently at anchor also made a beautiful scene: bathed in light with their watery reflections and the ghostly figures on the decks, it evoked a feeling of peace.

Afterward, I went to the ward for the night. The bunks here were four high, swinging on chains and springs; "gouser" bunks they called them. Mine was the fourth one just beneath the overhead steam pipes. It looked to be "close quarters," as there was not much room between. If a man raised his knees, he could push the man above out of his bunk—but then hospital patients weren't supposed to "horse-play."

January 8

When morning came, a C.P.O., called "Jimmie Legs" by the gobs, raised us by blowing on his pipe, and yelling, "Out you come! Let go ---- ---- and grab a sock! Hit the deck; out you come!" Whereon the low man pushed the man above with his knees, and the next the other, until I was raised into the steam pipes. I immediately went over the side and piled on the man in No. 3, and in turn we wrestled No. 2, who assisted us in grabbing No. 1; and then the four of us fell in a pile on the deck, all laughing. And we made our way into the head and washed and shined for the coming day.

After chow, there was an inspection by the ship's doctors, and aside from those Marines needing a change of bandages, we were through for the day. They were coaling the ship, so we made ourselves scarce for fear they would put us to work and to stay out of the dirt. We were told that we would have shore leave in the afternoon, so everyone tried to get the wrinkles out of his deloused uniform to look as a Marine should: but it was impossible.

After noon chow, the liberty party fell aft. We were told that the return boat would be at the pier at 9:00 p.m.; to be there or they would leave without us. After we got ashore, the men split up. I was in a doughboy uniform, with wrapped puttees, a short overcoat, and army hob-nails. The uniform was too small; it was wrinkled and stained from the "delouser," and the hob-nailed shoes were heavy. At every step the hob-nails drew sparks, and the clanking irritated me, until I gave it up and boarded an el.

People along the way stopped and stared, and that bothered me, not realizing that they were looking at an overseas "hero." For not many "heroes" were back yet, and they hadn't got used to the sight. On the el it was even worse. I had to stand and hang onto a strap while the people in the car stared. It was embarrassing; but the people loved it. A few tried to talk to me. They wanted to know if I had just returned; how many Germans I had shot; and what it was like. Had I been wounded? Did it hurt? And so on. I was glad when the car thinned out. When we came to the Battery terminal, I took another el, crossed the Brooklyn Bridge, went to Flushing Avenue, and got off.

A Marine I had met said I would find the Marine quartermaster sergeant in a National Guard armory on Flushing; so I headed there. I encountered drunkards and "dopes" on Flushing; every lounger there had his hands out begging a nickel "for something to eat." But I went on.

At the armory, I found the quartermaster in the basement, and he grinned and shouted to me to call out my sizes and he would toss the clothes out to me. I started with the underwear, and stripped for the change: new underwear, new hose, new shirt, new trousers, a blouse, a new pair of shoes a belt, a hat ornament, and an overcoat. I felt like a million.

And the sergeant who outfitted me asked, "How does it feel to be back in the country again?"

I replied, "I don't know; this is the first liberty I've had. I know one thing, though, I can't get used to these shoes; they lift my feet right off the ground." I bid the sergeant "so long" and retraced my path to 42nd Street and Broadway. I was completely newly clothed, except for my overseas cap, which I had retained to identify myself as an overseas Marine.

On Broadway I found an army and navy store and made my first purchase in the country: four chevrons, gold; one for my right sleeve, and one for my left, for both overcoat and blouse. Then I located a community house where I found a woman that would sew them on for me, and at the same time sit down to my first meal in the country (aside from the chow we had been served).

I roamed about 42nd and Broadway until it was time to return to the boat. And as I stepped down to the pier the fellows all hailed me with, "Where did you get them?" And I was kept busy giving directions to the Q.M. until the boat put away from shore.

And as we walked up the gangway and saluted the Officer of the Deck, he straightened up and returned a very stiff salute; then in an aside to me, he queried, 'You look fine: where did you make your haul?"

January 9

Not much happened on the *Solace*. Coaling the ship was the main activity, and it was a dirty job, so most of the Marines took advantage of the daily liberty ashore. We took the el downtown, and it was hard to get used to the stares of the people. They were unthinking, even rude, but then we were servicemen and were supposed to "like it."

The first el we boarded was crowded, and we had to stand and hang on to the straps in the orthodox method, swaying with the cars. We were an assorted group of wounded veterans; some were on crutches, some blind in one eye, one with his arm in a frame to support a wounded shoulder, and others with body wounds, all on liberty and headed for town. Not a man or woman aboard the el got up to their feet and offered the cripple a seat. All sat and stared. Some asked fool questions of us, and some remarked to another, "Ain't it terrible? Look, he's blind in one eye." Or, with reference to the man with his arm in the tractor, "I wonder if it hurts." It "hurt" all right; not the wounds, for they were about healed; but the unthinking American public who persisted in viewing us as Exhibits A and B, and not as one of their own who had feelings. We soon learned to ignore the rudeness, and lived apart from the people, and sought pastimes among ourselves.

One sight aboard the *Solace* made us glad that girls had not entered our military life. There was there a young, good-looking gob which had "strayed" and was the victim of syphilis. He was in the padded cell which had cushioned walls and floor. He was determined to kill himself, and his pitiful attempts were terrible to watch. We could look through a small window in the door, and he would "bridge" himself on his head and heels and rock back and forth, trying to break his neck. He kept this up for long periods of time, though unsuccessfully. His wrists were heavily bandaged from attempts to sever an artery; and although every precaution was taken to prevent his success, he still maintained a continuous attempt. The wages of sin are heavy, and his remorse knew no bounds.

January 12

Just before leaving New York, it became quite cold and the river became a floating sea of broken cakes of ice. Going ashore today on liberty, the ship's officers told us that a long boat was missing from a destroyer; it was a liberty party and it was presumed that ice had crushed their boat. We were asked to be on the lookout for it. On going ashore, we could see what was meant, for large ice fragments continually bumped the boat while the crew fought still larger ones away with the pike poles. We were glad to reach shore intact and dreaded the return to ship.

I had promised myself a feed in a high-class restaurant when in town, and a show to celebrate my return. I scouted east and west of Broadway and 42nd, and north and south, until I found the restaurant that met my requirements. The window was draped with a green plush curtain, and it looked the part. So I entered.

Inside, it was up to my expectations; several couples were dining quietly at tables, with waiters hovering in the background. One advanced to me, and I told him that in France I had promised myself a special dinner when I got

43. Hilarious Celebration

home, and this was it. He bowed, smiled, and led me to a table for eight in the center of the room, seated me, and waited for my order. I figured two could play this game, and I ordered filet mignon, French fries, and coffee. It was about two years since I had ordered this, and I was in great expectation.

After he served the entrée, I ate and finished it and glanced around; all eyes of the diners were on me and all were smiling. Just then a group of doughboys entered, and I heard one of them yell out—"Bullis—what are you doing here?!" It was Felnore, whom I had known in the military hospital in Paris. And I rose to greet him, and the waiter seated the group at my table. And six doughboys and a lone Marine had a hilarious time celebrating their return from war.

I am afraid we upset the decorum of the restaurant, but the people, waiters and management, all enjoyed it as much as we. After a grand time and a swell meal, it was time to go, and Felnore insisted on taking all the dinner checks; and we went out into the streets again. After seeing part of a musical, I left to meet the boat, and went aboard for the last time while in New York.

44

The Worst Battle

Today was a happy one, for the ship heaved anchor and steamed down the Hudson out to sea. We had a last look at the "Old Lady" in the harbor, and as she faded into the distance, we scanned the ocean hoping to see the missing boat and men.

While out at sea, all Marines who had no limbs missing were gathered together and told to go topside and move "rough boxes" to the hole of the ship. At the term "rough boxes," all the Marines refused to bear a hand and emphatically told the ship's officers that we had just missed wearing the "wooden overcoats," and had no intention of getting reacquainted. The officers grinned and put their own crew to work on them, and we were sent below to the ward where a C.P.O. would keep us busy.

We Marines were fed up by this time, and went to every means to get out of it; besides, the hospital orderlies and crew needed their exercise. A little C.P.O., who had a perpetual sneer and snarl, was our taskmaster, and the men delighted in making it rough for him. He gave me a pail of soapy water and rags, and growled, "Wash down the bulkheads." I took the pail and wandered away. After quite a while I returned, and said, "I can't find any bulkheads." He grabbed the pail mumbling into his teeth and dismissed me. I wandered off on my own, and as I went I noticed that the white bulkheads of the ward didn't need washing, anyway.

January 14

At the entrance to Chesapeake Bay, the ship idled while navy tugs swung the submarine netting out of the way to let us enter. We sailed up the bay and entered the Potomac River, where we ran into unbroken ice, and several of us went forward to watch at the prow of the ship. The ice looked to be four to six inches thick, and it was lifted up before the ship as it plowed forward, cracking with a great roar and slithering aside in a tumble of broken pieces: it was a spectacle to watch.

The ship forged ahead, but below Mt. Vernon ice jammed in the steering gear, and we swung wildly in a great turn and nosed into the bank. We thought we would be stuck there for some time, but after clearing the steering gear the ship was backed out from shore and we again forged ahead. We broke ice all the way to Washington, D.C.—and there drove into a mud bank. They finally got unstuck from that, and we were edged into a pier by tugs, and a gangplank was run down to shore.

There was a group of private cars to meet us, and, after we stepped ashore, I searched among the line of cars to make my selection. All the cars were driven by women, and I spotted one with a pretty girl, and climbed in. It was a roadster—but my elation was short; for two more Marines also crowded in.

We cruised slowly through Washington, passed the Capitol, drove up Pennsylvania Avenue passed the White House, and finally to the naval hospital, our new home. And we were soon hustled into the buildings and assigned bunks. It was a newly constructed building with nice new shiny floors and fixtures, and we were the first to occupy this portion of the hospital.

Naval Hospital, Washington, D.C.

January 16

After inspection this morning we were free to wander the hospital grounds and get acquainted. Small groups of Marines gathered here and there, but something was missing: all were hoping for letters and for sick leave and did not like the inactive life we were doomed to.

Across the street from the hospital was an open, weedy field, with a building under construction, and, being a curious group, we wandered over to view it. The building was to be the famous Lincoln Memorial, and had promise of being a very beautiful monument.

We were soon satisfied, and continued along to other sights in the vicinity. From the memorial we could see in the distance across the weedy, barren field the Washington Monument and the Capitol; and on the other side and across the Potomac, we could see Arlington Cemetery; all ours to visit and see while we were here in Washington.

Jan 19, 1919
U.S. Naval Hospital
Washington, D.C.

Dear Dad:

I am at the U.S. Naval Hospital here in Washington and feeling fine. I am in good condition now but the naval doctors want to give me a good examination. Then I will get about thirty days sick leave and come home. I am putting in for a discharge from the service and no doubt I will get it in time.... Today, Mrs. Daniels, wife of the Secretary of the Navy, came out to the hospital and said "Hello" to the wounded and sick. I and a couple of Marines had just left the hospital when a big Packard drew alongside and Mrs. Daniels invited us to ride into the city with her. Wow. If the President was here I might even go for a ride with him. Who knows?

Well, Dad, you can bet it will be a happy moment when I get a letter from each of you, telling me everything that has happened since Sept. 28th and how all of you are. I can tell you, it made me happy last night when I came in from liberty to get your telegram. That was the worst battle I ever had to fight was when I didn't hear from home. On Oct. 4th, while resting before going over the top, quite a few of the fellows got letters: imagine, we were going over in a few minutes and I didn't get any, and, of course, I was disappointed. But it did a fellow good to see the other boys get theirs. For some, it was the last home news they every got. And I am sure it helped them face the hell we went into a few minutes later, and where I got my "blighty."

Well, this will save until I get home and maybe will sound better then. I will probably walk in on you soon; will wire *when I leave*. There is always some doubt as to when in this man's army. Not kicking or finding fault; but the truth: you never know *when*, *where*, or *why*.

With "beaucoup" love to all, as ever,
Everard, or just plain "Bill"

45

Joe Erwin

Dear Mother:

I received your letter dated Jan. 13 today, and believe me, it was good. Am mighty glad to know everybody is well. We had a delightful trip on the USS *Solace* (naval hospital ship) from N.Y. to Washington and suffered no hardships. I believe I would rather have stayed in New York, but I guess it is better for my purse that I didn't. I have received all the telegrams and have sent you a couple. I wonder, did you get the one I sent when I landed on Jan.4th?

The first I knew of Joe Erwin's death[1] was when I got your letter and was sorry to hear it. I don't know anything about it, for I hadn't seen Joe since July. As you know, we went across on the same boat, and were in the same battalion, but not the same company. He received his first wound in Belleau Wood near Château Thierry in June. It was a serious wound, a piece of shrapnel hitting him in the back of the head. But I saw him at St. Aignan-sur-Cher in July and he then said he was going to return to his company. Since then, I have neither seen nor heard about him. If you can, let me know the date of his death and whether he died in action or in a hospital; I can probably tell something of the place and fight. It is too bad, but then I don't know of a more honorable death. It was for a great cause and in the line of duty; so what more can a man do? John 15:13: Greater love hath no man than this that a man lay down his life for his friends.

Well, Mother, the doctor came around this morning and asked me if I would like sick leave. Of course, I said *Yes*; so I will get about thirty days at home. All I have to do is await the "red tape," and then I will be on my way. So you can expect me soon. Will wire and let you know when I start.

Better not write after you get this, for I will be on my way home.

With "beaucoup" love,
Ev.
U.S.M.C.

46

Red Tape

Jan. 26, 1919
U.S. Naval Hospital
Washington, D.C.

Dear Dad:

Well, I am still in the naval hospital here and patiently (?) waiting for sick leave. I sure wish they could hurry up and forget their confounded red tape.

I suppose most of the Park boys are home now and starting in where they left off. With me, I don't know what I want to do. It is odd, being twenty-two years old and don't know yet what I want. Well, I suppose that feeling will wear off as soon as I get in "cit's" again. It was that way with me when I got in uniform. As soon as I got into uniform all I wanted to do was fight (and fight I did); so I suppose as soon as I don civilian clothes again it will be all business.

Well, Dad, I won't say much on paper, for I would rather tell it in person. And I expect (at least am hoping) to be home in a week. But you can never tell. I am well and having a good time but anxious to get home.

Hope everybody at home is well.

With love,
Everard

Feb. 1, 1919
U.S. Naval Hospital
Washington, D.C.

Dear Mother:

Well, I am still here, although it is not my fault. I put in a couple of weeks ago for sick leave but am still waiting for an answer. I tell you, I would rather, by far, be in the trenches over there, than in a hospital over here. Here I am well and able to be about, yet having to stay in the hospital, sitting around doing nothing, except standing one fool inspection after another. Yesterday was about the climax. We had to stand at attention while a bunch of young men, women, and a few buck privates of the army went past and asked fool questions. It wouldn't have been so bad if they had been officers, but to have to stand at attention while a doughboy private went past—and at that, he hadn't been across. Wow, I am beginning to see it all now: the glories of war.

I don't feel quite as bad as I sound, but I do wish they would give us the thing we want most of all—a furlough home. The Doc said that the papers would be ready Mon-

46. Red Tape 229

day. Monday, it will be the last of the week; and the last of the week, it will be—etc., etc. I will wire when I start so as to let you know the impossible has happened.

I always figure that one could have a pretty nice time in a city like Washington, but believe me, all the pleasure is taken out of it when it costs half of one's roll every time he makes a liberty. I don't believe there's a show I haven't seen. I was to the play "Why Marry" a week ago, and saw the famous Nat Goodwin,[1] and saw the "Passing Show of 1918." The most fun is to go to the movies and see these war plays. I think I will have to join a movie company and play in the war scenes; for they are far more thrilling than a real war and also one has more comforts and more to eat than we did.

This letter sounds as though I am in a bad humor this morning, but I am not. On the contrary, I feel fine, for we have liberty this afternoon, and I can go to another movie[2] and to Child's --? --somewhere in that piece of anatomy (maybe that's the right word, I don't know, though,) called memory. I have recollection of sitting down to a nice table, with a table cloth, too, and of having plenty of the right kind of food with plenty of butter for your bread (not oleomargarine, or none at all, but butter); plenty of sugar and cream for one's coffee, and etc. Well, believe me; I am waiting to do that again and soon.

Well, my pen is about dry, so will close for this time and hoping to see you all soon.

With lots of love,

Ev.

P.S. I got Dad's telegram O.K. but couldn't get out answering it.

P.S.S. This is being written with a "Heinie" pencil, captured at Soissons, July 19. When I get home I will have to start a side show and exhibit the only living Boche pencil in captivity, a relic of the Great War, and so on and so forth. I have also a purse full of German, French, Belgian, English, and Swiss money and also *No* American money (although I have some in my money belt). The end has come, so till we meet again—in German, *Auf wiedersehen*: in French, *Au revoir*. Ev.

UNITED STATES MARINE CORPS

To all whom it may Concern:

KNOW YE, That _____Everard Jay Bullis_____,

a _____private_____ of the U. S. Marine Corps, who was enlisted at __RD., Philadelphia, Pa.__ on the __27th__ day of __June__, 1917, to serve __Duration of War__ years, is hereby

HONORABLY DISCHARGED

upon report of medical survey, for disability.

Said _____Everard Jay Bullis_____ was born __October 10,__ 18 98, at __Minneapolis, Minn.__ and when enlisted was __72¼__ inches high, with __Blue__ eyes, __Dark Brown__ hair, __Dark__ complexion; occupation, __Clerk__; citizenship, __U.S.__

DELIVERED at __MB., NY., Washington, DC.__ this __30th__ day of __April__, 1919.

Character: __"EXCELLENT"__

Major (ret'd), U.S.M.C., Commanding Marines.

Everard's discharge paper (courtesy Robert G. Bullis).

Everard's service certificate (courtesy Robert G. Bullis).

Everard's grave marker in Wenatchee City Cemetery in Wenatchee, WA (courtesy Robert G. Bullis).

Notes
David J. Bullis

Introduction

1. gob, a sailor.
2. A "dick" in 1917 meant a detective. This usage went well into the 1930s, if not later.

Preface

1. Coublanc was a town in a valley of the Cote d'Or Mountains in France, and was a Forward Training camp of the 2nd Replacement Battalion. They went through very strenuous training here.
2. Nellie (Ralph Nelson) was a neighborhood friend from St. Paul, MN. He was in Grandchamp with his outfit. He was attached to the 6th Regiment, 4th Brigade Marines, 2nd Division upon reaching the front.
3. Suburb of Paris.
4. September 1914, the first battle of the Marne. The Germans were stopped short at Meaux. Meaux is over 40 km northeast of Paris.

Chapter 2

1. Captain George Hamilton was a heroic figure in the Great War. See Mark Mortensen's book, George W. Hamilton, USMC: America's Greatest World War I Hero.

Chapter 3

1. The Second Division was comprised of the 4th Marine Brigade, the 3rd Infantry Brigade, and other units. It was nicknamed the "Indianhead" Division in 1919.

2. Pieces, rifles.
3. The "Sho-Sho" was a French automatic rifle; in French, named *Chauchat*.

Chapter 6

1. This was in Utica, New York at the Savage Arms Company. He was staying at the Hotel Montclair. He was able to dismantle the machine gun and name each part blindfolded.
2. This is in reference to the Franco-Prussian War, 1870–1871. The Germans defeated France.

Chapter 7

1. Hiram Bearss: Medal of Honor, Croix de Guerre, Navy Distinguished Service Medal, Army Distinguished Service Medal, Distinguished Service Cross, and several others.

Chapter 10

1. Killed in action 7/18/1918, in the Soissons battle.
2. Captive balloons were large, elongated balloons, with fins in the rear, fastened by metal cables to the ground. The observers watched for enemy movements and as spotters for artillery fire.
3. Years later, Everard, a student in the University of Minnesota, working alone in a lab, a man came in, looking for someone. It turns out he was a fellow veteran. They reminisced about the war; and in the course of their conversation, the man became visibly

excited when Everard recounted the story of the balloon: he was the second observer. He received seven wounds. Then he stripped his outer clothes, and showed Everard the scars on his legs, arms, and body. He was decorated by both the French and American Governments.

Chapter 13

1. Smith survived his wound.

Chapter 16

1. Killed in action 11/02/1918

Chapter 23

1. Killed in action 09/15/1918

Chapter 25

1. In a letter home, when Everard and chums were in Chicago, new recruits on their great adventure, running down the streets of Chicago, carefree and shouting: what a difference war makes.

Chapter 29

1. Captain Hamilton of Belleau Wood was now Major Hamilton.

Chapter 31

1. Captain Frank Whitehead was awarded the Distinguished Service Cross for his heroism that day. He was severely wounded.

Chapter 32

1. This was the lieutenant that greeted him when he returned to his outfit on being gassed. He presented Everard with a new Sho-Sho, which was unwanted.

Chapter 37

1. Hemmingway was a volunteer, as were Robert Service and e.e. cummings. Other literary figures also served.

2. General John J. "Black Jack" Pershing was senior commander of all the American forces in France in World War I.

Chapter 41

1. The *Northern Pacific* was stranded off Fire Island until about the 18th of January, when it was pulled out to sea by tugs. It was in dock for months under repair, and then returned to service.

Chapter 45

1. The neighborhood boy that didn't come home. He was wounded October 3, 1918, and died October 4.

Chapter 46

1. Nat Goodwin died about a week after my grandfather saw this play.

2. When he says "movie," it must be remembered that these were Silent films, and would be for another nine or ten years, when "Talkies" came out. I have seen several scores of these films and many are quite good.

Index

AEF 53, 63
Albert, King 198
ambulances 17, 18, 200
American Red Cross Hospital No. 1 183
Ansauville 141
Argonne 63, 190
Arlington Cemetery 225
Armenians 127
artillery 18, 19, 26, 27, 30, 32, 33, 36, 38, 40, 47, 48, 58, 61, 65, 67, 76, 80, 83, 86, 88, 121, 125, 130, 131, 132, 133, 134, 136, 141, 150, 151, 159, 160, 162, 168, 195, 230
Autueil 91
aviators 46, 49, 57, 58, 63, 85, 91, 132, 150

Bar le Duc 147
battalion P.C. 44
batteries 27, 36, 156
Bazoilles sur Meuse 107
Beaumont, Major 6
Belgians 147, 183, 192, 229
Belleau Wood 1, 15, 26, 27, 31, 33, 36, 37, 41, 44, 46, 47, 48, 50, 52, 53, 54, 56, 57, 62, 84, 91, 95, 100, 101, 108, 133, 140, 143, 148, 157, 179, 180, 191, 193, 194, 199, 205, 217, 227, 231
Bernécourt 141
Berry, Major 83
Big Fight 12
billet 41, 42, 56, 57, 60, 111, 142
Blanc Mont 1, 146–155, 158, 159, 160, 161, 180, 199
"blighty" 91, 226
Boche 18, 57, 58, 62, 124, 137, 155, 174, 229
Bois de Belleau 43, 143
Bois de Bonvaux 138
Bois de Colombey 120
Bois de Fey 134
Bois de Hailbat 136
Bois de la Vipère 156, 159
Bois du Four 132, 133
Boone, Doctor 169
Border, Lieutenant 187
Boss, Andrew 3
Bowness, Sergeant 45, 88, 125
Bowser, Miss 188

Boxer Rebellion 7, 8
Boyd 12
Brack, George 3
bread 49, 50, 148, 149, 150, 229
Brigman, Corporal 191, 200
Broad Street 6, 12
Broadway 201, 221, 222
Brock, Robert 37
Brooklyn Bridge 219, 220
Brooklyn Naval Hospital 217, 218
Brooklyn Navy Yards 217
Bullard, Miss 190, 192
Bullis, Bill 184
Bullis, Celeste 14
Bullis, John J. 4, 14
Bundy, Omar 53

camions 61, 62, 65, 149
candles 38
captive balloon 58
Carter, Joe 161, 169
Casey, John 37
cemetery 83, 84, 85, 86, 135
centennial 1
Châlons sur Marne 147
Champagne 61, 147, 151, 193, 199, 205
Champillon 19, 31, 205
Charmes la Côte 143
Chasseurs Alpins 154, 182, 183
chateau 17, 56, 106, 124
Château Thierry 41, 66, 179, 227
Châtillon sur Seine 97, 100
Chauchat 111, 230
Chaudon 75
Chaumont 110
Chesapeake Bay 224
China 7, 8, 9, 100, 218
China Town 9
Choctaw 193, 198, 200
Coast Guard 209
cockney 90, 91
Colombey les Belles 15, 120
Comfort 111, 121, 136, 137, 138, 139, 152, 161, 164, 165
Commercy 147

235

Conley 148, 149
Conner 161, 162, 169
Connolly 111, 119, 121, 122, 133, 136, 137, 138, 139, 148, 152, 161, 164
Cooper 205
cooties 49, 50, 55, 146, 147, 217
Corbett, Lieutenant 34, 35, 70, 111, 112, 128, 129
Coupru 54
Crackle 188
Crépy en Valois 63, 64
Crouttes sur Marne 54

Daly, Sergeant Dan 100, 101, 102, 103, 105, 108
Daniels, Josephus 10
Daniels, Mrs. 226
Davidian 127
Davis, Sergeant 165
Denver 193
diary 5
Dodge 83
Dolcourt 117
Domgermain 142, 146
doughboys 34, 59, 76, 77, 79, 101, 108, 177, 191, 194, 216, 223
Duffy, Miss 172, 173, 174, 175
dugouts 70
Duke, Jimmie 57, 70, 71, 87, 88, 111, 125

East River 217, 219
Eiffel Tower 16
88mm 48
89th Division 188, 200
Elizabeth, Queen 198
England/English 7, 42, 62, 90, 95, 96, 115, 183, 188, 189, 229
Erwin, Joe 97, 227
Essen Hook 156, 157, 158, 159
Essen Trench 156

Fairmont Park 8
Feland, Logan 53
Felnore 188, 190, 191, 193, 200, 223
La Ferme Paris 18
Field Hospital # 15 175
15th Field Artillery 76, 133
5th Division 134, 136, 138
5th Marines 53, 113, 159
5th Regiment 56, 61, 193
1st Battalion 40, 113, 160
First Regiment 12
First U.S. Division 67, 75
Flirey 141
Flushing Avenue 220
Fontenay 123
Ford 34, 169
Foreign Legion 67
Forêt de la Reine 141
Forêt de Retz 65
Forêt de Villers Cotterêts 65

Fort Snelling 3
40/8 car 101
49th 28, 40, 147, 160, 193, 217
42nd Street 221
4th Army 153
4th Brigade 18, 109, 113, 230
4th Marine Brigade 53, 230
Fourth of July 53
Frazier, Mr. and Mrs. 12
Freeville 102, 106, 108, 109
French army 49, 150
French cavalry 79, 86
French First Moroccan Division 66
French Navy 14

galley 56, 86, 88, 122, 141
Galliford, Lieutenant 118
Gare du Nord 179, 200
Garvey, Claude 36
Gas 50, 87, 88, 128
gas shell 50, 86
Gavin, Bill 31, 37, 70, 71, 128
Germans 16, 18, 19, 20, 23, 24, 28, 29, 30, 32, 33, 36, 37, 38, 39, 44, 46, 47, 48, 49, 50, 51, 53, 54, 58, 59, 60, 61, 66, 69, 72, 74, 75, 76, 77, 78, 79, 80, 83, 84, 85, 86, 87, 90, 91, 92, 95, 115, 116, 127, 130, 131, 132, 133, 134, 135, 136, 137, 138, 139, 140, 141, 147, 149, 152, 153, 154, 155, 157, 158, 159, 160, 162, 163, 165, 166, 167, 168, 172, 173, 174, 178, 181, 193, 217, 220, 230
Gibson 31, 32
Giles 65, 66, 88
Gilligan, Sergeant 21
Gowdy 119
Grandchamp 15, 230
Great War 1, 5, 229, 230
Greek 198
Gridley 107

Haiti 8, 105
Hamilton, George 1, 22, 29, 88, 89, 230, 231
H&E 179, 180
Harbord, James 53, 83
hardtack 50, 61, 65, 161
Heinies 37, 229
USS *Henderson* 5, 12, 97
Hill, James J. 4, 31
Hinkey, Dinkey, Parlez Vous 109, 115, 124, 127, 149
Hiram, Col. 44, 45, 230
Hoboken 64, 206, 215
Hoffman, Charles F. 217
horsemeat, canned 34
Hospital Center, Kerhuon 202
Hotchkiss 29, 164
Hotel Waltonian 8
Hudson River 219

Indian Head 7
Ireland 176
Ireland, Bishop 4

Jiggs, Sergeant Major 7
Johnson, 2nd Lt. 30, 97, 141, 165
Joyce 32, 125

Kerhuon 200
Keville, Tim 37, 63
Kiser 12
Kopfa (clerk) 205

LeJeune, John A. 12
Leopold, Prince 197
Leviathan 215
Lewis Machine Gun School 41
Liffol le Grand 102, 107
Lincoln Memorial 225
Lindgren 165, 169
Long Island 207
Louis Pasteur Institute of Paris 182
Lowener, Emma 13
Lucy le Bocage 33, 34
Lugar 71, 74, 91, 92, 94
lyddite 38

"Mademoiselle from Armentières" 62
Mairie 18
Malay Peninsula 62
Marine Brigade 61, 205
Marine Corps 10, 11, 53, 63, 103, 187
Marne River 40, 55
Marne Valley 39
"La Marseillaise" 113, 114, 195
mascot 61
USS *Mauritania* 202
Mauser 168
Max, Lieutenant 83-86
Maxim gun 22, 30, 70, 74, 75, 76, 80
McAulliff, Corporal 66
McKinley, Mr. 126
Meaux 16, 62, 230
Medal of Honor 100, 217
Medford, Massachusetts, Police Force 37
Mênil la Tour 142
Mexico 3
Miller 19, 205
Minnesota 4, 9, 13
Moneypenny 135
monkey meat 34, 49, 50, 61, 102
Mont le Vignoble 142
Montreuil aux Lions 18
Moselle River 112, 122
Mt. Vernon 225

National Army camp 102
National Geographic 182
National Guard 45, 53, 109, 220
navy personnel 168
Nelson, Ralph "Nellie" 12, 15, 18, 21, 199, 230
Neuilly sur Seine 182, 188, 195, 198
New England 45, 53
New York 11, 13, 96, 182, 189, 192, 214, 215, 217, 219, 222, 223, 227, 230

Nicaragua 8
Nice 70
9th Infantry 75, 77, 79, 134, 156
Norris, Captain 11
USS *Northern Pacific* 202, 207, 213, 215, 217, 231
Norton-Harjes 192
No. 9 Lugar 30

Oklahoma 193, 197
103rd Infantry 53
Ophien, Leonard 188, 200
outpost 29, 30, 45, 47, 50, 69, 136, 138, 139, 140

Paris 16, 46, 59, 61, 62, 65, 91, 92, 94, 95, 96, 126, 176, 177, 179, 182, 190, 195, 196, 197, 198, 200, 204, 223, 230
Paris-Maubeuge road 65
Paris-Metz highway 46
Perkins, Sereant 70, 71
Pershing, John J. 1, 3, 4, 5, 14, 53, 110, 193, 231
Philadelphia 6, 7, 8, 9, 10, 12, 215
Philippines 44
pleurisy 151, 170, 187
Pont St. Vincent 122
Potomac River 224
Potter, Guy 37, 38
Powell, Major 193
Prussians 23, 134, 230
ptomaine poisoning 33
puking gas 50
pup tents 127
Purple Heart 1

Quantico 11
Quigley, Captain 32, 137
Quirk, John H. 34

ravine 76, 77, 79, 80, 81, 83, 84, 85, 86, 87, 133, 134, 136, 140
Red Cross 91, 174, 183, 202, 203, 208
Red Cross Hospital No. 5 91
Rembercourt 139
Rheims 61, 62, 147, 151
Rheims Cathedral 151
Rice Park 4
Rochester, New York 184
Rose, Madame 192, 193
runner 41, 60, 77, 78, 165
Rupt de Mad 135
Rusinow 33

Saâcy sur Marne 40, 62
St. Denis 15
St. Hilaire au Temple 148
St. Louis, Sergeant 88
St. Mihiel 1, 63, 121, 143, 157, 159, 193, 199, 205
St. Paul, Minnesota 3, 4, 9, 97, 98, 99, 187, 217, 230
Sainte Aulde 53
San Dominican troubles 8
Schroeder, Frank 37

Index

Schumaker, Miss 172, 173
Scotties 91
Second Division 18, 28, 114, 191, 230
2nd Engineers 113, 131
Second U.S. Division 67
Selaincourt 114, 115, 117, 120, 122, 139
Senegal 72
7th Regular Army Regiment 33
78th Division, 310th Infantry 140
75mm artillery 51
77mm artillery 48
Sho-Sho rifle 29, 30, 41, 51, 54, 71, 111, 118, 121, 132, 136, 141, 146, 152, 153, 164, 230, 231
USS *Siboney* 215
6th Engineers 188, 200
6th Marines 17, 53, 61, 86, 156, 159, 160
6th Regiment 40, 230
Smith, Bob 34, 35, 50, 52, 70, 71, 87, 188, 192, 230
Smith, Miss 188
Smith, Mrs. 192, 193, 194
Snair, Corporal 88
Soissons 1, 65, 95, 111, 140, 143, 147, 157, 180, 187, 193, 198, 199, 205, 229, 230
Solace 208, 219, 221, 222, 227
Sommepy 152, 158, 159
spies 33
Springfield rifle 74, 160, 161
Star shells 152
"The Star-Spangled Banner" 113
Stars and Stripes 12
Statue of Liberty 197, 215
Sterno 38
Stone, Senator 194
Suippes 150
Sullivan, Miss 180, 182
Sutherland, Miss 185
Sweet, M.L. 10, 11

tanks 65, 67, 81, 85, 113, 157
Thiaucourt 133
Thiaucourt-Regniéville road 141
3rd Battalion 44, 61, 160
3rd Brigade 113, 114
Third Division 33, 39
3rd Infantry Brigade 230
Thomas, Charley 193, 200
Thomason, Lieutenant 22, 24
Torcy 30, 34, 45
Tours 96
train 4, 7, 15, 16, 39, 61, 90, 91, 96, 97, 98, 100, 101, 102, 109, 110, 111, 144, 145, 146, 147, 176, 177, 178, 200
trench 20, 21, 22, 30, 42, 46, 57, 70, 74, 77, 78, 79, 112, 116, 125, 130, 131, 133, 136, 137, 142, 143, 146, 149, 153, 154, 155, 156, 157, 158, 159, 161, 164, 165
Trench des Prussiens 153
Tripe 125
Tritt, Private 88
trucks 17, 18, 40, 62, 63, 64, 67, 76, 90, 111, 149, 202
Tupa, Frank 97
Turkey 189, 203
Turrill, Julius S. 53
20th Company 32
26th Division 45, 53
23rd Infantry 80, 160
210mm 48, 76, 156
XXI Corps 153

United States Marine Corps 56
U.S. sailors 90
University of Minnesota 97, 230

Vanderbilt, Mrs. W.K. 182, 189, 195
Van Dyke, 1st Sergeant 11
Vaterland 215
Vaux Andigny 15
Vera Cruz 8
Verdun 143
vice patrol 9, 10
Vierzy 77, 78, 79, 83, 86, 87, 111
Villa 3
Vitry le François 147
La Voie du Châtel 19

Wagner, Captain 173, 175, 176
Wagner, Sergeant 50, 116, 123, 136, 138
Waller, Tony 7, 8
Washington, D.C. 219, 225, 228
Weyburn, Saskatchewan 93
White House 225
Whitehead, Frank 1, 164, 231
Wilson, Woodrow 200
Womack 65, 122, 123, 167
Woodard, Corporal 161, 162, 167
World War II 5

Y.M.C.A. 107, 126, 215

Zing 97